- 1988 年 10 月，袁伦渠教授在莫斯科国民经济学院劳动经济教研室演讲，右边是他的导师伊万诺夫教授。

- 1988 年 11 月，袁伦渠教授在莫斯科国民经济学院留学时，与其导师、苏联著名劳动经济学家伊万诺夫教授在一起。

- 1989 年 3 月，袁伦渠教授与其翻译的《劳动社会学》作者、民主德国的施托伯格教授在一起。

- 1999 年 10 月，袁伦渠教授在日本访问期间为立正大学博士生讲课。

- 2006 年 7 月，袁伦渠教授与本书序言的撰写者、我国劳动经济学的奠基人之一赵履宽教授在北京交通大学明湖前合影。

- 2006 年 9 月，袁伦渠教授在德国举办的学术会议上发言。

● 2007 年 7 月，袁伦渠、林玳玳教授带领学生在乌鲁木齐铁路局哈密工务段调研。

● 2008 年 9 月 11 日，袁伦渠、林玳玳教授与学生刘盾参加由国务院参事室和美国蓝十字蓝盾集团举办的“中国医疗保障体系运行机制国际研讨会”。

● 2009 年 10 月 1 日，袁伦渠教授应邀在天安门观礼台观看中华人民共和国成立 60 周年阅兵式后留影。

● 2010 年 11 月 14 日，袁伦渠教授在“中国人力资源强国战略高层论坛”上作主题发言。

● 2013 年 3 月 16 日，袁伦渠教授参加博士毕业生刘盾的博士论文答辩，该答辩会聚集了若干学界名家，左起依次为荣朝和、田小宝、林玳玳、刘盾、袁伦渠、曾湘泉、杨河清、赵坚。

2013 年 5 月 19 日，袁伦渠教授参加中国人民大学劳动人事学院的博士论文答辩会。

2016 年 3 月 10 日，袁伦渠教授列席全国政协十二届四次会议。

2017 年 9 月 25 日，袁伦渠教授访问母校俄罗斯国立经济大学（前身为莫斯科国民经济学院），与几名昔日同窗（如今已是该大学的教授）合影。

2013 年 6 月 13 日，袁伦渠教授参加首都经济贸易大学的博士论文答辩会。

2017 年 10 月 16 日，袁伦渠教授在俄罗斯高等经济大学圣彼得堡分校举办的金砖五国全球商业与创新国际会议上与林毅夫教授合影。

2010 年 4 月，袁伦渠、林玳玳教授与学生在校园合影。

2012 年 7 月 6 日，袁伦渠、林玳玳教授参加学生的毕业典礼后合影。

2017 年 12 月 4 日，在袁伦渠教授主持的“中俄劳动经济学科建设比较研究”项目的支持下，俄方专家造访北京交通大学，受到高艳副校长的接待。

2018 年 10 月 24 日，袁伦渠教授在俄罗斯科学院远东问题研究所主办的第二十三届国际学术会议上作主题发言。

北京交通大学哲学社会科学文库

改革开放以来我国劳动经济问题的理论与实践探讨

——袁伦渠劳动经济研究论文集

袁伦渠　著

北京交通大学出版社
·北京·

内 容 简 介

本书是一部作者对我国改革开放40多年来劳动就业、收入分配、社会保障和人力资源管理制度改革的理论研究和实践探索论文集，全书收录经作者精心挑选、梳理的公开发表论文30余篇，结集成为劳动经济问题、就业问题、收入分配问题、社会保障问题、人力资源管理问题、劳动关系问题、劳动社会学问题、苏联和东欧国家劳动问题研究等篇章，另附政策建议、回忆录、演讲稿及访谈实录若干，共同构成了各部分既相互独立又紧密联系的劳动经济问题研究体系。全书以劳动力市场运行为中心，运用涵盖劳动经济学、劳动社会学、劳动心理学和劳动法学的多学科研究视角，采用宏观与微观并重、定性与定量相结合的研究方法，对我国劳动就业、收入分配、社会保障和人力资源管理等领域的重大理论与现实问题进行了理论分析和实践探讨。

图书在版编目（CIP）数据

改革开放以来我国劳动经济问题的理论与实践探讨：袁伦渠劳动经济研究论文集 / 袁伦渠著. 一北京：北京交通大学出版社，2021.12

ISBN 978-7-5121-4639-6

Ⅰ. ① 改… Ⅱ. ① 袁… Ⅲ. ① 劳动经济－中国－文集 Ⅳ. ① F249.2－53

中国版本图书馆CIP数据核字（2021）第249886号

改革开放以来我国劳动经济问题的理论与实践探讨
——袁伦渠劳动经济研究论文集
GAIGE KAIFANG YILAI WOGUO LAODONG JINGJI WENTI DE LILUN YU SHIJIAN TANTAO——YUAN LUNQU LAODONG JINGJI YANJIU LUNWENJI

责任编辑：田秀青
出版发行：北京交通大学出版社　　电话：010-51686414　　http://www.bjtup.com.cn
地　　址：北京市海淀区高梁桥斜街44号　　邮编：100044
印 刷 者：艺堂印刷（天津）有限公司
经　　销：全国新华书店
开　　本：170 mm×235 mm　　印张：15.75　　字数：332千字　　彩插：2
版 印 次：2021年12月第1版　　2021年12月第1次印刷
定　　价：69.00元

本书如有质量问题，请向北京交通大学出版社质监组反映。
投诉电话：010-51686043，51686008；传真：010-62225406；E-mail：press@bjtu.edu.cn。

袁伦渠的学者人生

——中国改革开放以来劳动经济学的发展

（代序言）

最近，袁伦渠教授打算出一本论文集，将40多年来公开发表的文章结集成册，并请我写一篇序言，我欣然接受。

袁伦渠教授是我的同行和朋友，我对他非常熟悉。我们是1978年党的十一届三中全会后认识的。当时我国劳动经济学界同全国学术界一样，受“科学的春天”的鼓舞，对“文化大革命”破坏的劳动经济学研究和教学进行拨乱反正、正本清源的工作。当时，我正在由我主持的中国人民大学劳动经济研究室从事研究工作，并准备在此基础上筹建劳动人事学院。我听说北京经济学院（现首都经济贸易大学）袁伦渠老师工作勤奋，“文化大革命”结束不久就开始劳动经济学的翻译和写作，于是，在1980年夏季的某一天去看望他，提出希望他协助我完成劳动人事学院的筹建工作。他谦虚但又热情地答应了。虽然当时北京经济学院领导未予批准，但他为人热情、谦逊好学的精神深深感动了我，我们两人便由此结缘。在学术会上观点和兴趣的一致、会下的促膝长谈、研究生培养和答辩工作中的交往，对劳动经济学执着的喜爱，把我们紧紧地联系在一起，这种友谊至今已40余年。

袁伦渠是我国最早开办劳动经济学专业的北京经济学院的第二届劳动经济专业毕业生。1964 年毕业后，他先后在国家劳动部、北京经济学院、北京交通大学工作，直至2016年，他作为国务院参事卸任，在我国劳动经济领域工作了52

年。在我国改革开放后劳动经济学科恢复和发展的全过程中，做出了突出贡献。

首先，他对我国劳动经济学科的恢复、重建和发展做出了自己的贡献。“文化大革命”结束不久，他就作为劳动经济学界的教师代表在1977年8月4日出席了在人民大会堂举行的全国劳动工资工作会议，会上受到邓小平同志的接见。受到鼓舞的袁伦渠立刻参加劳动经济学的恢复和重建工作。1977—1978年他连续参加了四次由于光远教授主持的按劳分配理论研讨会，批驳了“文化大革命”期间将按劳分配诟病为产生资本主义土壤的谬论。20世纪80年代初，他在《经济学动态》《经济研究参考》《工业经济管理丛刊》等中国社会科学院主办的期刊上发表了数篇文章，为计件工资、奖励制度等分配制度正名，同时与人合作出版《劳动工作基本知识》《劳动经济学概论》《工资福利与社会保险》等著作，发行数十万册，为广大因“文化大革命”而荒疏业务的干部和读者详细介绍了劳动就业、收入分配和社会保险的基本理论和知识。他还受劳动人事部的聘请，担任劳动人事学科主讲教师，先后为天津、陕西、广东、浙江、辽宁、广西等省市的劳动人事干部和高校专修班讲授劳动人事课程，并通过录音、录像面向全国讲授。由于知识丰富、教学认真，受到全国各地学生的好评。

改革开放后，我国的劳动经济学科取得了长足发展，这其中袁伦渠做出了自己的贡献。他历时10年，边讲边写主编了我国第一部《中国劳动经济史》，并与人合著《新中国工资史稿》，填补了我国劳动科学研究的空白，并以此为教材开设了改革开放后首次劳动经济史课程。1981年他主译改革开放后我国第一部国外《劳动经济学》教材，发行量2万余册，成为广大劳动工资干部和师生的重要参考书。1985年他主译我国第一部国外《劳动社会学》教材，并在北京大学社会学系讲授，将该学科介绍给国内学术界。他主编的《劳动经济学》教材自2002年由东北财经大学出版社出版后，至今已出版六版，先后获得北京市精品教材、北京高等教育精品课程、“十二五”普通高等教育本科国家级规划教材等多项殊荣。他还曾提出由劳动经济学、劳动社会学、劳动法学、劳动心理学、劳动卫生学、劳动保护学、劳动统计学组成劳动科学体系的见解，从而为申请劳动科学为一级学科提供了理论依据。1994年，袁伦渠被北京交通大学（当时称北方交通大学）引进。他与夫人林玳玳教授携手带领大家申请了劳动经济和社会保障的硕士点与公共管理的一级学科，在此基础上组建了劳动经济系，填补了北京交通大学经济管理学院学科领域的空白。全系至今已培养博士、硕士研究生数百名，其中不少在政界及企业界身居要职、有所建树。

其次，他对劳动经济理论的传承、创新与发展做出了自己的贡献。袁伦渠曾公开发表论文百余篇，出版专著或译著10多部，主持或参与国家级和省部级课题20余项。20世纪80年代初期，他参与国家劳动部主持的《当代中国工资福利与社会保险》重大研究项目，担任该书编委和编辑部成员，他作为主笔编写的第一章被认为是本书最好的篇章之一。20世纪90年代中期，他参与国家劳动部主持的国际合作项目“中国养老保险改革与立法研究”，并主持其中关于企业补充养老保险制度研究的子课题，较早地提出补充养老保险的实施条件、资金渠道、鼓励政策、基金分配、待遇水平和发展对策，对企业补充养老保险政策的制定提供了理论依据和参考方法。该研究公开发表的成果受到上海劳动局和北京劳动局的好评，他也因此被劳动部聘为中国社会保险法起草咨询专家。他和林玳玳教授主持的国际合作项目“中国劳动立法对外资在华企业人力资源管理的影响”，受到惠普、三星、壳牌等跨国公司的欢迎，其成果以英文在美国出版。此外，他还曾主持多项铁道部关于用工制度和劳动组织的横向课题，为铁路部门提升劳动力配置效率起到了积极作用。

袁伦渠教授为我国劳动经济学界的国际交流也做出了自己的贡献。20世纪80年代末，他受国家教委派遣赴莫斯科国民经济学院（现为俄罗斯国立经济大学）留学和讲学，师从著名劳动经济学家伊万诺夫教授。访问期间他曾在莫斯科国际学术会上发表有关中国劳动工资制度改革的俄语演讲，这是中国学者第一次向苏联东欧学者介绍中国改革开放10年来在劳动就业、收入分配和社会保险理论上的突破与实践上的探索，引起当时苏联东欧学者的极大兴趣，此讲稿以俄、英、日、西四种文字在苏联科学院主办的《远东问题》期刊1990年第1期和第2期上发表。随着中外学者学术交流的日益加深，袁伦渠教授先后去俄、日、美、韩等国讲学，并被日本立正大学聘为客座教授。2017年后，他又两次去俄罗斯访问，就劳动经济学科建设问题与俄罗斯国立经济大学、国立圣彼得堡财经大学、莫斯科高等经济大学等多所知名学府合作，并和中国人民大学、首都经贸大学共同组建了“中俄劳动科学研究网络”，从而接续了由于苏联解体而中断了20多年的中俄高校劳动经济学界的联系。

袁伦渠教授是我国劳动经济学界唯一的国务院参事。他于2004年3月至2016年3月先后被温家宝总理和李克强总理聘任为国务院参事，成为我国劳动经济学界国务院参事第一人。在担任国务院参事的12年中，他勤勉敬业、恪尽职守，他牢记为国务院领导建言献策、咨询国是的宗旨，悉心投入参事工作的多种活动。他参加总理每年主持的座谈会，参与每年政府工作报告征求意见稿的修改，就国务院领导同志关心的问题，参加相应课题组，深入第一线调查研究。他曾就总理关心的生产安全问题，亲赴各地矿山调查研究，甚至深入井下看望采煤工人，为改善矿工的劳动环境向国务院领导建言献策。参事工作卸任时，国务院参事室领导在写给北京交通大学党委的信中对袁伦渠的参事工作业绩给予了高度评价。

最后，我认为，这本论文集收录的30余篇论文，反映了改革开放之后各个时期的代表性成果，具有较高的学术与实践应用价值。

其一，本书涵盖劳动就业、收入分配、社会保障和人力资源管理等既相互独立、又彼此联系的四个部分，并运用多学科交叉的劳动科学对这四个部分进行了综合性、整体性的研究，对建立劳动科学体系具有参考意义。本书收录的文章贯穿了我国就业从“统包统配”走向劳动力市场，收入分配从“大锅饭”走向按劳分配为主的多层次分配，社会保障制度从企业保障走向社会保障多层次全覆盖的改革过程，在理论价值之外还具有丰富的历史参考价值。

其二，本书对劳动经济问题采用了宏观研究与微观研究相结合、定性与定量研究、实证与制度分析相结合的方法，纠正了计划经济体制下偏重宏观和定性分析的现象，又不同于当前我国劳动经济学界普遍“食洋不化”，片面强调微观与定量分析，而忽略我国独特历史、制度背景的现象，对于建立中国特色的劳动经济理论具有一定的指导意义。

其三，本书在我国学术界第一次提出劳动科学的学科群概念，并重点介绍了劳动社会学的理论和研究方法，结合作者在北京大学讲学的经历，将西方这一年轻的学科引入我国学术界。本书全面系统介绍企业年金的论文，得到了劳动部和上海劳动局、北京劳动局的认可，为20世纪90年代我国企业年金制度的实行提供了理论和政策依据。

此外，本书还有较高的实践应用与政策指导价值。袁伦渠教授从事劳动科学教学和研究50余年，曾在劳动部等国家机关和国务院参事室从事工作多年，多次参加国家高层学术会议，并多次应邀参加国家劳动法和社会保障立法的讨论和调研活动，积累的实际经验也反映在本书中。

“就业是民生之本，收入分配是民生之源，社会保障是民生之基”。这本论文集涉及这些重大民生问题，其理论和政策建议对相关部门，尤其对我国实现“六稳”“六保”政策具有较大参考价值，对劳动经济学科的传承与发展也具有重要的理论意义。在此，我对袁伦渠教授这部论文集得以出版表示由衷的祝贺，也诚挚地将它推荐给广大读者。

赵履宽　现任中国人民大学荣誉一级教授 博士生导师

赵履宽

2021 年 1 月

自序：52 年工作生涯

教学科研伴随一生

我于 1960 年从北京市第九中学毕业，1960—1964 年在北京经济学院（首都经济贸易大学前身）劳动经济系就读，成为我国最早开办的劳动经济专业的第二届毕业生。1964—1971 年在劳动部（现为人力资源和社会保障部）办公厅工作（“文化大革命”期间 1969—1971 年被下放到河南省的“五七”干校劳动）；1971—1975 年在铁道部丰台桥梁厂子弟学校教书；1975—1994 年任母校北京经济学院劳动经济系讲师、副教授、教授，其间 1980 年参加“社会学讲习班”，师从费孝通教授学习社会学；1988—1989 年由国家教委选拔赴苏联莫斯科国民经济学院（现为俄罗斯国立经济大学）经济系留学，师从著名经济学家伊万诺夫教授学习劳动经济学。1991 年晋升为教授，1992 年享受国务院特殊津贴，1994 年 4 月至今任北京交通大学教授、博士生导师，2007 年晋升为二级教授，2004 年 3 月至 2016 年 3 月被温家宝总理和李克强总理聘为国务院参事。

我自 1964 年参加工作至 2016 年国务院参事卸任，一生工作 52 年，除“文化大革命”几年外，绝大部分时间从事劳动经济和劳动政策的教学和研究。劳动经济学是经济学的重要组成部分，它涵盖了劳动就业、收入分配和社会保障及人力资源管理各部分。就业是民生之本，收入分配是民生之源，社会保障是民生之基，这就注定了劳动经济学是一门关注民生的理论性、政策性、实践性都很强的学科。

党的十一届三中全会后，在科学春天的鼓舞下，我决心将“文化大革命”造成的损失夺回来。我先后撰写和牵头翻译有关劳动经济和劳动政策的著作和教材 10 余部，在国内外发表论文 100 余篇，1984 年担任了中宣部组织的由邓力群、马洪、武衡主编的大型“当代中国”丛书《中国职工工资福利和社会保险卷》的编委和编辑部成员，参与本书的编写并担任工资福利部分的统稿人。专著《中国劳动经济史》论述了1940年鸦片战争以来至1985年中国就业、收入分配和社会保障制度发展演变的历史规律，出版后被国内外多家学术团体和学者所引用，作为我国第一部劳动经济史专著，填补了我国经济史研究的空白。针对“文化大革命”后国内高校劳动经济学界缺乏教材的情况，我牵头首次翻译了国外《劳动经济学》《劳动社会学》两部著作，通过在北京大学社会系讲学及发表文章将劳动社会学这门新兴的学科介绍引进到中国学术界。几十年来，劳动社会学这门学科已经在中国落地生根，成为中国高校的一门主干课程和学科。在教学方面，先后为本科生、硕士生、博士生教授过新中国劳动经济史、劳动经济学概论、现代劳动组织学、社会保障学和劳动社会学等多门课程。

1994年4月，在我近54岁的年龄被北京交通大学引进任教授和博士生导师。作为学科带头人和责任教授联合同仁先后申请并经教育部批准成立了劳动经济和社会保障两个硕士点、公共管理一级学科点以及劳动与社会保障本科专业，在此基础上组建了劳动经济系，并开始了上述学科硕士研究生和博士研究生的招生工作。近二十年来，我先后为硕士生、博士生开设了不同层次的劳动经济学、社会保障学以及人力资源管理等多门课程，培养博士生30余名、硕士生100多名。这些毕业生在社会上声誉良好，大多在劳动人事和人力资源领域工作，其中不少成为企业的高管，有的成为高校教授和博士生导师，还有的担任了政府部门的高级职务。

在科研方面，我先后参与国家级和主持省部级科研课题20余项，包括社会保障体系研究和老龄产业研究等多个方面。例如：1999—2001年我主持了美国PDIGRC（全球人力资源咨询机构）的国际项目“中国劳动社会保险立法的发展趋势及其对外资在华企业的影响”，项目完成后在国际论证会上，得到了与会的国际跨国公司高管的肯定和赞誉，促进了外资在华企业家遵守中国劳动和社会保障法的意识，达到了国内外企业合作共赢的目的，该项目成果2001年在美国纽约以英文公开出版。1998—2000年我主持并带领学生完成的铁道部项目“人工成本与铁路职工减员增效研究”第一次创造性地以人工成本核算铁路职工应配备的人数，得到了铁道部验收组的肯定，对铁路合理配备劳动力、提高生产效率起到了积极作用。2002年我根据自己几十年教学科研的积累，总结了我国改革开放以来劳动就业和收入分配的最新研究成果，借鉴国外先进经济理论和研究方法，联合首都经济贸易大学王守志教授写出了一部新的《劳动经济学》教材（著名经济学家胡代光和高鸿业为总主编的六部经济学教材之一）。该书由东北财大出版社出版后，2005 年被评为北京高等教育精品教材，以此书为教材开设的课程，被评为 2007 年北京市精品课程，2014 年被教育部评为“十二五”普通高等教育本科国家级规划教材。该书出版后至 2021 年 3 月五易其稿，已出至第六版，13 次印刷，印数约达 6 万册。目前已被数十所财经院校选为本科生教材和研究生学习参考书。

在学术交流方面，2006 年在我主持下，劳动经济系举办了全国公共管理高层论坛，荣幸地邀请到清华、北大、人大和浙大的著名教授前来参加。同年我应邀出席中国管理学会在德国举行的“世界管理学论坛”学术会议。2009 年 7 月我参加了国务院参事室组织的关于中美医疗制度比较研究课题，赴美国考察。

国务院参事工作概述

2004 年 3 月，我有幸受国务院总理温家宝聘任为国务院参事，在国务院参事室工作。国务院参事室是国务院的直属机构，国务院参事是国务院工作人员。参事们由中央各部门的阅历广、知识丰富、知名度高的专家学者组成，他们作为政府智力的支撑力量，发挥个人专长，就宏观经济和社会管理诸方面以“直通车”的形式为国务院领导同志建言献策、咨询服务。遵照《国务院参事工作条例》规定，我每年列席和旁听全国人大和全国政协两会，定期听取中央领导指示和中央文件的传达，参与总理政府工作报告（征求意见稿）的修改和每年一度的总理召开的座谈会。为不负领导的重托，每次学习讨论我都认真思考、做好书面发言，并积极参加国务院交办和参事室组织的调研活动，就国计民生和社情民意问题进行调研。

我在调研活动中特别注意根据自己的专业特长，就劳动就业、收入分配和社会保障等民生问题提出自己的建议。例如：针对我国煤矿安全事故频发的问题，2005 年 5 月至 9 月，我随国务院参事室和国家安监局调查组深入黑龙江鸡西煤矿、河南平顶山煤矿、云南曲靖煤矿，组织当地干部和工人进行多次座谈，并深入平顶山煤矿 900 米深的井下看望第一线采煤工人。我参与撰写的《关于煤矿安全生产的调研报告》《关于解决矿工工伤工亡待遇的建议》《关于煤炭行业人才培养建议的调查报告》得到了国务院领导同志的批示，对加强煤矿企业人才建设和煤矿生产安全管理起到很大的推动作用，减少了伤亡事故，提高了工亡工人的赔偿和抚恤标准。2006年3月，我参与参事集体考察湖北经济发展期间，就湖北省所有制改革、经济结构调整、农业免税、新农村建设问题谈了自己的体会，对乡镇企业工人劳动合同的签订、工人劳动保护政策的执行、失地农民的就业和经济补偿问题向湖北省政府领导提出了自己的建议，并接受了当地媒体的采访。2007年4月，在参事集体赴广西考察期间，我在自治区座谈会上就落实科学发展观以人为本、关注民生建立和谐劳动关系等问题，向自治区领导提出了建议。2010年根据政府工作报告关于缩小居民收入差距的精神，收集整理多方资料，写出《发达国家缩小居民收入差距措施》一文，该文举出的措施包括三方面：一是通过初次分配，增加劳动收入在收入分配中的比重，通过再分配严格税收制完善社会保障体系，发展慈善公益事业，完善社会救助制度；二是通过立法和竞争约束垄断行业的收入；三是规范收入秩序，限制高收入，严格财产稽查制度等规范收入。此文发表在国务院参事室主办的《国是咨询》2010年第2期供中央政治局领导参考。2014年5月我根据2014年政府工作报告精神查阅多种资料五易其稿，写出《中国劳动就业、收入分配与社会保障事业》一文，全面系统地介绍分析了中国的社会福利政策，提供给参事室领导同志赴西班牙智库国际论坛上介绍中国国情，此报告得到了国外专家学者的兴趣和热议，反映良好。该文发表在《国务院参事袁伦渠咨询国是文稿汇编(2004年3月—2016年3月)》上。2013年我参与了国务院参事室社会管理调查组，走访了五个省市，参与写出了《进一步加强政府施政过程中群众工作的建议》，响应了当时开展党的群众路线教育实践活动。上述调研报告和建议，不少得到了国务院领导同志的批示和圈阅。

2012年"两会"期间，在国务院参事室与人民网联合主办的"两会论坛"上，我发表的《退休双轨制的历史背景和解决建议》一文得到了网民们的热烈响应，在网上有160条留言，177人分享，最高点击量突破3万，对我国退休待遇双轨制并轨改革起到了促进作用（见国务院参事室主办的《国是咨询》2012年第2期第20页）。2015年6—9月，我参加国务院参事室关于专业市场与电子商务调查组，调研报告《专业市场与电子商务融合过程中存在的问题及对策建议》得到李克强总理的圈阅和批示。2016 年 8 月至 2017 年 4 月，我参与了国务院参事室“我国高校科研评价体系改革研究”课题组，提出的七条建议获刘延东副总理的批示。

此外，我根据自己的专长，就国务院法制办交来的征求意见的法律法规文件，参与讨论和修改并提出建议。例如：2011 年“关于女职工特殊保护条例”，2010 年“企业职工带薪休假条例”“中华人民共和国劳动合同法修改草案”“中华人民共和国老年权益保护法”等条例和法规，我都参与了讨论并提出了自己的修改建议。

作为国务院参事，我尤其关注社情民意工作，每年定期参加有关劳动就业社会保障的学术会，在会上就劳动保障等民生问题发表意见并提出建议。2014 年 11 月 18 日，应邀请在陈竺副委员长主持的“分析 2014 年经济形势征求 2015 年经济工作会议建议”的座谈会上，提出了科技创新对就业和创业促进作用的建议，并提交了书面发言，得到了陈竺副委员长的肯定。2015 年应“中国国际经济交流中心”（曾培炎原副总理任主任）的邀请，出席了该中心举办的“我国应对老龄化战略研究专家研讨会”，发表了“养老保险基金不足应由国有资产填充的建议”，此建议与财政部部长楼继伟后来在媒体上发表的观点相同。

在 2004 年 3 月被聘任至 2016 年 3 月卸任的 12 年参事工作生涯中，我几乎参加了国务院参事室组织的所有集体活动。2016 年 3 月 21 日卸任时，国务院参事室主任王仲伟和其他领导同志专门为我举行了欢送会，会上对我十二年的参事工作给了很高的评价，并将我十二年的部分建言献策结成《国务院参事袁伦渠咨询国是文稿汇编》（2004 年 3 月—2016 年 3 月）一册。以下是参事室领导在该书前言中对我的评价：

袁伦渠参事自 2004 年 3 月受聘为国务院参事以来，严格遵守《政府参事工作条例》，模范履行参事职责，勤勉敬业，恪尽职守，始终围绕党和政府的中心工作，深入基层一线开展调查研究，向国务院提交多篇有参考价值的参事建议，为政府科学民主决策发挥了积极作用。

袁伦渠参事在从事参事工作的 10 多年中，围绕劳动就业、收入分配和社会保障等课题深入开展调查研究，上报十余篇参事建议，均得到了国务院领导同志的批示，对加强人才建设和煤矿生产安全管理等起到了积极作用。

袁伦渠参事谦和务实，责任心强，广泛参与社会活动，积极扩大政府参事的社会影响。10 多年来，他积极参加参事集中工作日活动，主动参与我室组织的重点课题调研等各类重要活动，多次参与《政府工作报告》(征求意见稿)的修改工作，积极旁听、列席全国人大和全国政协会议。担任参事期间，他还兼任北京交通大学经济管理学院教授、博士生导师，中国劳动学会常务理事、中国社会保险学会常务理事等职务。

袁伦渠参事品格高尚，治学严谨，始终坚持以参事工作为主业，十年如一日，默默耕耘，辛勤付出，为我国教育事业和政府参事事业做出了重要的贡献。

值此袁伦渠参事离任之际，我们特将由他牵头或者参与撰写的建议汇编成册，以志纪念。

目 录

主要论著概述

我的著作和研究成果大致分为两部分：一是社会保障理论与政策研究，二是就业和收入分配理论与宏观政策研究，现将成果的主要内容和社会意义分述如下：

就业和收入分配理论与宏观政策研究

党的十一届三中全会以后，受科学春天的鼓舞，各学术领域开始对过去三十年进行回顾总结，提出新时期的历史任务。1977 年 8 月 4 日，我作为我国劳动经济学界的代表，出席了在人民大会堂举行的第一次全国工资工作会议，会上受到邓小平等中央领导的接见。为此我深受鼓舞，开始了对我国就业和收入分配理论与宏观政策的研究。在当时缺乏文献和资料的情况下，我从查阅档案和积累卡片做起，经过数年艰苦努力，按历史的分期用夹叙夹议的方法写出了 5 篇长文，这是“文化大革命”后我国最早全面系统研究就业和收入分配问题的文章。其中一篇《我国国营企业职工计件工资制和奖励制的演变》发表在中国社会科学院《工业经济管理丛刊》1980 年 1 月创刊号上，其余 4 篇先后发表在于光远先生创办的《经济研究参考》上，它们分别是《新中国成立以来我国城镇劳动就业情况》[①]《我国国营工业企业实行计件、奖励制度的过程和看法》[②]《我国工资制度沿革资料（1840—1984）》[③]《新中国成立以来劳动工资工作的成绩经验和教训》[④]。其中前 4 篇重在历史的梳理和评论，

① 发表在《经济研究参考资料》1983 年第 40 期。

② 发表在《经济研究参考资料》1984 年 6 月 8 日第 86 期。

③ 发表在《经济研究参考资料》1985 年 8 月 16 日第 124 期。

④ 发表在《经济研究参考资料》1986 年 12 月 6 日第 188 期。

第5篇则在前4篇的基础上用详尽的数据和事实论证了我国就业与收入分配的宏观政策，指出了其中的成绩、经验和教训，并提出了建议。在就业的宏观政策方面提出：（1）解决好我国的劳动就业问题最根本的措施是大力发展生产和控制人口的增长。（2）实行符合我国实际情况的经济政策和就业政策：在所有制结构上，要实行多种经济成分并存的方针；在产业结构上，实行农、轻、重工业并举，重点发展商业、服务业、饮食业的方针；在企业结构上，采用大型和中型并举的方针，积极发展中小企业；在就业概念上，提出了只要参加社会劳动并取得相应的维持生活报酬或收入的都应视为是就业（实际上提出了非正规就业）。（3）在企业劳动管理方面，提出改变单一的固定工制度，实行多种形式的用工制度，包括由职工自谋职业。（4）注意统筹城乡劳动力。在收入分配的宏观政策方面提出：（1）确定职工工资水平要从我国国情出发、统筹兼顾、适当安排：处理好发展生产，提高劳动生产率与职工工资水平的关系；处理好国民收入中积累和消费的关系，不可脱离我国实际，不要在职工中过早提出"高工资、高消费"的口号；处理好工农关系和城乡关系，要考虑职工工资水平与农民的收入水平比例，差距不能过大，这种差距应随着农业劳动生产率的提高逐步减小；处理好工资水平和扩大就业的关系。（2）坚定不移地实行社会主义按劳分配原则：解放思想，逐步改革工资制度；要打破职工吃企业大锅饭，企业吃国家大锅饭的现象；按劳分配是个人消费品分配的主要形式，但不是唯一形式，允许其他分配形式的存在。以上研究成果受到国家劳动部的重视，并已经在政策制定中作为参考。

在以上5篇论文的基础上，我于1986年同庄启东、李建立共同撰写出版了《新中国工资史稿》，1990年独自撰写了《中国劳动经济史》。《新中国工资史稿》作为我国第一部工资史专著，曾引起我国著名经济学家何建章、王积业等同志的关注，有的学者在承担的国家课题中援引本书的重要内容。法国巴黎社会经济研究所学者认为"此书资料详实，数字准确，给人的印象深刻"，并收集整理了我1980年以来此一研究方向的所有论文和著作，作了目录和索引。该所学者 Angel Pino 多次来信并到我处造访，在其博士论文中有10多处援引了该书的数字和内容。《中国劳动经济史》采用历史法，按照不同历史时期研究分析了1840—1985年各个时期我国就业与收入分配及其宏观管理政策的产生、演变和发展的历史，揭示出劳动就业制度和收入分配制度进行改革的历史必然性，论证了按劳分配为主体，多种分配形式并存的理论和企业工资总额与经济效益挂钩的理论与实践，配合了当时国有企业工资制度的改革。

我在1988年与我的学生潘功胜、熊敏鹏所著，由中国财经出版社出版的《现代劳动组织学——宏观论与微观论》一书中对劳动组织制度提出了宏观管理和微观管理的两个层次。就业的宏观管理以全社会劳动力管理为对象，分析全社会就业的部门结构、产业结构、地区结构及其变化规律。宏观劳动力就业研究采取总量分析的方法，分析国民经济各要素的总量与劳动力总量之间的相互关系。微观管理采取个量分析的方法，研究单个企业劳动组织活动的各种关系，对于一般将劳动组织只作企业内部劳动组织研究的做法是一个突破。

1988—1989年在苏联留学和访问期间，我曾在莫斯科国民经济学院（现俄罗斯国立经济大学）和列宁格勒财经学院（现圣彼得堡国立财经大学）用俄语发表了“中国劳动工资管理改革的理论与实践”的讲演，后在莫斯科国际会议上宣读，并接受了塔斯社的采访。这是我国学者第一次向苏联和东欧国家学者系统地介绍中国改革开放十年来劳动就业与工资制度改革理论上的突破和实践上的进展，引起学者们的极大兴趣，受到苏联高校及东欧学者的欢迎，此讲演稿以俄、英、日、西班牙四种文字刊登在苏联科学院《远东问题》杂志1990年第1期和第2期上。

1993年以后，我开始关注我国社会主义劳动力市场的研究，发表了论文并参与主持有关就业、工资宏观管理方面的课题。1996—1998年主持铁道部课题“‘九五’期间铁路职工总量控制和用工制度研究”，1998—2001年主持铁道部课题“铁路企业实施减员增效与再就业工程研究”，这两个课题首次将人工成本理论引入铁路企业管理，设计出铁路职工工资总额和用工形式的框架，用人工成本直接控制职工总量，从而提出了“九五”期间铁路职工总量由行政手段直接控制转向由经济手段间接控制的思路和措施，探讨出一套具有铁路特点的灵活的多种用工形式，此研究成果在成都铁路局实施。2000年《有关中国劳动力市场的几个问题》提出了中国政府规范中介机构，实行工资指导线，对就业和工资进行宏观调控的政策建议。2002年，我结合几十年教学科研的积累，总结了改革开放以来劳动就业与工资管理的研究成果，写出一部新的《劳动经济学》，在本书中联系中国实际并借鉴西方的理论与方法对中国就业、工资的宏观控制和治理做了探索，力求做到中西理论的水乳交融，避免照搬照抄和“食洋不化”，为建立中国特色社会主义就业和工资理论做出了尝试。该书出版后，2005 年被北京市教委评为北京高等教育精品教材，2014 年 10 月被评审为“十二五”普通高等教育本科国家级规划教材。至 2018 年 3 月已出第六版，至 2021 年 3 月印刷 13 次。

社会保障理论与政策研究

社会保障是国家通过立法形成专门基金，对基本生活发生困难的社会成员提供物质保障的制度。它包括社会保险、社会救助、社会优抚、社会福利以及慈善事业。社会保障的核心是社会保险，包括养老、失业、工伤、医疗、生育等保险项目。社会保障是经济体制的重要组成部分，是社会发展的“安全网”和“减震器”，是建立社会主义市场经济和现代企业制度的重要保证。

我于 20 世纪 80 年代初开始研究社会保障问题，几十年来对社会保障进行了比较深入细致的研究，先后发表论文数十篇，著作多部，承担国家和省部级课题多项，内容涉及社会保障的理论、社会保障的管理、社会保障的中外比较，社会保障的改革与发展，在国内外产生了一定的影响。我主编的《中国劳动经济史》中对中国各个时期的社会保障制度进行了梳理和分析，揭示出中国社会保障的发展演变和规律性，这是我国改革开放以后对社会保障系统全面研究的最早著作之一。我作为编委和编辑部成员参与编著的《当代中国工资福利与社会保险卷》是中宣部下达的重大研究项目《当代中国丛书》（邓力群、马洪、武衡主编）之一卷。该书从纵的历史角度和横的理论角度分析和论证了中国社会保险制度的理论和发展路径。该书出版单位中国社会科学出版社总编室书面评价说：“我社出版的‘当代中国丛书’是中宣部下达的出版项目，袁伦渠同志参加了其中《当代中国工资福利与社会保险卷》的编写，为该书编委和编辑部成员。他起草并拟定向部党组汇报的编写提纲，他撰写的第一章结构严谨、选材精当、观点与材料密切结合，在征求意见时得到了好评，是本书编写最好的篇章之一。”

20 世纪 90 年代后，我有幸参与和主持了多项国家级和省部级重大课题。1994 年参与的首批国家级重大总体研究课题“中国社会保障体系的建立与完善”经国务院协调小组鉴定认为：“突出总体，注重实用性和可操作性，定性分析与定量分析相结合”，已作为中国社会保障改革的重要依据。1992—1995 年主持的国家教委课题“社会保障体系研究”，经专家鉴定为“处于国内同类研究的领先水平”，得到国家劳动部社会保险司和铁道部劳资司的重视和肯定。1996年参与劳动部主持的国际合作项目“中国企业养老保险改革与立法研究”是一个崭新的课题，已用中英两种文字出版，得到国内外较高评价。其中我负责的子课题“中国企业补充养老保险制度研究”，较早地提出了企业补充养老保险的实施条件、资金来源、鼓励政策、基金分配、待遇水平和发展对策，为中国企业补充养老保险制度的制定提供了理论根据，推动了企业补充养老保险的试点，完善了社会保险体系。该研究报告发表在《市场与人口分析》1998 年第 5 期上，后被数家刊物转载，得到了社会及上海市劳动部门等的好评。

1994 年我作为当时北京市的人大代表，在北京市两会召开前夕提出的“北京市社会保险制度改革的建议”成为优秀提案，并被北京市有关单位采纳。1997年北京市人代会期间，我针对养老保险制度改革中社会上流行的“青年人养活老年人”的说法，写出《不要忘记离退休人员的历史贡献》一文，从理论和数据上批评了这一不正确观点，指出“离退休职工应当分享社会经济发展成果”和“养老保险金的不足应由国企资产划拨”的建议，这一超前观点直到十八年后的 2015 年才得到财政部部长楼继伟的承认和肯定①。

1999—2001 年受国际 PDI Global Research Consortia 资助，我与林玳玳教授共同带领研究生完成了国际项目“中国劳动和社会保障立法对外国在华企业人力资源管理的影响”。通过大量国内外调研，查阅大量的文献法规，参加国际跨国公司的多次研讨会，系统全面地向国外学者介绍了中国劳动法和社会保险法规的内容，指出了外国在华企业执行中国劳动法和社会保险法的现状，论述了中国劳动法和社会保险立法的趋势及对外国投资和人力资源管理的影响。此一研究对外企熟悉和遵守中国法律、正确处理外企雇主和中方员工的劳动关系，达到双方互利共赢发挥了重要作用，受到惠普、三星、壳牌等跨国公司的欢迎，成为它们在华投资管理企业的重要指导书，对推进我国招商引资、国际合作的发展作出了贡献。本研究成果的英文版（约 30 万字）于 2001 年在美国以 *Labor and Social Insurance Legislation in China: Trends and Developments For Operating*

① 参见 2015 年 3 月 23 日新京报社论《弥补养老保险不足需国有资产补充》以及 2015 年 5 月 21 日光明日报李思辉文章《划转国有资产充实社保资金是正道》，2017 年 11 月 19 日北京青年报第 8 版《避免将基本养老保险基金缺口转移给下一代人，国企国有资本 10%划转社保》。

in The New Economy 作为题目公开出版，其结论性报告在《中国人力资源开发》2001 年 5 月特刊上发表。

我于 2003 年主持完成的教育部课题“我国老龄产业发展研究”，论证分析了中国老龄产业发展的理论依据，并提供了实际操作手段，对发展医疗保健护理、家庭服务业等老龄产业，满足老龄人口的特殊需要和服务起了重要作用，从而丰富了中国养老保险制度的研究。

作为我国改革开放后最早研究社会保障制度的学者之一，我的以上的成果对我国社会保障制度的理论和实践进行了较全面系统的研究，为国家社会保障政策的制定提供了一定的参考，我也因此被劳动部邀请为《中华人民共和国社会保险法》起草咨询专家。

人生写照

名师剪影

王想平

袁伦渠教授，58 岁，北方交通大学劳动经济学博士生导师，北京市人大代表，享受国务院特殊政府津贴。在从事劳动经济理论教学和科研的 20 多年时间里，袁教授已公开发表专著、译著 10 多部，论文 100 多篇，洋洋洒洒达 250 多万字。他历经 10年时间著述的《中国劳动经济史》，是我国第一部劳动经济史专著，填补了我国劳动经济研究的空白，为构建中国劳动经济完整的体系作出了重大贡献。作为中国社会发展与社会保障研究会副理事长，袁教授先后参与了国家级重大总体研究课题“中国社会保障体系的建立与完善”以及与联合国开发计划署国际合作项目“中国社会保障制度改革与立法”等重大课题的研究，并在一些权威经济理刊物上发表 20 多篇相关学术论文，受到学术界和有关政府部门的高度重视，被聘为《中华人民共和国社会保险法》起草小组咨询专家。

◆《光明日报 · 教育周刊》1999 年 4 月 14 日第 5 版

我为人民而工作

——记北方交通大学博士生导师袁伦渠教授

1998 年 9 月 23 日，北京市市长贾庆林亲自向我国著名劳动经济学专家、北方交通大学博士生导师袁伦渠教授颁发聘书，再次聘任袁教授为北京市特约审计员。这已是袁教授连续四届、长达 8 年担任这个职务了。作为特约审计员，每年要花相当多的时间监督市审计局的工作，对这份有苦劳没酬劳的差事，袁教授相当地看重："这可是政府对我的信任，我一定要为人民尽心工作。"

朴实的言语，正是袁教授甘于奉献的人生写照。

"国家需要我，我就该回去"

转眼已是十多年前的事了。1988 年，国家教委给北京经济学院一个前往苏联作高级访问学者的指标。已经 47 岁的袁老师经过严格考试，分别获得赴加拿大和苏联留学的资格。但当时校领导考虑校内缺少既懂俄语又懂劳动经济的教师，主张袁老师去苏联留学，他愉快地服从了组织安排，前往苏联莫斯科国民经济学院留学。

1988 年 11 月袁伦渠教授在莫斯科参加国际学术会议

苏联著名的劳动经济学术权威、博士生导师伊万诺夫教授就在该校执教。袁老师作为我国劳动经济领域派往苏联的第一位高级访问学者，一到那里，就将我国自十一届三中全会改革开放以来劳动经济和实践的进展，介绍给苏联同行，同时虚心学习和钻研苏联劳动工资模式。由于国内劳动经济领域的研究起步晚，又受到“文化大革命”的破坏，当时苏联学者认为中国在这方面充其量算是个“初中生”。但袁老师刻苦认真的态度和对劳动经济研究的建树，改变了他们的看法，也深深打动了伊万诺夫教授。在全苏联高校劳动经济教研室主任参加的研讨会上，他郑重地向大家宣布，决定破格招收袁伦渠为博士研究生，在一年之内完成博士论文，授予博士学位。并力荐袁老师到苏联最高经济研究机构——苏联科学院经济所讲学。这是苏联科学院接待的改革开放后第一位劳动经济领域的中国学者。苏联科学院公开发表的刊物还用俄、英、日、西班牙四种文字刊登了袁伦渠的简历和这次学术报告的全文。

袁伦渠本想抓紧时间，在一年里念完伊万诺夫教授的博士课程。可刚过了七个月，学校就来函，希望他能尽快回国，协助组建新的专业。已经着手做中苏劳动经济比较博士论文的袁老师再一次选择了服从。“国家需要我，我就该回去。”

临别时，伊万诺夫教授对袁老师的决定深感不解。多次劝他留下。看到袁老师深深的爱国之情，伊万诺夫教授感动了，破例亲笔为袁老师写了结业鉴定书，高度赞扬袁老师劳动经济研究的成就和他爱国敬业的精神。

著作等身，淡泊名利

仔细观察袁伦渠教授，你就会发现他的右手中指已弯曲变形，左侧突出一块老茧。这是袁教授笔耕不辍、潜心写作的结果。自从研究劳动经济理论以来，袁教授已公开发表专著、译著、论文达二百多万字。每一篇专著、论文的发表都凝聚着袁教授无数的心血。

改革开放之初，由于之前“文化大革命”的破坏，我国劳动经济史的研究基本上是空白。在无资料可以借鉴的情况下，袁教授从1978年开始，一点一滴收集资料，查阅大量历史档案，并走访数十位有关领导、专家学者，历经十年的时间，写出了我国第一部中国劳动经济史专著《中国劳动经济史》。这本专著的发表，引起了国内外专家的重视，高度评价该书填补了我国劳动经济研究的空白，为构建中国劳动经济研究完整的科学体系作出了重大贡献。法国巴黎政治研究所在刊物上为该书作了书评和介绍，并派学者到袁教授家作了访谈。

不断适应经济发展形势，进行开创性学术研究，是袁教授始终坚持的学术信条。“文化大革命”后，劳动人事干部培训没有一本理想的教材，为弥补这个缺陷，他与人合编了《劳动工作基本知识》一书，这是我国“文化大革命”后最早出版的劳动经济专业的书籍之一，由于该书简明扼要，浅显易懂，五年内连续八次重版，发行50万册。

20世纪80年代我国劳动工资制度改革是经济改革的重点。袁教授以敏锐的眼光较早地对我国劳动就业和工资制度改革等问题进行深入的研究，撰写了大量论文，并与他人合著了我国第一部工资史专著《新中国工资史稿》，获得了劳动部科技进步奖。

进入20世纪90年代，随着改革的不断深化，建立完善的社会保障体系成为改革顺利推进的重要保证。作为中国社会发展与社会保障研究会副理事长的袁教授，更是义不容辞地担当起追踪理论研究前沿的重任。他先后参与了首批被国务院列入国家级重大总体研究课题“中国社会保障体系的建立与完善”以及劳动部与联合国开发计划署国际合作项目“中国社会保障制度改革与立法”等重大课题的研究。同时在一些权威经济理论刊物上发表了二十多篇相关学术论文。

在劳动经济领域的不懈探索，他取得的突出成果得到了党和政府的肯定。早在1991年，他被破格提拔为教授。1992年，获得了国务院颁发的特殊政府津贴。先后被聘为国家劳动部高级职务评审委员会委员，《中华人民共和国社会保险法》起草小组咨询专家。在袁教授从事科研、教学的三十多年里，发表专著10多本，论文六十多篇，洋洋洒洒二百多万字。这其中的酸甜苦辣，袁教授曾有过一次感人肺腑的总结：

“1964年我怀着要为祖国做一番事业的抱负从大学毕业，但不久就赶上了‘文化大革命’，白白耽误了十年的宝贵光阴。进入中年以后，我越发产生了时间上的紧迫感。我要把全部精力都投入到劳动经济专业的科研和教学中。”袁教授如是说。

说起来，你也许不会相信，这样一位惜时如金、忘我工作的经济学教授，家里却颇为清贫。几年前学校分的房子。他至今没有装修过，家里只有几把用过多年的木凳、木椅，连一个沙发也没有。家里最像样的东西是满柜子的专业书籍。作为专家，他不是不能赚大钱，而是他常常放弃机会。

从 1986 年开始，袁教授就在中央电大担任主讲教师，他在认真给电大学生赶写教材、上好辅导课的同时，也录磁带作为讲义，可袁教授只拿十多元钱一课的课时费。

作为劳动部聘任的高级专家，他每年要参加大量学术会、课题鉴定会。每次参加会，无论多远，他都坐公交车去，他的理由很简单：减少别人的负担。参加完会，他经常不要报酬。

从不计较个人利益得失。这就是袁教授身为教授，著作等身，但仍然清贫的原因。

关心群众，当好人民代表

1987 年 9 月，当时任民建北京市委主委的浦洁修大姐请袁伦渠到办公室谈话，进一步了解这位年轻经济学家成长的经历。后来在浦大姐的介绍下，他被民建北京市委直接吸收为会员，并于当年底当选为北京市人大代表，至今已连选连任三届。

袁伦渠教授与前民建中央副主席浦洁修在一起

“浦大姐多次嘱咐我们，一定要珍惜组织上的信任，珍惜人大代表的无上荣誉，发挥专长，积极参政议政。浦大姐的殷殷期望，督促我每次参加人代会都要尽己所能为民鼓与呼。”袁教授是这么说的，也是这样做的。

1988 年，袁教授第一次参加北京市人大会议。他提出了在人行横道旁应设立机动车减速、缓行标志的建议，得到了市政府的采纳。当时公安交通管理局局长甚至亲自登门对他所提的建议表示感谢。这一建议在当时对保证行人安全产生了较大作用。

在改革开放不断推进的 20 世纪 90 年代，劳动经济领域的各项改革，成为关系亿万人民切身利益的大事，这为在这一领域学有专长的袁教授，更高质量地参政议政创造了条件。1994 年，他在人代会上提出了加快养老保险改革的建议，受到北京市有关部门的高度重视，对加快北京市养老保险制度改革起到了促进作用。由于袁教授对社会保险研究有较深的造诣，这以后每年人代会，袁教授都成为新闻媒体关注的焦点人物。1993 年他在北京电台对居民播讲了社会保险知识，1995 年 4 月人代会期间，北京电视台对袁教授作了专访。《北京青年报》作了专题报道，在社会上引起积极反应。

1997 年，袁教授受动物园社区 29 户居民群众的委托，到该区进行了为期半年的调研，协调了海淀区政府、北京市煤气公司和市有关单位，解决了该区六栋几十户居民多年来未解决的煤气做饭问题。该区居民给北京交通大学党委送来“人民的好代表——袁伦渠”锦旗一面。

由于工作突出，袁教授多次受到民建北京市委的表彰，被评为参政议政先进会员。

◆ 中共北京市委统战部、北京海外联谊会主办，《诤友》，1999 年第 9 期总第 69 期

寸心难表电大情

——访主讲教师袁伦渠教授

本报记者 赵向华

袁伦渠，1940 年生，原籍山东金乡人，北京经济学院劳经系教授、研究生导师。北京市第十届人大代表。1986 年起担任中央电大劳动经济学课程主讲教师。

“电大作为成人教育的一种形式，是顺应了世界教育发展趋势的。‘秀才不出门，便知天下事’的时代已经过去，在今天高科技飞速发展、知识不断更新的形势下，在职人员要想跟上时代发展步伐，就得继续学习，而电大为这种学习提供了最好的机会，这是普通高校所不能比拟的。”袁伦渠教授在接受本报记者采访时，首先肯定了电大这种办学方式的必要性。

正是基于对电大的这样一种认识，袁教授任电大主讲教师以来，一直兢兢业业，恪尽职守，以其令人瞩目的学术成果和认真负责的工作态度赢得了电大师生的好评。

袁教授是 1986 年开始为电大当主讲教师的，当时，他除担当着本校教学

工作，还在北京市《社会与社会调查》刊物任编委兼编辑。百忙之中，他仍积极为电大赶写教材，并认真做好广播录音课的所有工作。1987 年 4 月，袁教授应邀去天津，6 月又去大连为电大的辅导教师上培训课。每到一地，他常常顾不上休息就上课，200 多人的大课，一天连讲五六节，晚上还要为学生解疑答难，忙到深夜。短短时间内，袁教授不但广泛接触了电大人，更深深地了解了电大事业，1987 年底，袁教授当选为北京市第九届人大代表。工作更忙了，但为了及时指导电大学生学习，他仍坚持写了大量辅导文章，每年一次的复习录像课及出考题，他也是从形式到内容，一一细问，斟酌再三。

自从研究劳动经济理论以来，袁教授译著达 250 万字之多。由于常年写作，他的右手中指已弯曲变形。1991 年，他因出色的研究成绩被评为教授，成为当时全国屈指可数的最年轻的教授之一。多年来，袁教授只知著书讲学，从不计较利益得失。为电大授课这些年，袁教授倾尽了耗费一生心血所研得的学问，当他以几元钱一课的报酬为电大录课时，有人仅靠笔录他的讲课内容便赚取了数百倍的金钱。当人们以此向他开玩笑时，他却很不以为然。想到自己将知识传给后人，袁教授自问无憾。并且，他认为通过电大这种特殊的授课方式，在使学生接受知识的同时，也扩大了劳动经济专业在全国的影响，为学科以后的发展创造了条件。为此，他还要感谢电大。

袁教授著书一生，清贫如水，然而对自己有缘登上电大讲坛，袁教授却看作是此生一大荣耀。袁教授热爱电大，信任电大，他认为，电大是进门容易出门难，教师学生不见面，考试出题库，没有真本事别想走出校门，为这样的学生讲课，袁教授说“值”。自从为电大讲学以来，袁教授结识了许多学生朋友，至今还与他们保持着联系。他含笑告诉记者，现在去外地出差，有时会遇路人以“袁老师”相称，那都是些在电视上认识了他的学生。

作为电大工作了多年的主讲教师，袁教授十分愿意继续为电大工作，他让记者转达他对电大学生的期望：努力进取，积极向上，力争达到和超过普通高校学生的水平。

◆《中国电大报》1994 年 4 月 22 日第 3 版

劳动经济问题[①]

REFORM, WORK, SALARIES AND WAGES

The Chinese economic reform whose main objective, among others, is to improve the people's living standards and fully satisfy their basic requirements, is now more than ten years old. These objectives can be achieved only through rapid scientific and technical progress, higher labour efficiency, development of commodity-money relations, and a transition from administrative to economic methods of running the economy. Restructuring society's production relations so as to harmonize the interests of the state, the collective and the individual through the development of commodity and money relations and greater independence of individual producers, is an important condition for the achievement of these objectives and the main direction of economic reform.

In this context, a labour and wages reform is an essential component of the overall reform in China. The socio-economic policy of "self-reliance", which originated in the 1950s and was epitomized in such slogans as "Learn from Daqing in industry" and "Learn from Dazhai in agriculture", led to the appearance of economic units that had weak mutual ties and were managed directly from the centre. The reduction or a complete lack of direct economic links between enterprises erected higher social barriers and impeded social mobility. As a result,

① 本文源于 1988 年 11 月本人在莫斯科国际学术会议上做的题为"中国劳动工资管理改革的理论与实践"的演讲；该演讲稿经过修改完善，以俄、英、日、西班牙四种文字刊登在苏联科学院《远东问题》期刊上，英文稿发表在 1990 年第 2 期上。

the Chinese work force was rigidly fixed to its production units (factories, institutions, people's communes, etc.) and denied the opportunity to make independent economic decisions as to its next place of residence, job, purchases of goods above the established norms and so on. At the same time, the job inheritance system came into being when young blue- and white-collar applicants could find employment only when their next of kin retired. Moreover, the standards of living declined from 1957 to 1978. According to the State Statistical Agency of China, the average employee's wages dropped from 637 yuan in 1957 to 602 yuan in 1977, the rationed consumption of staple foods also went down: from 203 kg per capita in 1957 to 195.5 kg of grains in 1978, and from 2.4 to 1.5 kg of vegetable oil, respectively.[1] This considerably diminished the labour activity of the masses which were not interested in increasing their labour efficiency. The system of production relations failed to combine the interests of the state, the collective and the individual, seriously aggravating the economic crisis by the late 1970s in China.

The practice of economic reform showed that many measures designed to develop society's commodity and money relations, increase enterprises' economic independence and ensure a transition from administrative to economic methods of management could not be implemented without a comprehensive reform of labour and remuneration. Only a departure from the 1960-1970s system of the "big pot" and the "iron rice bowl" can provide the requisite material and moral incentives for every enterprise and employee to boost the material and technical level of production, to raise the level of education and vocational training, improve the quality of products and labour productivity of every worker, every enterprise and on a nationwide scale. By stimulating the interest of every employee in his labour, the labour and wages reform can help achieve the main objectives of the economic reform.

The labour and wages reform is acquiring particular significance for the PRC, which has the biggest population, making it the world's richest country in labour resources. By the end of 1986 China numbered 510 million of economically active population, with the work force of cities and villages amounting to 130 million (or

25.5 per cent). Some 93.33 million (72.9 per cent) were employed by state-owned enterprises, 34.21 million (26.1 per cent) by collectively owned enterprises, and 550,000 (0.4 per cent) by enterprises belonging to other forms of ownership. In the Seventh five-year plan period (1986-1990), the number of employees in towns and the countryside is to approach the 100-million mark, including 30 million in towns and settlements, i. e. the average number of job applicants will be 6 million per year. As the economic reform gains momentum in urban areas and productivity rises, enterprises will face a mounting redundancy problem. The share of redundant employees at enterprises is estimated at 15-20 per cent, and another 15 million jobs have to be created. Furthermore, as the household contract system developed in the countryside it released a great number of workers that have to be placed in the non-agrarian sphere. Selective surveys indicate that the redundant work force in the countryside amounts to over one-third of the total (or over 100 million persons). It is an important task of the labour reform to provide jobs for this mass of job applicants.

THE WORK FORCE MANAGEMENT REFORM

The work force management system reform in the PRC started after the Third Plenary Meeting of the 11th CPC Central Committee (December of 1978). It included a reform of the system of job placement, the use of work force at enterprises, labour planning and establishment of labour services companies.

Under the highly centralized system of economic management, China for a long time applied the system of "single hiring and distribution" (*tongbao tongpei*). It boiled down to the following: graduates of universities, specialized secondary and vocational schools, as well as demobilized men and officers of the People's Liberation Army from cities and villages were sent by the state to state-owned enterprises; the rest of the work force of cities and villages was sent by local labour agencies to state-owned or collectively owned enterprises; relatives of retired workers of state enterprises "inherited" their jobs.

The system had played its active role in history, but time revealed its drawbacks such as: (1) excessive personnel at many enterprises and declined labour productivity; (2) its inability to provide broad job opportunities; (3) the undermining of people's morale; (4)inducing some cadre workers to cheat.

The main reasons for those drawbacks lay in excessive concentration of power in the hands of the state, centralization of the management system. Using absolute indicators the state determined the number of white- and blue-collar workers in all areas and sectors. Regions, sectors and enterprises had no say in management which was based exclusively on administrative orders, methods of economic regulation being non-existent. This gave rise to a gap between planned targets and the production reality and economic efficiency; nobody was interested in cutting the number of employees.

To meet the requirement of revitalizing the economy and pursuing the "open policy" China carried out a reform of the work force management system. Its main direction was a transition from the labour force plan formed according to the number of employees to the plans based on the wages and salaries fund.

In 1980 the CPC Central Committee called a national conference on employment in Beijing, in 1981 the Central Committee and the State Council developed "Some Decisions on Opening Wide Opportunities of Employment, Revitalizing the Economy, Job Placement in Cities and Villages" and laid out a policy with regard to the job-placement reform, namely a combination of different forms of developing the economy, conducting the course of "combining three approaches" (*sang jiehe*) in employment (i. e. job placement by the state and on recommendation of local employment agencies; independent search for a job, and independent creation of a job). [2]

A characteristic feature of the course was a transition from reliance on state-owned enterprises as the only opportunity of finding employment to a variety of employment in the state, collective and individual sectors; job opportunities were thus substantially broadened. The job-placement activity was considerably developed within the framework of this course. In 1979-1987 some 70 million residents of cities and villages were given jobs and 98 per cent of those on the waiting list obtained jobs. The structure of employment underwent considerable changes, the share of those employed in the collective and individual sectors was constantly growing. For example, in 1987 of all those who found employment at enterprises of cities and villages 32.7 per cent went to the state sector, 45 per cent to the collective sector, 9 per cent to the individual sector, and 13.3 per cent obtained temporary jobs.

The course meant a breakaway from the traditional employment theory and policy in the PRC, it became an important landmark in the history of employment. Its introduction stimulated the job-placement effort.

For a long time Chinese enterprises applied the system of "permanent" workers. A worker would be hired for life if he was put on the personnel roll of an enterprise; he could get a discharge only in exceptional cases, and the enterprise could not fire him. As a result, the work force became the property of an enterprise or a department, while the enterprise could not select those it needed for production, and the workers could not choose the enterprise that would suit their training and desire, which affected the effectiveness of both the workers and enterprises.

A number of changes were introduced in the use of the work force at enterprises after the Third Plenary Meeting of the 11th Central Committee to eliminate these shortcomings. The employment System abandoned the system of hiring relatives of retired employees (*zinu dingti*), "turned its face to society", declared free hiring, comprehensive examinations and selection of the best candidates. The new hiring procedure raised the requirements for skills of selected workers, helped to overcome the "wrong style" of hiring and to promote young people.

A recently introduced system of labour contracts led to a reform of the system of "permanent" workers. With society owning the means of production, the system of labour contracts that meant equitable agreements between an enterprise and its employees, clearcut rights and duties of both sides, regulates a new type of employment. The main features of the new system of labour relations are: the signing of a labour agreement on a voluntary and equitable basis by both sides, mandatory observance of the agreement by the sides; an equal political and economic status of contracted and permanent workers; the creation of a system of social insurance for contracted workers to guarantee their living standards; severance or extension of the contract on its expiry by agreement of the sides; during temporary lay-offs contracted workers become the responsibility of labour services companies.

Practice has shown that the system of labour contracts which is being introduced now is a major reform in the use of the work force at enterprises. It helps to eliminate the defects of the system of permanent workers and takes care of the interests and mutual choice of both sides—the enterprise and the worker. It promotes closer ties between the workers and means of production and improves economic efficiency. In April of 1988 7.51 million of contracted workers (or 7.8 per cent of all white-collar and blue-collar workers) were employed at state-owned enterprises.

In addition to contracted labour, a reform has recently been carried out in the system of permanent workers employed at many enterprises. Since 1984, in addition to contracts, some enterprises have created teams with improved organization of work (*youhua laodong zuhe*) to change the system of permanent workers. In spite of the overall administrative management of the enterprise, such teams are created by office and shop-floor workers on a voluntary basis. The workers elect team-leaders from among the established staff, and the team-leaders select workers for their teams. Under the system, labour contracts are signed at different levels—between the plant and shops, between shops and teams, and between teams and individuals. Labour contracts clearly spell out the rights and duties of both sides, the duration of contracts, wages and salaries, as well as penalties for violations of contracts, and so on. Workers with a good performance record can extend their contracts. Those with a poor record see their contracts severed or are offered lower-paid jobs and smaller bonuses. If any changes are introduced in a contract during the expiry period the contract is extended.

Two factors merit attention in the system of teams with improved organization of work: assignments are distributed with regard to the health and age of employees; surplus labour is redistributed at the enterprise, e. g. it may set up a new shop, a services division, a new unit which is fully self-sufficient. An enterprise may also organize advanced training and retraining courses, create new jobs and so on.

By late August of 1988 there were 26,000 state-owned enterprises at which 9.6 million permanent workers formed teams with improved organization of work (or 12 per cent of permanent workers and office employees). The reform has produced initial results: labour discipline has improved, office and shop-floor workers have become more active, excessive personnel has been cut, and all of these enterprises have performed better.

Labour services companies are an important form of job placement. They are responsible for organization, training, relocation, and regulation of functions of economically active population, and are a so-called reservoir of society's work force. Labour services companies developed fairly rapidly in the 1980s and managed to alleviate the employment problem in many cities and towns where school leavers formed a major part of excess labour. During the economic reform the companies performed the following functions: issued recommendations for placement of the unemployed; directed them to local enterprises to fill temporary slots; set up their own production facilities and services and offered jobs there. They became an important part of the reform of the system of labour management in the PRC which helps solve the employment problem and ensure the most effective use of workers according to skills.

The work force management reform attaches great importance to a reform of the managerial and administrative cadre system whose main objective is finding able, gifted professionals and managers and their most rational use.

The creation and introduction of a system of civil servants have been the main aspect of this reform. The system is a coherent scientific system of managing the personnel and includes categories of posts, examinations, a system of fines and bonuses for performance, promotion and demotion mechanism, training and retraining programmes, salaries and social insurance benefits scales, retirement schemes and dismissal rules, guarantees of rights, discipline regulations, and other management tools. It is characterized by equality, competitiveness and selection of the best candidates. All civil servants have to pass open examinations. Everybody is granted equal opportunities to take such exams whose results enable the state to select the best. An important feature is the use of bonuses for good performance which is the main criterion of assessing their work. Strict inspections will be carried out to assess the work of civil servants, with the results affecting their promotion, salaries, bonuses and fines.

Another essential factor is legal regulation of employment and use of the work of civil servants. Selection, promotion, salaries, retirement and other instruments of managing the work of civil servants must abide by law, and nobody has the right to violate existing laws and by-laws. During the reform strict demands were made of the performance, discipline, etc., of civil servants.

The main aim of the above-mentioned reform is to create, within five years, a skeleton of the system which is to be introduced on a wide scale. The policy documents were the Instruction on Civil Servants and a set of resolutions that were gradually implemented by central authorities and at the level of provinces and cities, Administrators were made civil servants through examinations and inspections, state and local administrative schools, were set up, and a system of training civil servants was gradually developed.

At present Temporary Instruction of Civil Servants and another series of resolutions are being discussed in the PRC, personnel is intensively trained, experiments are made in some provinces, cities and departments.

The system of personnel management is expected to include competition and selection; a mechanism of competitions is gradually created also for managers in cultural, scientific, educational and health establishments. For example, if the system of personnel management is or can be used it should be adopted, if it cannot, competition-based invitations should be utilized. Officials for international organizations should be selected on the basis of openness, equality and competition, outside their own departments, uniform rules of hiring and examination should apply.

Intellectuals have an important role to play in training and selecting professionals with higher and secondary specialized education. The new system of hiring to special technical positions is based on competitive invitations. Gradual improvement of a system of remuneration received by intellectuals, in accordance with specific features of science, education and health care, creates a relatively independent system of payment. The question of creating a system of remuneration for civil servants is also under consideration. A "double choice" approach is gradually introduced in the PRC: professionals choose organizations, and organizations select professionals; this makes for a better choice, the specialists are promoted more quickly, their salaries and social insurance benefits increase.

THE REFORM OF WAGES AND SALARIES IN THE PRC

The system of wages and salaries inherited from the old China was dismantled after the formation of the PRC. By 1956 a new system had been created which later evolved into a nationwide system of remuneration to workers and office employees. Its main feature is a uniform scale of pay, a single form of compensation, uniform criteria of compensation established by the state for workers and office employees of state-owned enterprises, staffs of scientific, educational, health care and cultural establishments; a system of gradual increases in pay was also introduced. The system had existed for about 30 years before the nationwide reform in 1985. Since 1985 the PRC has started to gradually change the system in order to dovetail it with the overall economic reform and production requirements.

Prior to the wages reform in 1985 most enterprises applied an eight-category pay scale, with some using a seven-category scale (e. g. in capital construction) and a six-category scale (in some sectors of the light industry), the textile industry paid for a job. Office workers, technicians and engineers are paid according to their grade. The predominant forms of compensation at enterprises are pay by the hour and a system of bonuses, some enterprises employ piece-rate pay. Special benefits, in addition to regular wages and salaries, are paid to factory and office workers who work under special conditions, e. g. miners, prospectors and construction workers. Those working in remote areas (e. g. in SUAR or Tibet) draw additional pay for working in such areas and for their household needs.

Yet the old system did not meet the needs of the economic reform. Its main defect was that enterprises drew from the "big pot of the state", and factory and office workers from the the "big pot of the enterprise". The former caused particular concern. There was no interdependence between staff costs and an enterprise's performance, all workers and office employees of the same category drew the same pay irrespective of how badly or well their enterprise worked. This led to wage levelling, and each pay rise was determined in accordance with norms and directives issued to enterprises to raise the categories of their employees. Enterprises suffered great losses, yet wages and salaries remained stable.

Enterprises thus had no say whatsoever in determining the pay of their employees, neither did they have sufficient incentive for better performance, which drastically reduced the activity of both employees and enterprises.

To eliminate the shortcomings of levelling and to boost economic performance of enterprises it was decided to launch a gradual reform of wages and salaries in 1985. At present it is in the stage of discussion and experimentation.

Most enterprises apply what is called "floating" bonuses that are contingent on effective management, with the employees' material interests being combined with production management. The former system of uniform distribution of bonuses by the state irrespective of management performance was changed. However, an enterprise will have to pay a tax if it exceeds the sum allocated for bonuses. The limit now is an average of four months' pay per employee, in this case the tax is not paid. While a progressive tax is paid on sums in excess of this limit.

About 14 million employees of over 3,300 big and medium enterprises (26 per cent of the total number of industrial enterprises, capital construction, and transport, and 38 per cent of all employees) are paid on the basis of their performance.

One of the main forms of remuneration is payment on the basis of the output, for example, at coal mines the fund of wages and salaries is calculated on the basis of one ton of coal mined. Another form makes the fund dependent on the cost of products, e. g. the size of the fund is proportionate to each 100 yuan of products on capital construction projects. Moreover, the fund depends on profits, taxes and so on.

A regulatory tax is levied on enterprises whose wages and salaries funds grow too quickly, this is done to ensure the state's effective control over the consumption fund and to prevent excessive disparity between the funds of different enterprises. Enterprises at which the fund grows at an annual rate of not more than 7 per cent are tax-exempt. A regulatory tax is levied on the surplus, and a progressive tax is applied to the rest of the fund.

The scale of rates of office and shop-floor workers of enterprises is being simplified. Uniform wage rates have been established for workers of state-owned enterprises. The former 300-odd wage rates were replaced by 11; each district has only five wage rates. The new wage-rates were applied to increase the pay of first-category workers, the ratio of wages of the first and eight-category workers is now one to three.

Office employees of enterprises are paid according to their grade, with each grade divided into several categories. All in all, there are nine norms of pay in the PRC, with only three in each district. The lowest pay of workers equals that of office employees. The highest pay of managers is twice that of the highest wages of workers, at big enterprises it is 1.9 times higher, and 1.7 times at medium-size enterprises. Categories of workers and office employees are raised in accordance with the new wage-rates. The pay at small state-owned and collectively owned enterprises is set by districts, in accordance with their specific conditions.

Enterprises now have more freedom to distribute wages, salaries and bonuses among their employees, since they have become contingent on the economic effectiveness of enterprises. For example, they can now decide on the use of their bonuses funds, fix piece-rate wages, raise categories of workers and so on.

The pay system for employees of state-owned scientific, educational and health care establishments is being changed for the first time since 1956. The system of position-related salaries existed for 30 years, until 1985: there were 28 categories for administrators, 18 in higher educational establishments, 21 in the health care sector, and so on. Bonuses were also paid.

A reform of salaries in state organizations and institutions started in 1985: a system of structured salaries has been introduced with a pay for position as its core (i. e. a salary consists of four parts: basic salary, pay for position, for seniority, and bonuses).

The basic salary ensures minimum living standards for personnel—from managers to technicians. The rates are identical for all. This is not to be confused with a so-called "rationally low salary" introduced in the late 1950s which included a basic salary plus pay for position.

Pay for position is the main part of the structured salary reflecting the principle of payment for the work done. The pay is fixed on the basis of duties, responsibility and complexity of work. Office employees are paid according to their duties and change in pay corresponds to that in position. Each position is subdivided into several categories to assure promotion according to performance.

Pay for seniority increases every year of an office employee's service for an organization. In addition to pay for seniority, teachers of primary and secondary schools, secondary specialized educational establishments and vocational schools, educators and nurses of kindergartens and creches are paid increments for pedagogical seniority and increments for that work.

Bonuses are paid for contribution to work, it is not recommended to divide bonuses equally among the staff. As a rule, average annual bonuses amount to 1.5 basic salary.

The structured salary which is based on pay for position is a big step forward compared to the previous system. It has the following advantages. First, each of its four parts that reflects different functions of remuneration plays a different role. A part of the structured salary may be increased or decreased when necessary during current changes. Second, it emphasizes the relationship between remuneration and position, as well as categories that determine pay rates; that is why there is a balance between remuneration and duties and contribution to work, which makes it possible better to implement the principle of pay according to work. Third, a system of increments was devised for seniority, work in education and health care, as well as a system of raising the categories, which entailed gradual increases in salaries.

The reform of salaries in state organizations and institutions is only in its initial stage, it will probably not be able to solve all problems of remuneration that must be gradually resolved during China's economic development.

SOME SOCIAL ASPECTS OF THE REFORM OF LABOUR AND WAGES AND SALARIES

The reform of labour and wages and salaries has not yet brought about drastic changes in the social structure of Chinese workers and office employees. The working class is still dominated by "permanent" workers, office employees, by cadres of state institutions and enterprises, and their incomes only marginally depend on the quantity and quality of work. One hundred and seventy-two state-owned enterprises of Pinggu county, a Beijing suburb, dispensed with the eight-rate system and pay their employees according to their labour contribution; for instance, in trade and construction wages and salaries depend on revenue and the amount of work done. In sectors that have no tangible criteria-science, design bureaus, etc., remuneration depends on the position. Structured multi-factor wages and salaries are paid to old cadre workers, technicians and engineers in the services, in supply and procurement cooperatives, and catering facilities. Thus, during the reform China started a transition from a rigid system of pay by the hour to concrete accounting of the quantity and quality of work done by each employee. [3] The reform of labour and wages that began in the late 1970s could not but affect the social structure of Chinese society, primarily the social structure of the working class.

China's working class has preserved from the late 1950s different forms of employment—"permanent" workers (*gudinggong*), "temporary" workers (*linghsigong*), "contracted" workers (*hetonggong*), workers "above the plan" (*jihuaiwai yonggong*), "seasonal" workers (*jijiegong*), and "workers-cum-peasants" (*yi gong yi nong*). Neither contract labour, nor "teams of improved labour" and "labour markets" have yet brought about any dramatic changes in the 30-year old social structure of the working class. "Permanent" workers predominated among Chinese blue- and white-collar workers in the mid-1980s, the share of "temporary" workers was rather high, while the share of "contracted" workers remained small. In 1985 out of 86.6 million workers, in the state sector 73.3 million (84.6 per cent) were "permanent" workers and office employees, 2.0 million (2.4 per cent)—"contracted" workers, 2.3 million (2.6 per cent)—"temporary" workers, and 9.0 million (10.4 per cent) — "workers above the plan". [4]

Yet the reform of labour and wages has made it possible to take important steps towards removing social barriers that evolved in the 1960s and 1970s between different groups and strata of the country's working class, between different categories of office employees and between blue- and white-collar workers. The introduction at enterprises, in organizations and institutions of the new forms of employment and the use of the new forms of payment, depending on the performance of the enterprise and of the individual worker, stimulated labour activity related to the introduction of a mechanism of competition for both retaining jobs and for employment opportunities. Yet employment problems have become more acute in many districts, especially along the coast, with a higher level of production mechanization and automation, and a higher equipment-to-worker ratio. This applies in particular to Guangzhou where over 100,000 persons are looking for jobs. The main reasons are as follows: (1) the creation of "teams of exemplary labour" ousted some workers out of their jobs; (2) the natural increase in the work force by 80,000 persons in 1989; (3) growing unemployment caused by structural changes in production (more investment is now poured into one job); (4) the expansion of the system of contract labour. Every year this increases the number of dismissed workers, as well as workers whose contracts expire; (5) the law on bankruptcy of enterprises has entered into force. [5]

On the whole, the growing social mobility which is largely due to the reform of labour and remuneration, is designed to generate in the future a noticeable growth in social activity of the working class and improved labour productivity, which eventually will be an important prerequisite for achieving the main goals of the economic reform in China.

NOTES:

[1] Zhongguo tongji nianjian. 1981 (China's Statistical Yearbook), Beijing, P. 426; Zhongguo shehuei tongzi ziliao (Chinese Social Statistics), Beijing, 1985, p. 76.

[2] Employment on recommendation of an employment office means being hired by state-owned and big collectively owned enterprises and organizations under a state plan; independent search for employment—employment at all types of collective enterprises; independent creation of a job is self-employment.

[3] *Renmin ribao*, March 5, 1989.

[4] *Tongzi*, 1985, No. 9, p. 47.

[5] *Renmin ribao,* April 2, 1989.

新中国成立30多年以来劳动工资工作的基本经验①

新中国的劳动工资工作，从1949—1985年30多年的发展历程来看，既有丰富的经验，也有教训。因此，认真总结一下经验教训，分清一些重大问题上的是非，对于解决我国劳动工资工作面临的理论和实际问题，开创这一工作的新局面，具有重大意义。要完成这一任务，远非我的能力所及。在这里，我仅试图从劳动管理和工资分配两个方面谈一些自己粗浅的看法。

一、我国劳动管理方面的基本经验

我国人口数量居世界首位，是世界上劳动力资源最丰富的国家。如何把这么多的劳动力组织起来，在国民经济各部门之间合理分配，并不断提高劳动者的政治文化技术素质，以适应建设社会主义物质文明和精神文明的需要，是一项长期而艰巨的任务。

新中国成立初期，面对旧社会遗留下来的大批失业人员，国家在积极恢复和发展生产的基础上，通过介绍就业、转业训练、以工代赈、组织生产自救和回乡生产、发放救济金等多种措施，帮助失业人员就业和解决就业前的生活困难，同时鼓励失业人员自谋出路。由于生产建设事业发展得快，并采取了较灵

① 本文选自1990年北京经济学院出版社出版的《中国劳动经济史》一书。

活的就业政策，到1956年，旧社会遗留下来的400多万失业人员绝大多数得到安置，基本上解决了失业问题。以后城镇劳动就业的重点，便转移到对新成长的劳动力的安排方面。30多年来，先后安排了城镇大量新成长的劳动力就业。特别是党的十一届三中全会以来，调整了所有制结构和产业结构，实行劳动部门介绍就业、自愿组织起来就业和自谋职业相结合的方针，全面加强了对就业工作的领导，使劳动就业工作取得了更大成绩。1978—1985年全国城镇新安置近6 000万人就业。1985年全国全民所有制单位职工人数达到8 990万人，比1952年增加了4.68倍；城镇集体所有制单位的职工人数达到3 324万人，比1952年增加143倍；城镇个体劳动者人数达239万人，比1956年增加13.9倍。1985年我国职工队伍由1949年的800万人增加到12 358万人，失业率仅为1.8%，使我国成为世界上就业最充分的国家之一。

30多年来，我国职工队伍的文化技术业务水平有了明显的提高。新中国成立前，工人中文盲半文盲占很大比重。现在一般具有初中毕业文化程度，不少人受到高中或中等专业教育。培养中等技术工人的技术学校得到迅速恢复和发展。1984年全国共有技工学校3 400多所，在校学生50多万人，新中国成立以来技工学校毕业生累计达到230多万人，其中大多数都已成为生产建设的骨干。企业普遍建立了学徒培训制度，进厂从事技术工作的新工人，一般要经过2～3年的学徒培训，掌握一定技能以后才能转为正式工人。随着高等和中等专业教育的发展，全民所有制单位中拥有的中等以上工程技术人员的比重不断提高，从而改变了新中国成立前那种大量产品不能制造，许多建设项目不会设计和施工，大批技术设备不会操作使用的状况。我国基本依靠自己的职工力量，建立了比较完整的国民经济体系以及门类比较齐全的工业体系和科学研究体系。与此同时，我国普遍建立了各项劳动管理制度，如劳动就业、劳动计划、劳动力招收调配以及进行企业内部劳动管理的定员、定额制度等。这些制度的制定和实行，有利于生产建设事业的发展，促进了劳动生产率的提高。

但是，30多年来，我国在劳动管理工作上也有值得吸取的经验教训，这就是：只有坚持统筹兼顾、适当安排的方针，把社会和企业劳动力管理搞好，才能推动城镇劳动就业工作的顺利开展。

第一，要解决好我国的劳动就业问题，安排好人民生活，最根本的措施是大力发展生产和控制人口的增长。社会主义制度的建立，为生产力的发展和实现充分就业创造了条件，但是如果发生了认识上的错误，举措不当，也会产生待业问题，这已被20世纪60年代和70年代的历史事实所证明。要解决好我国城镇劳动就业问题，最根本的措施是发展生产和控制人口的增长。

第二，在城镇劳动就业方面，还必须从我国人口多、底子薄的国情出发，实行符合我国实际情况的经济政策和就业政策。长期以来，由于“左”的错误思想的影响，包得过多，统得过死，束缚了各方面的积极性，损害了建设事业的发展。在劳动管理方面，从多种就业方式逐渐演变为国家对城镇劳动力实行“统包统配”的制度，城镇劳动就业的多种渠道被堵塞，只剩下政府统一分配，路子越走越窄。鉴于这些教训，在所有制结构上，要实行多种经济成分并存的方针，在保证国营经济占领导地位的情况下，积极发展各种类型的集体经济，并发展适当数量的个体经济。在产业结构上，要实行农业、轻工业、重工业并举和物质生产部门与非物质生产部门协调发展的方针，特别要重点发展商业、饮食业、服务业、修理业等为生产、生活服务的各种事业，改变重工业畸形发展，农业、轻工业，特别是为人民生活服务的各种事业严重落后的状态。在企业结构上，采取大型和中小型并举的方针，在保证国家拥有必须的大型企业的同时，积极发展中小型企业，使大中小企业成龙配套，协调发展。总之，要发展多种经济成分和多层次的经济结构，这样既可以促进生产较快发展，又能提供更多的劳动岗位，有利于就业问题的解决和劳动生产率的提高。

在就业问题上，要破除那种多年来形成的只有国家“统包统配”，安排到全民所有制和大集体工作才算就业的思想。应当明确承认，只要参加社会劳动并取得相应的维持生活的报酬或收入的，都应看作是就业。只有在城镇居民有就业要求、具有劳动能力，但没有机会参加取得相应报酬或收入的社会劳动的情况下，才能称为失业。没有就业要求、缺乏劳动能力，或已经参加有报酬或收入的劳动和其他类似情况，都不应当称为待业。为了发挥各方面的积极性，创造更多的就业机会，必须坚持贯彻执行1980年中央劳动就业会议提出的政府介绍就业、劳动者自己组织起来就业和个人自谋职业相结合的就业方针，以便动员各方面的力量，搞好就业工作。

第三，在企业劳动管理方面，要改变单一的固定工制度，实行多种形式的用工制度，把企业劳动管理搞好。由于长期“左”的错误，企业原来实行的比较灵活的用工制度被改变为单一的固定工制度，企业劳动力只能进不能出，一经录用，终生在职，企业之间劳动力合理流动十分困难，影响了劳动者个人和企业的积极性，不利于改善企业管理和提高劳动生产率，弊病很多。因而有必要实行多种形式的用工制度，把企业劳动管理搞活。企业除了对新招收的工人实行合同制以外，对原有的固定工制度也必须进行相应的改革，将它纳入劳动合同制的轨道，逐步做到合理使用，人尽其才。企业要建立健全定员定额管理制度，根据生产发展变化，随时改进劳动组织。机构设置、人员配备要力求精干，少用人多办事。因客观情况发生变化而出现劳动力多余的时候，应及时将多余人员调离原岗位，妥善加以安排。

第四，大力发挥劳动服务公司的作用。为了搞活社会劳动力管理，需要有一个社会机构加以保证。近年来各地陆续发展起来的劳动服务公司就是一个较好的形式。各地劳动服务公司要办成城镇新成长劳动力和社会闲散劳动力的组织管理中心、技术培训中心、生产活动中心和社会救济中心，发挥组织和社会管理的双重职能，以推动就业工作和生产建设事业的顺利发展，巩固安定团结的局面。

第五，要注意统筹城乡劳动力。马克思说："从事加工工业等而完全脱离农业的工人的数目，取决于农业劳动者所生产的超过自己消费的农产品的数量。"①对于这个问题，我们多年来也是有沉痛教训的。1958—1960 年的 3 年中，在"大跃进""反右倾"的影响下，生产建设急于求成，只顾工业生产的发展，不顾农民提供劳动力的可能性，造成了职工人数的大增大减，城乡劳动力大进大出，劳动就业受到重大损失。在"大跃进"的 3 年中，全民所有制职工人数猛增 2 500 万人，其中从农村招工占 55%；"文化大革命"中再次出现不顾实际可能，乱上项目，盲目扩大生产建设规模，随意增加职工的现象，1970—1972 年 3 年中全民所有制单位净增职工近 1 275 万人，造成职工人数、工资总额、商品粮销量的"三个突破"和挖了粮食库存的严重局面。在"文化大革命"中，采取了不适当地缩小城乡差别的办法，一方面动员城镇知识青年到农村"扎根"，另一方面又从农村招收大量农民进城做工，结果形成了城乡劳动力大对流，给国民经济造成很大损失。

1985 年底，城乡社会劳动力近 5 亿人，其中农村劳动力 3.7 亿人。我国经

① 《马克思恩格斯全集》第 26 卷 I，第 22 页。

济不发达，目前城乡劳动力都有多余。据有关资料测算，到2000年，我国城乡劳动力将达7.6亿人，约占全国人口总数的63%，平均每年进入劳动年龄的约为2 000万人。新中国成立30多年的经验教训是，农民大量进城不行，城镇劳动力大量下乡也不行，城乡劳动力交流也不行。从我国的实际情况出发，切实可行的办法应当是：城镇劳动力主要应在城镇寻找出路，当然也可以积极动员和采取经济手段吸引一部分城市人口走工农结合、城乡结合的道路。例如，到大城市郊区、林区、工矿区和小城镇去，发展农林牧副渔业，办农工商联合企业。县以下城镇由于就业门路不如大城市多，更应提倡走工农结合、城乡结合的道路。至于农村多余的劳动力基本上应就地安排，就地消化。其办法一是发展农林牧副渔多种经营；二是因地制宜，调整农村经济结构和劳动力结构，发展乡镇企业；三是随着农村建设事业的发展，就地发展中小城镇；四是在农村逐步建立一支强大的科技专业队伍，吸引和培养农业现代化所需要的人才。

关于农业人口向非农业人口的转化，主要受两个条件制约：一是农业劳动生产率的高低；二是城市生产的发展程度，即是否需要农业劳动力进城。目前这两个条件都不具备。因此，不能离开我国的客观条件，急于消灭城乡差别，大讲农民进城是客观规律，而应当继续执行控制农民进城的方针。

二、我国工资分配方面的基本经验

新中国成立后，人民政府在全国范围内，进行了两次全国性工资改革，废除了旧中国不合理的工资制度，基本上实现了按劳分配原则。同时，随着我国生产的发展和劳动生产率的提高，多次提高了职工的工资。1984年全国全民所有制单位职工的平均工资达1 034元，比1952年的446元提高了1.3倍。据典型调查材料，由于城镇就业不断扩大，每一就业者平均赡养的家庭人口，从1952年的3.6人（含本人）减少到1985年的1.74人。职工家庭按人口平均收入由1957年的235元增加到1984年的660元，提高1.6倍，扣除价格上涨因素，仍然提高89%。

但是，1958年以后，由于“左”的思想指导，重积累、轻消费，在经济建设上靠投入大量资金，扩大基本建设规模，铺新摊子的办法发展生产。表面上看来生产的发展速度不慢，但实际经济效益很差，社会财富增加不多，人民所得实惠很少，职工工资增长缓慢。从1958—1980年，人均国民收入每年递增

4.3%，社会劳动生产率每年递增 3.7%，工业全员劳动生产率每年递增 2.8%，而职工的平均工资每年只增加 1%，如果考虑城镇生活费指数上升的因素，则 1958 年以后，每年职工实际平均工资一直低于 1957 年的水平，直到 1980 年以后才稍有增加。

新中国成立以来，我国的工资工作有哪些经验教训呢？我认为，以下几点值得考虑。

（一）确定职工工资水平，要从我国国情出发，统筹兼顾、适当安排，坚持“一要吃饭二要建设”的方针，在发展生产、提高劳动生产率的基础上，使职工工资有计划、按比例地增加。为此，要注意处理以下几个方面的关系。

第一，处理好发展生产、提高劳动生产率与职工工资水平的关系。生产决定分配，职工工资水平的提高，生活的改善，最终取决于生产发展水平和劳动生产率水平。职工工资水平对生产发展水平和劳动生产率提高的依赖关系，在新中国成立以来三个不同历史时期看得十分明显：第一个五年计划时期，生产发展较快，劳动生产率较高，我国在保证完成国家重点项目的同时，职工工资水平提高也较快，职工生活有了明显改善。在此时期，全国工农业总产值平均每年递增 10.8%，工业劳动生产率平均每年递增 8.7%，社会劳动生产率平均每年递增 6.5%，全民所有制职工的平均货币工资，每年平均递增 7.4%，实际工资递增 5.4%，劳动生产率和职工工资的增长两者的关系是合理和恰当的。但 1958—1976 年的近 20 年期间，除“大跃进”和“文化大革命”之间一段短暂的国民经济调整时期外，我国的生产水平和劳动生产率水平大幅度下降，致使全民所有制单位职工 1976 年的平均货币工资比 1957 年还降低了 5%，每年平均递减 0.3%。粉碎“江青反革命集团”以后，国家在较快发展生产的基础上，较快地提高了职工的工资水平。从 1978—1984 年，全国全民所有制职工的平均工资，每年平均增加 65 元。扣除价格上涨因素，实际平均工资年平均增长 5%，成为新中国成立以来货币平均工资与实际平均工资水平增长最快的时期。

在这方面，我们的教训是：生产决定分配，分配反过来又影响生产的发展。因此，要纠正重生产、轻消费，只抓生产，不抓生活的错误倾向，应当把职工的生活放在应有的地位，防止在生产发展和工资水平增长之间只顾一头的偏向。

第二，处理好国民收入中积累与消费的关系，既要保证国家生产建设对资金的需要，又要保证人民生活的不断改善。因此，我们要防止两种倾向，一是片面强调积累，忽视消费；二是强调消费，忽视积累。多年来，由于“左”倾思想的影响，我国一味强调高速度，强调优先发展重工业，没有把改善人民和职工的生活放在应有的地位，造成积累率一直偏高。我国的平均积累率，除了“一五”期间和三年经济调整时期分别为24.2%和22.7%，较为合理外，其余各个时期多在30%以上，积累率过高，大大超过了合理的界限，影响了人民消费水平的提高和职工生活的改善。党的十一届三中全会以后，已经基本上纠正了重积累、轻消费的倾向。当前应当注意防止第二种倾向，不能盲目地要求实行较高的工资和消费标准。我们必须看到，我国当前工农业水平毕竟还较低，就是20世纪末，我国工农业生产水平能够在现有的基础上翻两番，由于人口众多，国民收入也只能达到小康水平。如果脱离我国的实际，在职工中过早地提出“高工资、高消费”的口号，是不适宜的，也是行不通的。

第三，处理好工农关系和城乡关系。我国有11亿人口，其中8亿多人在农村，在社会劳动力中，农业劳动力占70%以上。因此，在确定职工工资水平时，应充分考虑到这一国情，要考虑职工工资水平与农民收入的关系问题。职工的工资水平与农民的收入水平相比，差距不能过大，并且，这种差距还应随着农业劳动生产率的提高逐步缩小。

新中国成立以来，在工农关系和城乡关系方面，我们曾经比较注意兼顾二者关系，国家采取有力措施，组织工业大力支援农业，尽量避免扩大工农收入和生活水平的差距。例如，职工和农民生活水平的差距，按城乡每人平均收入计算，1957年工农差距为1:3.2，1965年缩小为1:2.1。但是，在“文化大革命”期间，农业生产发展缓慢，农民收入多年来没有增加，因此，工农收入和消费水平的差距又有所扩大。党的十一届三中全会以来，政府一方面通过几次调整工资和增加奖金、津贴，较多地增加了职工的工资收入；另一方面，又在农村落实了一系列经济政策，较大幅度地提高了农产品收购价格，普遍实行了各种形式的经营承包责任制，使农民劳动积极性提高，农民收入逐年增加，工农生活差距正在缩小之中。1984年，按工农人口平均收入计算，两者的比例缩小为1:1.85。但是，我们也应看到，1984年我国农村中人均收入500元以上的农户，只占全部农户的11.9%，按平均每户常住人口5.43人计算，每户不超过3 000元，其中“万元户”是极少数。个别农村地区的温饱问题尚未完全解决。另外，职工还享受许多农民所没有的劳动保险和生活福利待遇，农民在生产经营中还要承担比职工大得多的风险，收入也不稳定。因此，我们处理工农关系和城乡关系时，还不得不考虑到这些情况。

第四，处理好提高工资水平和扩大就业的关系。我国每年新增加的工资总额，一部分要用来提高原有职工的工资水平，一部分用来支付新增职工的工资，即扩大就业。由于我国国民收入较低，每年新增加的工资总额不可能太多。这样，如果过多提高原有职工的工资水平，势必影响扩大就业，影响城镇每年几百万新成长劳动力的安排，影响安定团结的局面。当然，职工长期不增加工资，多劳不多得，也会挫伤他们劳动的积极性。因此，提高原有职工工资水平和扩大就业这两头，必须同时兼顾。据统计，1953—1980 年的 28 年间，在新增加的工资总额中，约有 45%用于提高职工工资水平，55%用于扩大就业。这个比例值得今后借鉴。

过去我国曾提出“低工资、多就业”的口号，新中国成立以来也一直实行“合理的低工资制”的政策，正是考虑到我国人口多、底子薄、工农业生产水平比较低的情况以及上述兼顾提高工资水平和扩大就业之间的关系问题。从我国国情出发，这一政策是正确的，今后应当继续实行。但是，在实行中，应认真贯彻执行党的十一届三中全会以来所制定的一系列就业方针，打破只有在全民所有制单位工作才算就业的观念，实行多渠道就业。决不能把“低工资、多就业”理解为“三个人的活五个人干”，更不能理解为吃“大锅饭”。在实行这一政策时，也应注意贯彻按劳分配原则，允许一部分劳动好、技术高、贡献大的职工，一部分生产好、经营管理水平高，对国家贡献大的企业，工资适当高一些。

（二）坚定不移地实行社会主义的按劳分配原则。新中国的工资史，在某种意义上可以说是不断探索对个人消费品如何实行按劳分配的历史。新中国成立 30 多年以来，我国对按劳分配的认识和实践经历了一个曲折和不断前进的过程。

在国民经济恢复时期和第一个五年计划时期，随着生产资料社会主义公有制的建立，我国初步建立了基本上符合按劳分配原则的全国统一的工资制度。这一时期，由于注意按照按劳分配规律办事，政治思想工作也做得比较好，职工学习科学技术的积极性和社会主义劳动热情十分高涨，有力地促进了国民经济恢复和第一个五年计划任务的完成。

在1958—1960年的“大跃进”时期，在分配领域开始否定按劳分配原则，取消了计件工资和奖励制，并且批判所谓资产阶级法权，大肆宣传吃饭不要钱和供给制的优越性，在少数企业和事业单位试行半供给半工资制度，企图用共产主义的按需分配代替社会主义的按劳分配。这样，就使初步实行的按劳分配原则受到很大冲击和削弱，在一定程度上挫伤了职工群众的劳动积极性。

在1961年以后的国民经济调整时期，在贯彻“调整、巩固、充实、提高”的八字方针过程中，又重新确认了按劳分配原则。在企业中恢复了计件工资和奖励制度，1963年还进行了一次职工工资调整，并在调整中坚持以生产和工作需要、劳动态度、技术业务水平和生产成绩作为职工的升级条件。这一时期，尽管对前一阶段否定按劳分配原则的“左”的思想没有认真总结经验教训，肃清影响，按劳分配原则恢复得还不够，但还是在一定程度上调动了职工的积极性，促进了生产的恢复和发展。

在“文化大革命”期间，劳动工资工作受到空前破坏，计件工资和奖励制被当作修正主义批判和取消。新中国成立后建立的工资制度被全盘否定，升级工作长期停止。在分配中出现了干多与干少、干好与干坏、干与不干一个样的平均主义现象，个别单位甚至出现了多干不如少干、少干不如不干、不干不如捣乱的荒唐局面。这些做法，严重挫伤了职工群众的积极性，再加上其他方面的原因，使我国国民经济濒于崩溃的边缘。

“文化大革命”以后，我们在理论和政策上进行了拨乱反正、正本清源的工作，恢复了按劳分配原则的名誉，逐步恢复了计件工资和奖励制度，对职工进行了多次升级，并进行了国家机关、事业单位的工资改革和企业工资改革。这些工作，对于改进我国的按劳分配制度，调动职工群众的积极性，推动社会主义经济建设，发挥了一定的作用。

新中国成立以来我国工资工作经历的上述三起两落的过程，反映了我们对按劳分配原则的认识过程。我们应当从中吸取什么经验教训呢？

第一，按劳分配是不以人的意志为转移的客观经济规律。在社会主义制度下，如果我们能够比较正确地认识和运用这一规律，并做好其他工作，国民经济就能发展，社会主义制度就能得到巩固；如果违背了这一规律，就要受到惩罚，再加上其他工作失误，国民经济就会垮下来，社会主义制度就要受到损害。过去30多年来，我们对按劳分配原则总的来说是认识不清、坚持不力、运用不活，有时还企图用平均主义来改造它和替代它。这是我们应当接受的一个基本教训。

第二，必须解放思想，逐步改革工资制度。新中国成立以来我国实行的工资制度，是由国家统一规定的工资等级和工资形式，按照统一的标准，考核劳动者所提供的劳动量，并在全社会范围内，对劳动者进行直接的分配。从工资分配同职工个人提供的劳动量有所联系来看，可以说是基本上贯彻了按劳分配原则。长期以来，我们对按劳分配原则的认识，也正是停留在这一程度上。但是，我们也不能不看到，这种工资制度从根本上说，不符合社会主义制度下有计划商品经济的要求，致使工资分配上的许多问题，诸如职工吃企业“大锅饭”，企业吃国家“大锅饭”的问题，统得过多、管得过死的问题，都无法解决。因此，为了适应社会主义有计划商品经济的要求，必须发展马克思主义的按劳分配理论，解放思想，对我国现行的工资制度逐步进行改革，逐步做到，在国家同企业的关系上，使职工工资同企业经济效益挂钩；在企业内部，使职工工资同个人的劳动贡献挂钩，以打破两个“大锅饭”。在分配上确立国家同企业，以及企业同职工个人之间的正确关系，既调动职工个人的劳动积极性，又调动企业经营管理的积极性。

（三）在社会主义初级阶段，在个人消费品的分配体制上应实行以按劳分配为主体的多种分配形式。个人消费品的分配方式，是由生产资料所有制形式决定的。社会主义生产方式的基础，是生产资料的公有制，这就决定了社会主义个人消费品分配原则必须实行按劳分配。但是，在社会主义社会，由于生产力发展水平还不够高，还不能实行单一的生产资料公有制，因此也不能在全社会实行单一的按劳分配原则。正是在这个意义上，我们说按劳分配是社会主义个人消费品分配的主要形式，但不是唯一形式。

新中国成立初期，生产资料所有制呈现多种形式，即以国营经济为主导，多种经济成分同时并存。与此相适应，在分配方面，实行按劳分配为主，同时允许其他分配形式存在，其中包括在民族资本主义企业中，允许资本家在一定限度内对工人的剥削。以后，随着对国营经济以外的各种非社会主义经济成分的社会主义改造，使按劳分配的范围逐步扩大。这是符合建立、巩固和壮大社会主义公有制，开展社会主义建设事业要求的。

但是，1956 年以后，脱离了我国生产力发展水平，过急过早地改变多种所有制形式并存以及与之相适应的多种分配形式并存的局面。在三大改造基本完成之后，多种经济成分就被单一的公有制经济所代替，同时，除按劳分配以外，其他各种分配形式被取消，并且按劳分配的形式也趋于单一化。尤其在1958—1960年的“大跃进”期间，又进一步强调所有制形式的“一大二公”，并急于用按需分配代替按劳分配。以后的很长一段时期内，盲目地进行“小集体”向“大集体”“大集体”向“全民”的所谓“升级”“过渡”；集体所有制的分配制度也向全民所有制看齐。分配上的这些不妥当做法，都给我国经济的发展造成十分不利的影响。

目前我国经济体制改革的一个重要内容，就是重新合理地调整生产资料所有制结构和与之相适应的分配结构，使之与我国现阶段的生产力水平相适应。在所有制方面，我们在坚持生产资料公有制占统治地位的前提下，重新允许和提倡多种所有制形式并存和一定的发展，例如，允许个体经济的存在和发展，以作为社会主义经济的补充。在经济特区建立中外合资企业，并允许外商独资企业的兴办等。这样，我国就又出现了国营经济、集体经济、个体经济、国家资本主义经济（中外合资企业）等多种所有制形式。与此相适应，在个人消费品的分配方面，我国又出现了一个以按劳分配为主体的多种分配形式并存的局面。

劳动经济学的形成和发展①

内容提要：200年前英国古典经济学家亚当·斯密和大卫·李嘉图对劳动问题进行研究；20世纪40年代美国制度学派建立以工会与雇主谈判工资为主的独立的劳动经济学；马克思批判吸收西方研究的合理内核，奠定了马克思主义劳动经济学的理论基础；苏联十月革命后建立了他们称之为社会主义的劳动经济学；当前我们广泛吸收我国改革开放以来最新研究成果，同时吸收借鉴外国劳动经济学先进的理论和研究方法，力图建立符合我国新时代要求的具有中国特色的劳动经济学。

① 本文发表在2011年第6期的《中国流通经济》上，作者为袁伦渠、林原，本书出版时作者对本文进行了修改。

劳动经济学是研究市场经济制度中劳动力市场现象及劳动力市场运行规律的科学。作为经济学的重要分支，劳动经济学从萌芽到产生、发展已有二百多年的历史，经历了曲折、复杂的过程。

一、国外劳动经济学的形成和发展

1. 古典经济学家将劳动和工资问题作为经济学研究的重要内容

劳动经济学是从经济学分化出来的，是经济学的一个分支，其萌芽和产生与经济学的发展有着密切的关系。17 世纪中叶至 19 世纪 70 年代，是古典经济学产生、发展和完成的时期，古典经济学派将劳动和工资问题作为经济学研究的重要内容。

早在 200 多年前，以英国亚当 • 斯密和大卫 • 李嘉图为代表的古典经济学派就对劳动与工资问题进行了深入的论述。亚当 • 斯密提出劳动决定价值的理论，明确提出"劳动是衡量一切商品交换价值的真实尺度"[①]，商品的价值是由劳动创造的，生产商品时花费的社会必要劳动时间是商品价值的尺度。大卫 • 李嘉图更明确提出了劳动时间决定价值量的原理和"工资、利润、地租"三位一体的分配形式，认为"如果体现在商品中的劳动量规定商品的交换价值，那么，劳动量每有增加，就一定会使在其上的施加劳动的商品的价值增加，劳动量每有减少，也一定会使之减少"。[②]

因为劳动是生产过程的基本要素，工资是国民收入的组成部分，每个经济学家都不得不对这个问题进行理论探讨，所以长期以来劳动经济理论一直是经济理论的重要组成部分。

2. 20 世纪 20 年代制度经济学建立了独立的劳动经济学

劳动经济学作为一门独立的学科产生于 20 世纪 20 年代。根据美国劳动经济学家麦克纳特的考证，劳动经济学是由美国制度学派的经济学家首先建立起来的，该派学者认为各种制度（如家庭、公司、同业工会、政府机关等）对经济发展起着重要作用，因此他们研究经济问题时，特别重视这些制度的结构和活动。

---

① 斯密. 国民财富的性质和起因的研究：上册 [M]. 北京：商务印书馆，1972.

② 李嘉图. 政治经济学及赋税原理[M]. 北京：商务印书馆，1976.

第一次世界大战后，美国经济发展异常迅速，成为经济最发达的国家之一。伴随着经济的发展，工人阶级队伍不断壮大，工会力量日益增强，劳资双方的关系日趋紧张，工会领导下的大罢工给社会经济发展造成了严重的负面影响。当时有些制度学派的经济学家专门从事劳动问题的研究，用制度不完善来解释劳资双方的矛盾，用工会和雇主组织之间的关系来分析美国的劳动问题，并把自己的理论体系称之为劳动经济学。在第一批以劳动经济学命名的著作中，最早的一本是1925年出版的素罗门·布拉姆的《劳动经济学》。同时，美国一些大学（如芝加哥大学、维斯康辛大学等）先后在经济学系单独开设了劳动经济学课程，出现了一批专门研究劳动经济学问题的学者。从此，劳动经济学便被承认为一门独立的经济学科。

早期的劳动经济学强调制度的作用，主张工会与雇主通过谈判提高工资待遇，改善劳动条件，使这门学科的研究集中于工会运动，范围过于狭窄，理论性也很薄弱。

3. 20世纪40年代芝加哥学派的“劳动经济学革命”

20世纪二三十年代的资本主义世界经济大危机，给刚刚发展起来的劳动经济学带来了严峻的挑战。失业和贫困的加剧使劳动关系更紧张，资本主义世界陷入了困境之中。但早期的劳动经济学由于范围狭窄，无法对现实起到有效的指导作用。到20世纪30年代末，劳动经济学几乎陷入了无人问津的境况。

现实引发了经济学家对宏观劳动力市场问题的深入思考。进入20世纪40年代以后，美国芝加哥学派发动了一场“劳动经济学革命”，重新肯定19世纪新古典经济学的传统，反对凯恩斯主义的政策，认为市场机制可以自发调节经济，使其趋于平衡，不需要政府采取措施进行干预。具体到劳动问题上，他们强调劳动力市场的自发调节作用，因而把劳动力市场的论述增加到劳动经济学中，并成为这门学科的主要内容。此后，劳动经济学的研究内容不断增加，除了原有的工会运动和劳资关系外，还包括劳动力的供给与需求、工资的决定与结构、失业问题、劳动政策等内容。这次革命以后，劳动经济学在美国有了很大的发展，各大学的经济系几乎都开设了劳动经济学的课程，研究劳动经济学的学者也大大增加。

4. 20 世纪 60 年代以来劳动经济学的新发展

20 世纪 60 年代以来，劳动经济学在西方发达国家得到进一步发展。以新古典经济学为代表的劳动经济学家，努力将劳动经济学与主流经济学即新古典经济学的研究方法相融合，更加注重经济分析方面。

1961 年，美国劳动经济学家舒尔茨发表了《人力资本投资》的演讲，提出普通教育、培训、健康、保健、流动等形成和增加人力资本，并且人力资本投资带来的收益大于成本的理论。于是人力资本成为劳动经济学研究的新内容。随后，从劳动力市场的现实问题出发，劳动力市场中的性别、种族和民族歧视、通货膨胀与失业率、人口老龄化和生活质量问题也被纳入了劳动经济学的研究领域。

与此同时，劳动关系（产业关系）这一劳动经济学研究的传统领域则出现了逐渐从劳动经济学中分化出来的趋势。研究劳动关系的学者，除重视吸取劳动经济学的内容，将劳动经济学作为劳动关系领域的基本理论分析之外，越来越重视与社会学、法学、组织行为学和政治科学等不同学科领域学者的互动和交流，从而使劳动关系成为一个跨学科研究的领域。在澳大利亚和英国，劳动关系成为一个独立的学科领域。在德国等其他一些欧洲大陆的国家，劳动关系则更多的从属于法学或社会学学科领域。

5. 马克思主义劳动经济学的产生与发展

马克思和恩格斯批判吸收了前人关于劳动经济学论述的合理内核，在《共产党宣言》《英国工人阶级状况》《资本论》《哥达纲领批判》等著作中，对劳动经济问题作了精辟论述，如关于价值、劳动二重性、剩余价值理论、生产价格理论以及利润、地租、工资理论和劳动与劳动力的科学区分等，这奠定了马克思主义劳动经济学的理论基础。

俄国十月革命与第二次世界大战后，苏联在批判西方劳动经济学的基础上，建立了他们称之为马克思主义的劳动经济学，或称为社会主义劳动经济学。与西方劳动经济学不同，他们主要研究社会劳动组织、企业劳动组织与按劳分配等，成为计划经济体制下的劳动经济学，形成了与西方劳动经济学相对立的局面。

二、劳动经济学在中国的发展

1. 新中国成立前劳动经济学相关著作的出版

新中国成立前，我国学者就出版了劳动经济学的相关著作。20 世纪 30 年代，商务出版社出版了著名社会学家陈达教授的著作《中国劳动问题》。1931 年，朱通久教授在黎明书店出版了《劳动经济概论》。1935 年，陈振鹭先生在上海大学书店出版《劳动大纲》。这些学者的研究主要针对劳工社会问题，以制度分析为主，与主流劳动经济学有很大区别。在该阶段，劳动经济学主要是作为一门课程在社会学和经济学中讲授，没有成为一门独立的学科。

2. 计划经济体制下劳动经济学的产生与发展

新中国成立后，劳动经济学成为一门独立的学科和专业。但受到计划经济体制的束缚，我国的劳动经济学在相当长的一段时间里背离了主流劳动经济学的研究范式，其发展也限于停滞不前的状态。20 世纪 50 年代初，我国邀请苏联专家来华讲学，全面吸收了苏联劳动经济学理论，翻译出版了柯斯津和梁思尼科夫的《劳动经济学》《劳动经济》。1981 年，三联书店出版了袁伦渠等翻译的他的导师苏联伊万诺夫所著的《劳动经济学》。这些著作成为当时我国劳动经济学学生和劳动干部的参考书，它们与计划经济体制相适应，论证了劳动工资政策的合理性。

我国的劳动经济学理论与实践长期受苏联的影响，脱离中国实际，而且起步不久就受到"左"的错误干扰和长达十年的"文化大革命"破坏，再加上高度集中的计划经济体制的影响，其内容与研究方法相当落后，甚至处于停滞不前的状态。在研究对象方面，偏重于劳动关系和劳动政策的研究，研究的主要目的是论证劳动政策的适应性，劳动制度、工资制度的合理性。研究方法偏重于规范的方法。

3. 我国社会主义市场经济体制下劳动经济学的新发展

党的十一届三中全会后，随着改革开放的逐步深入和社会主义市场经济体制的逐步建立，我国经济学界对劳动经济理论的研究出现了重大的突破，主要体现在以下几个方面：

（1）劳动力具有商品性质属性的理论。劳动力作为商品是通过劳动力市场与用人单位谈判成交，实现劳动力使用权的让渡，实现就业。

（2）劳动力产权归个人所有的理论。劳动力的生产费用由个人和家庭负担，劳动还是谋生手段。劳动力产权归个人所有，劳动者有权支配自己的劳动力，有选择职业、转换岗位的自由。

（3）企业用工主体理论。由国家用工主体转换为企业用工主体理论。

（4）企业与劳动者双向选择的理论。

（5）工会与集体谈判理论。

（6）按劳分配与按生产要素分配理论。

（7）劳动力市场理论。

三、我国劳动经济学科研与教学发展

1950 年，在清华大学、燕京大学、辅仁大学社会学系设立了劳动组。1952 年院系调整时，以上三所大学的劳动组合并为劳动专修科，先设在中央财经学院，后迁到中国人民大学。1955 年，劳动干部学校成立，设立了劳动经济和劳动保护专业。1958 年，劳动学院成立，后改为北京经济学院，设立劳动经济、劳动保护和物资管理本科。1979 年，中国人民大学成立了劳动经济研究室，并于 1983 年成立劳动人事学院。1994 年，中国人民大学劳动人事学院设立博士点。2001 年，首都经济贸易大学（原北京经济学院）成立劳动经济博士点。当时全国已约有 200 余所高校开设劳动经济学课程，其中不少高校获得了劳动经济学博士点、硕士点的授予权，培养了一大批劳动经济学领域的科研和应用型人才。

与此同时，劳动经济学的科研机构纷纷建立起来。1956 年，国家劳动部成立劳动经济学研究所。1982 年后，一批专门的科研机构相继成立，包括劳动部工资研究所、国际劳工研究所以及国家发改委人力资源开发研究所等。这些科研机构的研究涉及劳动经济学的基本理论、劳动力市场、劳动关系、就业与失业等，进一步推动了我国劳动经济理论与实践的发展。

四、劳动经济学与劳动科学体系之间的关系

劳动是一种普遍的社会现象，是人类最主要的实践活动。劳动和人是分不开的，凡是有人的地方都有劳动问题。正因为劳动如此重要，许多学科都从不同角度对劳动加以研究。从经济学的角度研究劳动，则形成劳动经济学；从社

会学的角度研究劳动，则形成劳动社会学；从法学的角度研究劳动，则形成了劳动法学（包括劳动保护学）；从统计学的角度研究劳动，则形成劳动统计学；从历史学的角度研究劳动，则形成了劳动史学；从生理学的角度研究劳动，则形成劳动生理学；从卫生学的角度研究劳动，则形成劳动卫生学；从心理学的角度研究劳动，则形成劳动心理学①。这样便形成了一个劳动科学学科体系②，如表1所示。

表1　劳动科学体系表

<table>
<tr><td rowspan="8">劳动科学体系</td><td rowspan="5">劳动的社会经济科学</td><td>劳动经济学</td><td>劳动科学体系中发展最早，影响最大，成熟度最高的一门主干学科，是劳动科学体系中的基础理论学科</td></tr>
<tr><td>劳动社会学</td><td>劳动社会学是从社会学分化出来的一门年轻学科，既是社会学的一个分支，又是劳动科学体系的一个组成部分。它是运用社会学的原理和方法，研究人的劳动活动的科学，其特点包括两个方面：一是从社会总体的角度对劳动进行综合性、总体性的研究；二是注重实地调查研究</td></tr>
<tr><td>劳动法学（包括劳动保护学）</td><td>研究调整劳动关系的法律规范的科学，既是法学的分支，又是劳动科学体系的组成部分，包括劳动法、劳动保护法等</td></tr>
<tr><td>劳动统计学</td><td>研究劳动统计的理论与方法的学科，着重研究劳动现象的数量方面，在劳动经济方面研究劳动生产率统计、工资统计、员工人数统计等</td></tr>
<tr><td>劳动史学</td><td>研究劳动科学产生及其发展演变规律的历史</td></tr>
<tr><td rowspan="3">劳动的自然科学</td><td>劳动生理学</td><td>研究人体在劳动过程中技能活动变化规律的科学，为消除或减少人体过度生理疲劳、改进劳动方法和劳动工具等服务</td></tr>
<tr><td>劳动卫生学</td><td>研究劳动者在劳动过程中的安全和健康的保护</td></tr>
<tr><td>劳动心理学</td><td>研究劳动过程中劳动者与工作环境、劳动者之间相互作用而产生的心理活动及其规律的科学。狭义的劳动心理学包括工效学、人体工程学、工业心理学；广义的劳动心理学包括管理心理学、职业心理学等</td></tr>
</table>

由此可见，对劳动问题的研究既涉及社会经济方面，又涉及自然科学方面。劳动是一种非常复杂又涉及多方面的现象，涉及经济学、社会学、法学、心理学、生理学等学科。劳动科学体系是一个多学科的知识群，而劳动经济学则是

① 伊万诺夫. 劳动经济学[M]. 袁伦渠，等译. 北京：三联出版社，1981.

② 曾湘泉，袁伦渠，等. 我国高校设立劳动科学一级学科势在必行[N]. 光明日报，2009-11-12（12）.

劳动科学体系中发展最早，影响最大，成熟度最高的一门主干学科，是劳动科学体系中的基础理论学科。

中国的劳动就业、收入分配和社会保障事业①

内容提要： 本文全面系统地介绍了改革开放后中国劳动就业、收入分配和社会保障的现状、理论和政策，使外国政要和学者对中国经济、社会、民生问题有了全面了解。

中国是一个有 5000 余年文明史、13 亿多人口、960 万平方公里的社会主义国家。改革开放 30 多年来，经济社会发展获得长足的进步，2011 年国内生产总值已经跃居全球第二大经济体。

近年来，世界经济形势复杂多变，国内经济下行压力加大，多重矛盾交织。我国在习近平为总书记的党中央领导下，在党的十八大和十八届三中全会全面深化改革政策的指引下，稳住脚步，处变不惊，统筹稳增长、调结构、促改革，坚持宏观政策要稳、微观政策要活、社会政策托底、创新宏观调控的思路和方式，采取了一系列既利当前、更惠长远的举措，圆满完成了 2013 年全年社会经济发展的主要经济指标，改革开放和社会主义建设取得了瞩目的重大成就。2013 年经济运行稳中向好，国内生产总值达到 56.9 万亿元，比 2012 年增长 7.7%，居民消费价格涨幅为 2.6%，城镇登记失业率为 4.1%，城镇新增就业 1 310 万，创历史新高，城镇居民人均可支配收入实际增长 7%，农村居民人均纯收入实际增长 9.3%，农村贫困人口减少 1 650 万人，城乡收入差距继续缩小。2014 年我国面对国内外错综复杂的经济形势带来的挑战与机遇并存的局面，看到了处于大有可为的重要战略机遇期，提出了经济和社会发展的主要预期目标：国内生产增值 7.5%左右，居民消费价格涨幅控制 3.5%左右，城镇新增就业人口 1 000 万以上，城镇失业率控制在 4.6%以内，努力实现居民收入增长和经济增长同步。

① 本文是 2014 年 4—5 月为国务院参事出国交流撰写的发言稿，数易其稿，受到国外政要和学者的一致好评。收录在国务院参事室编《国务院参事袁伦渠咨询国是文稿汇编（2004 年 3 月—2016 年 3 月）》。本文参阅和引用了人力资源社会保障部和中国劳动科学研究院公布的资料。

由于我们采取了宏观调控思路和方式，从而圆满完成了2013年社会经济目标和2014年经济社会预期完成目标的设定，保住了稳增长保就业的下限和防通胀的上限，确保了经济运行处于合理区间。

但是中国仍然是一个发展国家，我国的经济发展水平与发达国家的差距依然很大，我们的人均收入水平还很低，我们的教育、社会保障、收入等方面与美国、日本、欧元区等发达国家还有很大差距，我们发展的任务还很重。我们的经济实体虽然排序第二，但我国追求的是经济社会的全面均衡和可持续发展，不以GDP论英雄。我们关注的是全国人民体面的就业、不断提高的收入和覆盖面大的社会保障等民生福利问题。

李克强总理在今年两会的政府工作报告中指出：就业是民生之本，收入是民生之源，社会保障是民生之基。就业、收入、社会保障三者共同构建成了中国的社会福利安全网，惠及了全国人民，保障了全国人民劳动和生活。以下我将中国社会福利构建的以上三个组成部分，逐一向与会者介绍。

一、就业——民生之本

就业是民生之本，保证公民就业是我国一项重要的社会任务。所谓就业是指符合劳动年龄的劳动者从事一定的社会劳动并以此获得劳动报酬和经济收入的经济活动。就业是公民的一项基本权利，中国宪法规定：“中华人民共和国公民有劳动的权利和义务。”国务院新闻办公室公布的《国家人权行动计划（2012—2015）》提出，“实施更加积极的就业政策，完善工资制度，全面实行劳动合同制度，改善劳动条件，强化劳动安全，保证劳动者的工作权利”。

中国有13亿多人口，9.2亿劳动力，长期面临严重的就业压力，劳动力供给大于需求的基本格局没有改变，就业总量压力仍然很大。就业总量压力主要集中在三大群体上。

1. 农民工就业质量不高，存在权益保障问题

2013年我国农民工有2.69亿人，其中外出者1.66亿人，本地就业者1.03亿人。广大农民工是我国的产业大军，对国家经济的快速和持续发展做出了杰出贡献。但是他们的劳动环境差，工伤事故多，被拖欠工资和超时劳动现象比较普遍，他们的劳动合法权益往往得不到保障，这是长期困扰我国政府的重要问题。

2. 以高校毕业生为主体的青年就业难问题突出

2013 年应届高校毕业生 699 万，2014 年达到 727 万，如何把这部分新成长的劳动力安排在就业岗位上，并合理有效配置，任务十分繁重。

3. 失业人员再就业和帮助就业困难群体实现就业难度依然很大

一些年龄偏大、教育程度低、缺乏就业技能的劳动者群体，经常处于半失业状态或面临失业风险，帮助他们实现就业和再就业是一项长期而艰巨的任务。

为了做好就业工作，政府坚持就业优先战略和更加积极的就业政策。2008 年《中华人民共和国就业促进法》正式施行，首次将积极的就业政策纳入法律，明确了扩大就业的政策规定，与此相配套还制定实施了《促进就业规划（2011—2015)》，这是中国首部国家促进就业的专项规划。就业优先战略与更加积极的就业政策制定和实施以来，中国的就业工作取得了巨大的成效。

（1）成功解决了数千万国有下岗职工再就业问题，使 3 000 多万国有企业下岗职工得到妥善安排，还先后使 2 800 多万下岗失业人员实现了再就业。

（2）成功化解了新一轮青年就业高峰的压力，由于经济持续增长的强力拉动和积极就业政策的有效支持，就业规模不断扩大，有效缓解了就业高峰压力。2003 年迎来我国高校扩招后第一批大学生就业高峰，当年高校毕业生突破 200 万人，达 212 万人，之后一路攀升，2014 年预计达到 727 万人。今年我国政府提出，要优化劳动环境，以创新引领创业，以创业带动就业，对今年 727 万高校毕业生将要开发更多就业岗位，实施不间断的就业服务体系，提高大学生创业比例。

（3）成功提高了农民工就业数量和质量。近年来，我国加大了中西部开发的支持力度，使中西部经济获得较快的发展，同时国家又施行了引导 1 亿人在中西部地区就近城镇落户的政策，使得本地农民工增长快于外出农民工的增长，农民工总量呈现出持续回流的态势。与此同时农民工素质也在提高，2013 年农民工初中以下教育程度占 6.1%，初中教育程度占 60.6%，高中教育程度占 20.5%，大专教育程度以上占 12.8%，接受技能培训的占 32.7%。农民工工资水平也不断提高，人均月收入比 2012 年增加了 319 元，达到 2 609 元。与 2008 年相比，2013 年农民工的权益保障取得了明显进展，参加养老、工伤、医疗、失业和生育保险的比例分别提高了 5.9%、4.4%、4.5%、5.4%和 4.6%。工资被拖欠的外出农民工的比重由 2008 年的 4.1%降为 2013 年的 0.8%。不过超时劳动、签订劳动合同的比例仍然不高，拖欠工资现象时有发生，这是今后我国进一步努力克服的问题。

（4）成功应对了国际金融危机对就业的巨大冲击，中国快速扭转了 2008 年下半年城镇新增就业下滑的局面，2010 年城镇新增就业人数达到了 1 168 万人，城镇失业率始终保持在 4.3%以内。2013 年登记失业率为 4.1%，城镇新就业人数达到 1 310 万。2014 年登记失业率控制在 4.6%以内，城镇新增就业人口 1 000 万以上。对就业困难人员加大帮扶力度，确保零就业家庭至少安排一人就业。做好淘汰落后产能企业职工的安置和再就业工作，努力实现更加充分和高质量的就业，使劳动者的工作更加体面和有尊严。

二、收入分配——民生之源

在中国不劳动者不得食，有劳动能力的公民必须参加劳动，以获取工资收入维持自己和一家人的生活。对工资收入，中国实行按劳分配和按生产要素分配相结合的分配制度，劳动者根据自己劳动产品或服务的数量多少和质量高低获取工资，凭借自己的技能、管理才能获取薪酬，在中国资本也可以参与分配。中国机关事业单位和企业工资分配制度稍有差别。机关、公务员实行职级制和结构工资制，按职务高低和工资结构的比重取得报酬，优秀工作者还可获一部分年终奖；科教文卫工作人员参照机关工资制度实行结构工资制和绩效工资制；机关事业单位工资基金主要来自国家财政。国有企业实行自我发展、自我约束、自负盈亏、自主分配的市场化的收入分配制度，企业根据各自经营的好坏和经济效益的高低确定工资总额，并按照预先规定的工资等级制度进行分配，职工们依照贡献的大小取得不同的工资报酬。在非公有制企业，则根据国家有关法规自行确定员工工资。为了保证劳动者的基本生活，国家还依法对各用人单位规定了最低工资保障制度。如北京市 2014 年规定最低工资标准每月不得低于 1 560 元。最低工资标准是一个底线，违者要受到处罚。

改革开放后，我国经济社会获得长足发展，全国劳动者的工资收入不断提高。5 年来，全国城镇单位就业人员年平均工资由 2008 年的 28 898 元增至 2012 年的 46 768 元，增长 61.8%。2012 年全国城镇非私有企业员工年均工资达到 46 769 元，扣除物价因素较 2011 年实际增长 9%。2012 年北京市职工年均工资 62 677 元，月均 5 223 元，处于较高水平。根据国家统计局数据，2013 年中国城镇居民人居年收入为 29 457 元，农村居民人均年收入为 8 896 元。

中国劳动者工资收入大幅度提高的同时，也存在一定问题。

（1）行业之间收入差别大。金融、石油、电信等行业收入特别高，农、林、牧、渔业和商业、饮食业、服务业收入低。例如：北京市 2013 年金融业人年均工资为 184 612 元，是全市平均工资水平的 2.18 倍；农林牧渔业人年均工资为 39 334 元，仅是北京市平均工资的 46%；商业、饮食业、服务业人年均工资为 38 838 元，还达不到北京市平均工资的 50%。北京市最高与最低行业平均工资之比达到 4.74:1。

（2）地区之间收入差别大。根据国家统计数据 2013 年我国东部地区城镇居民可支配收入为 32 789.6 元，中部地区为 22 391.8 元，西部地区为 21 847 元，东部地区收入为西部地区的 1.5 倍。与此同时东部地区农村居民人均纯收入为 13 503 元，中部地区为 8 490 元，西部地区为 6 819 元，东部地区为西部地区的 1.98 倍。

（3）城乡之间收入差别大。根据国家统计局数据，2013 年中国城镇居民人居年收入为 29 457 元，农村居民人居年收入为 8 896 元，城镇居民收入是农村居民收入的 3 倍。

为缩小劳动者的工资差别，体现社会公平，我国采取了一系列的措施：第一，在国民收入中扩大居民收入的比重，在国民收入初次分配中，扩大劳动收入的比重。第二，在国民收入的再分配中通过税收制度将高收入者的部分财富转向低收入者，国家通过强制性互济性的社会保障制度构筑覆盖弱势群体的安全网，让低收入者受益。

为缩小劳动者收入差距，党的十八届三中全会和今年李克强总理所作政府工作报告提出了深化收入分配制度的改革，其中包括：健全企业职工工资决定和正常增长机制，推进工资集体协商，构建和谐劳动关系；加强和规范国企负责人的薪酬管理；改革机关事业单位工资制度；增加边远地区福利津贴；多渠道增加低收入者收入，不断扩大中等收入者比重。最近经国务院批准，由发改委牵头的深化收入分配制度改革的部际联席会议正式成立，将对我国收入分配制度进行系统研究，提出改革实施的具体措施。

三、社会保障——民生之基

社会保障是我国福利的重要组成部分，它由社会保险、社会救助、社会优抚、社会福利和社会慈善事业构成，各自担负着为不同困难劳动者群体排忧解难的任务，为丧失劳动能力和贫困劳动者编织成了一个安全网。

党的十八大确定我国社会保障到 2020 年目标是社会保障覆盖城乡全部居民，这一目标可归纳为 4 方面：一是人人享有，二是水平提高，三是公平合理，四是安全可靠。

1. 社会保障全覆盖

近 10 年来，我国先后建立了新型农村养老保险、城镇居民基本医疗保险和养老保险等重要的保障制度。2011 年 7 月 1 日颁布施行《社会保险法》以后，社会保障覆盖人群迅速扩大。2012 年底，医疗保险覆盖了城乡 13.4 亿人，全民医保基本形成。城乡基本养老保险覆盖了 7.88 亿人，失业、工伤、生育保险分别覆盖 1.5 亿人、1.9 亿人和 1.54 亿人。下一步，一是努力实现新型农村养老保险和城镇居民养老保险对城乡居民的全覆盖，基本实现应保尽保；二是持续推进扩大城乡职工社会保险覆盖面，重点是非公单位职工、劳务派遣工、灵活就业人员、城镇个体户，尽可能引导进城务工农民工参加水平较高的社会保险，同时对家政服务、网络创业者抓紧制定社保政策；三是对城乡居民“自愿参保”调整为“全民参保”从而形成“全民参保”的局面。

2014 年 2 月 21 日，李克强总理发布《社会救济暂行办法》，其中规定：人均收入低于当地最低生活保障标准的共同生活的家庭成员给予最低生活保障；对无人抚养的困难老人、未成年人、重病患者给予特殊供养；对受灾人员及其他特殊困难人员给予医疗救助、住房救助、临时救助等救助。

2. 社会保障水平稳步提高

1998 年全国企业退休人员养老金只有 413 元，2005—2014 年，连续 10 年上调养老金，最近国务院常务会议决定，2014 年 1 月 1 日起，将全国企业退休人员养老金再提高 10%，并向特困群体适当倾斜。北京、青海、新疆、河北、甘肃、江苏、云南 7 省份人均月退休金分别为 3 050 元、2 593 元、2 298 元、2 100 元、2 065 元、2 027 元、1 820 元，其中北京市最高，这次上调使全国 7 400 多万企业退休人员收益。职工和居民基本医疗保险建立，“看病难”“看病贵”等问题得到缓解。今后我国稳定提高社保水平的措施是：第一，建立社保待遇随经济增长的调整机制；第二，完善社保与缴费更紧密联系的激励机制；第三，推进多层次社会保险制度，使政府组织实施的基本社会保险、企业施行的企业年金和商业保险相结合。

3. 社会保障公平

公平正义是中国特色社会主义的内在要求，社会保障作为国民收入再分配的手段，更要注重公平。当前突出的问题是养老保险待遇的双轨制，即企业退休人员与机关事业单位同类人员存在待遇差，后者远高于前者。双轨制是我国经济转型期存在的矛盾。20 世纪 90 年代，实行计划经济向市场经济转轨，率先在企业建立了社会统筹和个人账户相结合的基本养老制度，实现了单位保障向社会保障的转变。机关事业单位养老保险改革则相对滞后，总体上仍实行单位退休制度，形成待遇上的差别。导致差别的原因：一是企业基本养老金与职工缴费年限长短挂钩；二是机关事业单位退休金按退休最后工资的一定比例打折扣计算，并随机关事业单位工资的调整而调整，社保基金主要由国家财政负担。这就造成了退休待遇分配的不公，为此 2005—2014 年，连续 10 次提高企业退休人员养老金待遇，但差别仍然很大，而根本的解决办法是改革机关事业单位的基本养老保险制度，最终实现二者并轨。

4. 社会保障制度安全可靠

我国社会保障经过多年的改革和发展资金规模不断扩大，监管措施不断完善，总体安全可靠。2012 年城乡各项基本保险基金总收入、总支出和累计结余规模分别达到 3.14 万亿元、2.39 万亿元和 3.75 万亿元。同时也要看到老龄化高峰迫近、城镇化加速、经济结构调整等给社会保障运行带来的挑战。为使社会保险基金长期稳定运行，我国采取的措施是：一是完善多渠道投资，拓宽投资渠道，依法严格征收社保费，调整财政支出结构，加大社会保障投入，通过国有股转持，国企经营利润和国有土地出让金划转，开征专项税收等增加社会保障战略储备；二要推进基础养老金全国统筹；三要实现社保基金保值增值。目前社保基金只能存入国有银行和购买债券以确保安全的同时，也要拓宽基金投资渠道，坚持多元化投资，保证投资安全。

就业问题

我国20世纪50年代是如何解决失业问题的[①]

在新中国30年的劳动就业史上，有一个阶段为人们所称道，那就是在20世纪50年代，我国经过国民经济恢复时期和第一个五年计划时期，只用了七八年的时间，就基本上解决了旧中国遗留下来的失业问题。在这一时期，安置失业人员的工作为什么搞得比较成功？采取了哪些做法？有些什么经验？温故而知新，认真进行一番回顾，对于解决当前社会上存在的失业问题，具有很重要的现实意义。

在旧中国，由于帝国主义、封建主义和官僚资本主义的压迫、掠夺和剥削，经济凋零，民不聊生，大批失业人员流离失所，衣食无着，成了失业大军。在农村，一批批因受地租、高利贷残酷剥削而破产的贫苦农民，纷纷背井离乡，流入城市，扩大了城市的失业群。到新中国成立前夕，城市失业人员达到400万人，相当于1949年末职工人数的一半。

新中国成立后，党和人民政府把解决失业问题当成一项中心任务，随着经济的恢复和发展，积极认真地加以解决。这样，在恢复国民经济的三年中，就约有一半以上的失业人员重新获得了职业；第一个五年计划开始以后，生产建设事业有了更大的发展，就业机会增多，每年都有一大批失业人员走上工作岗位，到了1956年，失业问题就基本上得到了解决。

在我们这样一个人口多、底子薄、经济十分落后的国家里，所以能在短短的七八年时间里基本上解决旧中国遗留下来的严重失业问题，从根本上说，是

① 本文发表在1981年第2期的《经济与管理研究》上。

由于当时较好地发挥了社会主义制度的优越性，同时，也由于党和人民政府采取了一系列行之有效的措施和符合客观实际的方针政策。具体来说，就是：

第一，努力防止产生新的失业人员。

首先是在对国民党军政机关和官僚资本主义企业的接收接管过程中，对原有人员实行“包下来”的政策。其中，对在国民党反动政府中工作的几百万公教人员，全部给以安置。官僚资本主义企业收归国有后，对其全部职工实行“原职原薪”政策，使之在原来的岗位上继续生产和工作。这样，就避免了几百万人的失业，同时也稳定了社会秩序，巩固了人民政权，对生产的恢复和发展起了推动作用。

其次，对城市的私营工商业进行“公私兼顾，劳资两利”的政策，使之在原材料分配、加工订货、产品收购包销、资金贷款等方面享受与国营企业基本相同的待遇，以保证其生产的恢复和发展及工人的就业。同时规定资方不得为单纯追求利润盲目招收和无理解雇工人，并教育私营企业的职工团结资方，共同克服困难，以免企业倒闭，造成新的失业。在私营工商业实行全行业公私合营时，人民政府各有关部门对企业的资金、财产、生产经营和人员等方面，采取“分口包干、统筹安排”的方法，保证正常的生产秩序，不使一个人由于这场大变革而失业。因此，在对私营工商业进行“利用、限制和改造”的全部过程中，没有发生任何失业现象。

第二，广开就业门路，实行介绍就业和自谋出路相结合的就业方针，安置失业人员。

这是解决失业问题的根本办法，它主要包括社会招收、介绍就业和自谋出路三个方面。

新中国成立初期，为了恢复和发展生产，稳定人民政权，解决失业问题，政府允许一些企事业单位和国家机关从社会上自行招收失业人员。例如，东北和华北的一些厂矿企业就曾根据自己的需要，直接吸收失业的技术人员和技术工人参加生产建设，补充本企业劳动力的不足。各大城市还举办人民革命大学，招收大量失业和无业的知识分子，经过短期政治训练后分配到国家行政机关和文教单位工作。许多失业的技术人员和知识分子就这样应招而被选择录用了。

所谓介绍就业，就是各地劳动部门对失业人员进行普查登记，将适合企业需要的人员介绍到有关企业去工作。这是安置失业人员的主要方法。起初，介绍就业的范围只限于失业的技术人员和技术工人，随后扩大到一般劳动者和知识分子。从1950年上半年介绍就业工作开始至1951年底，经过劳动部门介绍就业的就有100万人以上。1952年以后，登记和介绍就业的范围更广，进一步扩大到失业和求职的旧军官、旧官吏、独立生产者、行商摊贩、资方代理人及小工商业主、家庭妇女等。

介绍就业的工作全面开展以后，取得了很大成绩，通过普查登记，基本上弄清了各类失业人员的情况，同时采取了边登记边安排的办法，使大批失业人员获得了职业，一时未能就业的也得到适当的救济和安置，减轻了生活困难。

除了政府介绍就业以外，当时还对失业人员实行自找职业，自谋出路的政策。这是由于，一方面我国经济基础薄弱，第一个五年计划的经济建设开始以后，国家每年也只能安排一部分劳动力，不可能一下子吸收全部失业人员；另一方面，在20世纪50年代前半期，我国多种经济成分并存，城市中除了国营企业外，还有大量的私营工商业和个体工商业户，都可以容纳一定数量的劳动力，一部分失业人员也可以通过他们自己的社会联系进入这些部门去工作。因此，1953年5月，在中央就业委员会、中央劳动部和中央内务部召开的劳动就业座谈会上，正式提出了“介绍就业与自行就业相结合”的方针，这一方针避免了失业工人产生单纯依赖国家，一切由政府包下来的想法，鼓励了他们自谋出路的主动性和积极性，数以万计的失业人员通过这条途径走上了工作岗位。由于这一方针对短期内解决我国的失业问题起了重大作用，因而受到了广大群众的热烈拥护，被形象地称作劳动就业工作的“两扇门”。

第三，组织失业人员进行劳动生产自救或发放救济金。

对经过失业登记后暂时不能就业的人员，则采取救济措施。这里所说的救济措施，并不仅仅是发放救济金，主要是将失业人员组织起来，实行生产劳动自救，即以“以工代赈”为主，同时采取生产自救、转业训练、资助还乡生产以及发放救济金等办法。

以工代赈是失业工人1950—1951年生产劳动自救的主要形式。所谓以工代赈，就是工人不坐等国家的救济，而是通过自己的两手，参加劳动，代替国家的救济。具体做法是：失业工人在自愿的原则下，组成工赈队，参加政府兴办的市政工程建设，如翻修马路、疏浚河道、修整下水道和公园等，完成工赈任务获得赈济。工赈工程的费用来自国家拨给的救济基金，其中绝大部分用于工赈工资，少部分用来购置原材料和生产工具。工赈队员的福利待遇一般高于失业工人领取的救济金，低于在业职工的工资水平。

实行以工代赈的办法，有很多好处。首先，它解决了失业工人的生活困难。据统计，1950—1952 年，全国参加以工代赈的失业工人达 200 多万人次。由于工赈工资一般能维持失业工人及其家属的生活，因而能使他们安心等待就业。其次，工赈队员做了许多有益于社会和城市居民的事情，促进了市政建设，受到了群众的赞扬。例如，北京、上海、天津、武汉、南京等几个大城市用以工代赈的办法，翻修了将近 100 万平方米的道路，整修了近 30 万米的下水道。经过工赈队员的劳动，北京的破烂不堪，荒冢累累的陶然亭变成了美丽的公园，上海年久失修、臭泥淤塞的苏州河水变清并恢复了航道，促进了城乡的物资交流。最后，失业工人经过以工代赈，提高了觉悟，锻炼了体力，学会了修路、架桥等简单技术，为以后的就业创造了条件。总之，由于以工代赈发挥了失业工人自力更生的精神，国家收到了少花钱、多办事的效果。后来，不少工赈队为城市建筑部门所接受，工赈队员也就成了建筑工人。

生产自救也是失业人员就业前的一条出路。失业人员中，有些原是手工业者和小商贩，具有一定的技术专长和经营管理知识。对于这一部分人，在自愿的原则下，国家出资扶持他们组织集体所有制的合作社，或进行个体生产，从事陶瓷、小五金和竹木器、玩具的生产，进行针织、缝纫、制鞋、制绳的劳动。他们或者自产自销，或者接受加工订货，从中获得一定的利润，维持生活。生产自救的形式大体上有三种：一是由劳动部门从失业救济基金中拨出一笔款项，贷给手工业生产单位，增添设备，扩大生产经营，吸收一部分失业人员参加劳动。二是劳动部门拨款，组织失业人员单独成立集体生产单位，自产自销或者为其他单位加工订货。获得的利润，一部分归还劳动部门的贷款，一部分用来扩大再生产。三是劳动部门与商业部门合作，组织和领导失业人员参加城乡的物资收购、储运和销售工作，由商业部门支付一定的报酬，维持生活。四是政府补助生产资金，扶持个人独立生产经营。

由于劳动部门坚持了生产自救原则，调动了失业工人的积极性，生产自救单位的生产经营情况一般都较好，参加人数也不断增加，仅国民经济恢复时期就有 15 万人左右。以后随着国家经济建设的发展，一部分生产技术条件和经营状况较好的生产自救单位就逐步纳入国家计划，有的转为集体所有制的手工业合作社或地方国营企业，在其中参加劳动的失业人员也就正式就业。一些规模小、人数少的单位，则由失业人员自己管理，成为独立的手工业者和小商贩。

转业训练是国家为失业工人创造就业条件而采取的一项措施，即国家选择有培养前途的失业人员，负担其伙食和学费，对他们进行技术训练，提高其文化技术水平，以满足经济建设对技术工人的需要。

转业训练的形式多种多样，大体来说有三种。第一种是劳动部门委托国营或私营企业以学徒或训练班的形式代为培训，失业人员学习期满后，代培的企业可优先录用，其余由劳动部门介绍给别的用人单位。第二种是劳动部门和用人单位共同组织训练班，由用人单位挑选失业人员参加训练并负责学习期满后的分配工作。训练班的设备、工作人员和经费由双方共同负担。第三种是劳动部门自己举办专业训练班，对社会上需要量大的专业和工种，如汽车司机、简单的机械加工、打字、会计和保育、炊事等进行技术训练，学习期满后由劳动部门介绍工作。

1951 年国家经济情况好转后，转业训练形式有了很大发展，国民经济恢复时期，参加的人数达到 20 万人左右。这不仅为当时国营和私营企业输送了质量较高的劳动力，而且为国家有计划的经济建设开始以后所需要的大量新技术工人的培训工作奠定了基础。后来，劳动部门举办的技工学校就是在转业训练班的基础上发展起来的。

对于未能参加生产劳动自救，生活又确实困难的失业人员，则实行发放救济金的办法。起初，由于国家经济困难，救济的重点只限于失业工人和失业知识分子，救济金的发放标准大致以能维持失业人员及其家属的最低生活水平为原则。半失业工人，其所得工资低于失业人员所领救济金而无法维持生活的，酌情给以补助。1952 年 9 月，全面劳动就业工作开展以后，救济的范围扩大到所有登记的失业人员，救济金的发放标准也有所提高，许多地区还增加了一次性的冬衣和医药费补助。

失业救济基金是调动各方面的积极性，由国家、企业和人民群众共同筹措的，其来源包括三部分：一是国家拨款，1950 年人民政府从财政经费中一次性就拨出 4 亿斤粮食来救济失业工人，以后每年都拨出失业救济专款；二是企业和在业职工的缴纳（国营和私营企业按月缴纳所付实际工资的 1%，在业职工按月缴纳实得工资的 1%）；三是社会各界的自愿捐助。特别值得一提的是，在业的工人阶级还发扬团结友爱精神，纷纷把一日劳动所得和一部分工资、实物等捐献给失业工人。人民解放军也节省伙食费支援失业工人。据统计，在全部失业救济金中，社会各界和职工群众缴纳和捐助的就占 60%左右。

此外，在失业人员中，还有些原是离开农村不久的农民，他们有的家属在农村，有的与农村有比较密切的社会关系。对于这部分人，人民政府发给旅费和一部分生产资金，动员其自愿还乡生产或移民垦荒。这些失业人员回乡后都得到当地人民政府的妥善安排，从而摆脱了失业之苦，成了安居乐业的农民。据统计，到 1952 年 9 月，被安置还乡的失业人员就有 10 多万人。

浅论我国社会主义初级阶段的失业问题[①]

不少社会主义国家并没有实现全部就业，我国也如此，很长一段时间里一直存在就业问题。党的十一届三中全会以来，我国劳动就业工作取得了显著成绩。但是，据有关部门预测，在第七个五年计划期间需要安排就业的城镇人员仍有近 3 000 万人，平均每年 600 万人。随着城市经济体制改革的深入发展、劳动制度的改革和新技术的采用，国营企业还会富余一大批职工。据调查，全国工业企业在职“失业”大军有 1 500 万～2 000 万人。据最近的抽样调查，上海市“隐性失业”人数占职工总数的 14%～25%，为 70 万～120 万人，这些富余人员需要另辟就业途径。与此同时，随着社会主义商品经济的发展，因市场和生产条件等因素的变化，以及企业经营管理不善等原因而破产或濒临破产的企业，也将会出现一些暂时失业的职工。在农村，随着家庭联产承包责任制的普遍推行和商品经济的发展，农业劳动生产率的提高，大批剩余农业劳动力也要向非农业部门转移。据典型调查，全国农业劳动力剩余 1/3 左右，约 1 亿人。以上富余人员所形成的就业压力，不可能完全依靠国家来解决。凡此种种都向传统的就业理论提出了挑战：在社会主义初级阶段，能不能完全消灭失业？是

① 本文发表在 1988 年第 4 期的《中国工运学院院报》上。

否有必要完全消灭失业？

一、在社会主义初级阶段不可能完全消灭失业现象

在社会主义初级阶段，不可能完全消灭失业现象，只可能把它限制在一个较小的范围内。这是因为，在社会主义制度下，下述规律仍然发生作用。

（一）生产过程两要素的比例协调规律

劳动就业的实质是指劳动者和生产资料的结合。这种结合客观上要求建立一定的比例关系，即劳动力和生产资料要相互适应。如果劳动者和生产资料之间的比例失调将会出现两种情况：一是劳动力过多而生产资料不足，即劳动力供大于求，从而使社会上一部分劳动者处于失业状态，造成人力的浪费；二是生产资料过高而劳动力相对不足，即劳动力求大于供，使生产资料处于闲置状态，造成物的浪费。因此，劳动力和生产资料之间建立合理的比例关系，实现劳动力供需平衡，是一切社会生产发展的客观要求。在社会主义社会里，同样要求劳动力和生产资料之间建立一定的比例关系。

长期以来，理论界不敢触及失业问题的重要原因之一，就是马克思主义关于两种生产之间的相互关系原理没有得到应有的重视。恩格斯曾指出："生产本身有两种：一方面是生活资料即食物、衣服、住房以及为此所必需的工具的生产；另一方面是人类自身的生产，即种的繁衍。一定时代和一定地区的人们生活于其下的制度，受着两种生产的制约。"[①]恩格斯关于"两种生产"的理论，是马克思主义人口和劳动力资源理论的基本观点，也是社会主义国家实行计划生育的重要理论基础。可是，在我国长期以来，马克思主义两种生产理论并没有得到应有的重视，也没有把人口出生计划列入国民经济计划，而且在指导思想上片面强调人多好办事，结果使我国人口的高出生率和高自然增长率持续了20多年。到目前为止，我国人口已达11亿多，劳动力资源日益增多，形成巨大的就业压力。另外，我国又处于社会主义初级阶段，商品经济发展起步晚，基础差，物质资料的生产十分落后，国家资金积累，扩大生产规模来创造新就业岗位的能力受到限制，无法从根本上改变两种生产不相适应的情况，致使劳动力和生产资料之间比例不协调，劳动力的总供给大于总需求，从而必然产生

---

①《马克思恩格斯选集》人民出版社1972年版，第4卷，第24页。

失业问题。

（二）技术进步规律

社会主义经济是商品经济，商品经济必须建立在技术进步的基础上，因此，科学技术的进步和劳动生产率的提高会带来劳动力的节约。由于技术的发展和技术有机构成的提高，物质生产会发生质的飞跃，同时，相对减少了对劳动力数量的需求。生产力内部的这种矛盾运动，在社会主义时期依然存在。马克思所揭示的相对人口过剩规律在社会主义条件下仍然起着作用，因为“各种不同的生产方式有着各种不同的人口增长规律和剩余人口规律”。[①]

随着新兴工业部门的出现，技术进步所创造的就业岗位比起技术进步所消灭的就业岗位要多，但是，技术进步还会产生结构性失业问题。也就是说，即使社会提供的就业岗位数量大于劳动力数量，失业依然有可能存在，从而形成“失业与职业空位并存”的局面。原因是全部就业不仅取决于就业岗位的供给与劳动力供给之间量上的平衡，而且取决于两者之间质上的平衡，失业往往是由于就业岗位对劳动力素质的要求与劳动力所具备的素质不一致造成的。我国目前尚处于社会主义初级阶段，劳动力素质较低，对劳动岗位变动及其要求的适应性较差，不可避免地会产生结构性失业问题。

（三）经济发展的动态规律

由于工业生产的技术基础是革命的，它使社会内部的分工不断发生变革，在经济发展上表现为：各个行业、各个部门的发展产生了不平衡，一些部门、行业规模扩大了，而另一些部门、行业的规模缩小了；一些新的部门、行业产生了，而另一些老的部门、行业被淘汰了。

一国经济结构的变化，不仅包括部门结构的变化，而且包括地区结构的变化。国内原来经济不发达的地区在经济增长过程中可能以较快的速度增长，而原来经济比较发达的地区的经济增长速度可能会减缓，或者以相对慢的速度增长。某个地区从落后走向繁荣，某个地区由于资源枯竭或者自然的变迁、从繁荣走向衰落，这类例子是经常存在的。这样，经济增长较慢的地区，或者经济增长较快但主要依靠增加技术投资来实现经济增长的地区，劳动力将会多余；而经济增长较快的地区，则有可能吸收更多的就业者。

---

①《政治经济学批判大纲》第 3 分册，第 24 页。

部门经济结构和地区经济结构的变化，必然造成劳动力的转移问题，要求劳动力按照经济发展的方向相应地流动。劳动力的及时转移，是保证社会再生产正常和迅速发展的重要条件。某些部门、行业或地区如果不能把多余的劳动力及时排出而滞留下来，就会出现隐性失业，造成劳动效率的降低；另外，需要增加劳动力的部门、行业或地区，如果不及时得到满足，生产的发展就会受到限制。但是，在实际工作中，从某些部门、行业或地区游移出的劳动力和另一部门、行业或地区需要吸收的劳动力，在时间上不可能正好吻合，在数量上不可能完全一致，在质量上不可能完全符合要求。正是由于这种时间上、数量上和质量上的差异，使劳动者在部门、行业或地区间的流动总存在一个“时差”问题，从而在这段时间可能出现失业现象。

二、社会主义初级阶段没有必要完全消灭失业现象

由于上述规律的作用，社会主义制度不可能完全消除失业，也没有必要完全消除失业。这是因为：

（一）部分人暂时失业是劳动力合理流动的必然结果

劳动力流动是指劳动力在国民经济各个行业，部门以及各种职业间所进行的各种形式的位移，其目的在于使劳动力的总供给在空间和时间、质量和数量两方面动态地满足社会对劳动力的总需求，从而保证社会劳动力资源与社会经济资源、物质资源和自然资源的最佳结合。在社会主义有计划的商品经济中，社会劳动力只有在流动中才能得到合理配置，而劳动力的合理流动，就必然产生部分人的暂时失业现象，其原因是：

首先，社会主义经济是建立在公有制基础上的有计划的商品经济，而商品经济的正常运行，必须具备完善的市场体系，作为市场体系组成部分的劳动力市场也必然形成，从而出现劳动力的流动现象。其次，作为商品经济细胞的企业，在自身利益动机的驱使下，必然要求根据企业的内部条件和外部环境对劳动力吐纳自如，真正成为一个具有自我调控的全面开放系统，从而使劳动力流动不可避免。最后，人的全面发展，劳动者主人翁地位的体现，人与人之间的关系以及分配关系的完善，也需要劳动力流动。由上述几方面原因造成的劳动力流动的起点和终点之间，存在一个劳动者与用人单位之间的互相选择的过程，在这个过程中，部分劳动力的暂时游离，在业和失业共存将难以避免，局部的

劳动力短缺和局部失业将同时存在。

（二）部分人暂时失业是建立社会动力激发机制的必要手段

我国传统的就业模式是普遍就业。这种就业模式不考虑经济活动和市场变化对劳动力的合理需要，只想求得一个让人人都有“铁饭碗”的“社会公平”，其结果是把社会性失业转嫁到企业头上，造成企业内部的“隐性失业”，从而扼杀了企业经营管理的积极性和劳动者的进取精神。

要激励劳动者的积极性和进取精神，就需要建立劳动者的社会动力激发机制，而开展就业竞争则是其中的一个重要方式。就业竞争可以促进失业者勤奋努力，竞相提高自己的劳动技能和知识水平，以适应用人单位的要求和选择，同时，就业竞争所形成的社会压力还会不断地传递给在业者，使之进入竞争的行列。因而，就业竞争能有效地调动全体劳动者的积极性、主动性和创造性，使人们经常处于自强不忽的最佳状态。开展就业竞争，就必然有落伍者，从而出现失业现象，而部分人暂时失业的存在又会造成就业竞争的环境。因而，一定的失业人员的存在是建立社会动力激发机制的必要手段。

三、改革劳动就业制度走就业市场化道路

由上面的分析，我们可以看出，由于现代化大生产的共同规律的作用，社会主义条件下有计划商品经济的要求，我国部分人员失业将是一个必然存在和不断出现的问题。因此，我们应当打破传统就业理论的局限性，承认社会主义初级阶段部分人员失业的不可避免性，正视我劳动就业问题的现实，使当前企业的隐性失业显性化。在此认识的基础上，实行劳动就业制度的改革，逐步使就业制度走市场化的道路。

要使就业制度走市场化的道路，首先是将竞争机制引入企业内部，在推行劳动合同制的同时，重点搞活固定工制度，通过优化劳动组合和合同化管理等多种形式把企业富余人员撤离工作、生产岗位。

其次，对于企业富余人员，应先以企业内部消化为主进行安置，并形成企业“内部失业”人员。同时尽快建立社会保险制度和劳动力社会调节体系，该体系应具有失业保险、职业培训、职业介绍和组织自救等功能，承担容纳、消化和分解企业向社会排放的富余人员任务，从宏观上调节剩余劳动力的流动和保障失业者的基本生活。

最后，尽快制定出劳动法，明确劳动力供求双方的关系和各自的责、权、利。进一步完善劳动仲裁机构，妥善处理各种劳动纠纷。立法、司法和公安系统要支持企业劳动就业制度的改革，保护企业家和改革者的人身安全，为改革创造安定的社会环境。要做好舆论宣传工作，以促进人们观念的转变和社会心理承受能力的提高。

通过以上措施，逐步消除“铁饭碗”式的劳动就业制度，做到竞争就业，真正把用人权交给企业，把择业权交给劳动者，从而走向就业市场化的道路。

注：当时叫待业，实际就是失业。由于认识的局限，当时认为失业是资本主义的伴生物，待业是社会主义国家的临时现象，可以克服的。

科学技术进步与劳动就业关系①

科学技术是生产力，它是人类改造世界的伟大力量。当今世界，正面临着一场新的技术革命，这场革命不仅对国民经济增长及经济结构产生影响，而且会对我国的劳动就业结构产生巨大影响。所谓科学技术进步，是指科学的发展和技术的变革互相促进、相互转化的过程。它有两层含义，一是国民经济各部门、各产业使用的生产技术本身的进步，这是科学技术的现代化过程；二是国民经济各种技术手段之间的比例和联系的改善，这是技术结构的合理化过程。这两个过程紧密联系，共同对社会生产和劳动就业产生影响。

我们知道，一国的就业水平，取决于社会当时所能提供的就业机会总量以及社会当时所具有的劳动力规模总量两者之间的协调关系。就业机会总量通过两种机会获得，一是外延型的国民经济增长，即通过国家的固定资产投资，扩大生产规模而增加对劳动力的需求；二是通过技术的进步和科学的发展这种内涵式的国民经济增长取得，这种方式在现代生产中具有越来越重要的作用。劳动力的规模总量则是包括一国所拥有的劳动力数量和质量两个方面。劳动力的数量如果多于或少于一国所能提供的就业机会总量，则有可能直接出现失业或

① 摘自1988年12月袁伦渠、潘功胜、熊敏鹏所著的《现代劳动组织学——宏观论与微观论》（中国财政经济出版社）。

者劳动力不足的现象；劳动力质量对于职业的满足程度，则在更高层次上影响国民经济的发展和合理就业的实现，所谓结构性失业便是一例。同时，外延型扩大再生产更强调劳动力的数量，内涵型扩大再生产则更重视劳动力的质量，随着技术进步的不断深化，对劳动力质量的要求也越来越高。

一、技术进步对劳动过程的影响

所谓劳动过程，就是劳动者使用生产工具对劳动对象（原材料等）进行加工，生产出物质产品的过程。技术进步对劳动过程的影响，主要表现在它使生产工具、劳动对象和劳动者在物质生产过程中的地位发生的变化。

在生产工具方面，机器的发展和变化受科学技术的影响最为直接、最为显著。马克思详尽分析了近代机器大生产体系的发生、发展和它的特点后指出，任何机器体系都由三个本质上不同的部分组成，即提供动力的发动机，直接进行工作的工具机，操纵机器的传动机。第二次世界大战后的科学技术革命，使机器体系由过去的三个组成部分发展为包括自动控制装置在内的四个组成部分。由于使用了电子装置，特别是电子计算机，原先由人直接操纵控制机器动作的机构，变成了操纵机器运行的自动机构。

一切机器都是人类劳动的模拟。如果说机器工具的使用补充和延伸了人类的双手，电子计算机的应用则补充和延伸了人类大脑的功能，脑力劳动在直接生产过程中的作用越来越重要，从而使人类的劳动形态发生了重大变化。在生产构成中，操纵机器、控制机器、修配机器的职能增加了，直接操作加工的职能减少了；从事科学研究的职能增加了，从事直接操作的职能减少了；脑力劳动的比重增加了，体力劳动的比重减少了。

在劳动对象方面，科学技术进步的影响主要表现在三个方面：一是把传统劳动对象（各种形式的天然原料和材料）的利用提高到一个更高水平，如由于新的物理化学加工方法的产生和推广，为煤、石油等的综合利用提供了可能。二是人类不仅能够利用人工再生产出自然界已有的物质，而且能够制造出自然界中没有和具有一定的预先规定性能的物质。三是劳动对象的来源在不断扩展，呈现出从陆地向海洋、从地球向茫茫宇宙扩张的趋势。

在劳动者方面，第二次世界大战后的科学技术革命改变着人在生产过程中的作用。在大机器工业出现之前，人们的劳动主要是使用手工工具，劳动力的素质主要表现在人的体力、经验和技巧上。大机器工业产生之后，机器逐渐替代了人的部门体力劳动，体力因素的作用开始下降，智力因素的作用开始上升。特别是以电子计算机控制为中心的自动化技术的出现，使人从直接参加生产周期转变到控制整个生产过程——为生产做准备、设计、规划和根据规定的程序维持生产的运转。显然，劳动者如果没有一定的文化、科学技术水平，就无法与现代化的生产资料相结合，当然也不能持续提高劳动生产率。

二、技术进步对劳动就业的影响

技术进步对劳动就业的影响，应该辩证地看待。也就是说，技术进步对就业的影响存在增加就业机会与减少就业机会的两种可能性，或者说两者同时并存，其中增加就业机会是主要的方面。

（一）技术进步对增加就业的促进作用

第一，技术进步扩大了人类经济活动的范围。因为技术进步，可以使以前由于费用太高和费时过多而放弃的工作变得现实可行，如过去由于人工处理能力限制，大量的信息和资料没有得到充分利用，而电子计算机技术的发展，就为人们迅速、有效、低耗地处理这些信息提供了可能。新的技术装备，使得潜在需求变成了现实需求，就业机会也就因此而增加。

第二，技术进步开辟了新的行业、职业，扩大了就业机会。传统工业的前景越来越暗淡，但同时，新技术正在微电子学、激光、航天和遗传工程之类的一些新领域创造无限的良机；此外，技术进步也带来了一系列新工种、新职业的产生，弥补了旧工种的消失，如美国航天工业的发展，带来了一系列同航天工业相关的新职业。技术进步，就是通过新行业的兴起和新职业的产生使扩大就业机会成为可能。

第三，技术进步创造了新的社会需求，从而扩大了就业。这是因为，新技术会带来新产品，新产品会自动地刺激起新的需求，从而使人们扩大消费，扩大的消费再促使企业生产规模扩大，进而扩大了就业机会。例如：计算机产品，在它出现之前，人们就不会对它有需求，但计算机产品一旦投入市场，人们对它的需求就随之产生，甚至对生产提出新的更高要求，这样就扩大了整个社会的总需求，从而增加了就业机会。

第四，技术进步导致了传统工业固定资产的更新改造，一方面创造了固定资产的需求，另一方面也提高了国内产品在国际上的竞争力，扩大了国际市场，增加对国内产品的需求，从而扩大了国内的就业。

（二）技术进步对劳动就业的消极影响

上面分析了技术进步对增加就业岗位的促进作用，然而，它又在以下方面对增加就业形成威胁：

第一，技术进步使得一些传统行业逐渐衰落，从而减少了在这些部门就业的机会，如当今西方发达国家，钢铁、汽车、造船等传统工业，正在迅速走向衰落。技术进步正是通过这种产业结构的变化，减少传统产业对劳动力的需求，从而影响整个就业水平。

第二，技术进步导致劳动生产率的大大提高，从而减少用人量，如机器人与工业自动化设备在企业的使用，将在很大程度上取代就业者。

第三，技术进步将使现有的原材料、制成品消耗大大降低，如以塑料代替钢材，以集成电路代替晶体管，从而使社会减少对这些材料和制成品的需求，引起这些行业就业人数的减少。

第四，技术进步对劳动力素质提出更高的要求，给劳动力的部门转移带来困难。由于技术进步，国民经济内部结构将不断发生变革，这就要求劳动力按照经济发展的方向相应地流动。但是由于技术进步，劳动力的技术结构并非与技术进步相适应，从而导致这部分被转移劳动力的失业，这就是所谓结构性失业。

在社会主义社会，技术进步的根本目的在于满足人民群众日益增长的物质和精神需要。因而，技术进步更有可能促使社会充分而合理地利用劳动力，改善劳动条件，扩大就业。但是，要将这种可能变为现实，还有许多具体的工作要做。

三、技术进步与我们应有的态度

面对技术进步对就业的双重影响，我们要持积极的态度，而不是持消极、悲观的态度。结合我国的国情，目前需要注意以下几方面：一是要建立合理的技术结构，走多层次技术发展的道路；二是要加速发展新兴产业，改造传统产业，增加就业机会；三是重视智力开发，提高劳动者素质，不断适应技术进步。

首先，建立合理的技术结构，走多层次技术发展的道路。也就是说，要使不同水平的技术装备之间、工艺过程的自动化、半自动化、机械化、半机械化、手工劳动之间保持合理的比例关系。当前尤其要重视建立技术密集型与劳动密集型相结合的产业结构，大、中、小型企业比例适宜的企业结构，以及实行合理的技术政策，即先进技术与一般技术并举的政策。只有这样，才能既促进科学技术的进步和劳动生产率的提高，为扩大就业提供物质基础，又能解决现实中劳动力过多与生产资料不足的矛盾，充分利用劳动力资源，安排更多的劳动者就业。

其次，加速发展新兴产业，改造传统产业，增加就业机会。发展新兴的物质生产部门，是当代科学技术进步的必然结果，也是积极有效地解决劳动就业的重要手段。据美国商务部1979年和1980年出版的《美国工业展望》中有关资料，美国的钢材、汽车、造船及修理三个传统工业部门1973年的就业总人数为103万人，1982年减少到80.2万人，而同期，美国的电子计算机、测量控制用仪器、宇航（包括飞机、导弹和太空飞船）三个新兴工业部门的就业总人数由50.2万人增加到116.9万人。扣除传统工业排斥出的22.8万人，新增就业机会43.9万个。同样，发展新兴的非物质生产部门，也是积极有效地解决就业问题的重要途径，如第三产业中新兴的信息服务业，就是最强有力的劳动力吸收器。

用新技术改造传统工业，防止传统工业的进一步衰落，提高他们的市场竞争能力，可以保持这些部门的就业水平，如美国一些经济学者认为，美国并不是在传统工业和高技术工业之间进行选择，美国面临的真正挑战是如何在传统工业中使用尖端技术。这对我们是有启示的。我国工业发展不平衡，劳动力多，如果一味贪大求洋，选用高、精、尖技术，不仅资金没保证，大量劳动力也无从安置。同时，我们又不能只求维持现状，而必须采用新技术改造传统产业，提高其市场竞争力。只有这样，才有可能更好地解决就业问题。

最后，要重视智力开发，提高劳动者的素质。技术进步所开拓的新的就业领域，对求职者的文化技术素质有着较高的要求，而且随着生产技术构成的普遍提高，各种新工艺、新设备的发明和使用的周期缩短，一个人所具有的文化程度、专业知识、劳动技能已日益成为就业的必不可少的条件；因此，只有大力发展教育事业，提高劳动者的文化科学素质，才能使劳动者在产业结构和就业结构不断变动的情况下，增强对职业和技能变换的适应能力。

总之，科学技术的进步对劳动就业的影响，既有积极的一面，又有消极的一面。但是，人类社会总是要发展的，科学技术是不断进步的，我们应当采取积极的态度，进一步提高科学技术水平，在大力发展新兴工业和劳动力的合理转移过程中，求得劳动就业问题的动态解决。

加入世界贸易组织对我国就业的影响[①]

内容提要： 本文在我国加入世贸组织前夕，针对加入世贸组织对我国劳动力市场的影响进行预测。通过分析加入世贸组织对劳动力就业以及劳动力由第一产业向第二产业和第三产业转移的影响，提出了加强劳动力培训和人才培养，以及加强劳动立法、执法，规范劳动力市场等应对措施。

随着我国与美国、加拿大关于世贸谈判协议的签订和与欧盟谈判的进一步展开，我国加入世贸组织的进程已大大加快。虽然我国加入世贸组织的谈判工作还没有结束，有关申请程序还有待最终审议通过，但是我国近期加入世贸组织已成定局，指日可待。“中国需要加入世贸组织，世贸组织同样需要中国的加入”已成为共识。

世贸组织是我国企业参与国际竞争的一个世界舞台，加入世贸组织意味着中国与世界 135 个国家相互开放市场，开放的领域将扩展到包括农业、银行、保险、零售、旅游、电信等在内的第一产业和第三产业。加入世贸组织对我国来说机遇和挑战并存，希望与困难同在。从短期来看，长期受到国家保护（包括监督或计划）的行业将面临严峻的考验，面对激烈的竞争，部分运作机制不灵活的国有企业将破产或重组，这将影响我国经济生活的方方面面；从长远来看，加入世贸组织将使我国经济真正融入全球经济之中并获得最佳的发展，使市场资源进入国际间进行优化配置。我国的优势资源如劳动力、土地、自然资源和外国的优势资源如资金、技术、管理等进行优势互补，从而为中国经济在 21 世纪的发展奠定更为稳定的基础。总之，加入世贸组织将使我国经济融入世

① 本文发表在 2000 年第 5 期的《经济界》上（作者为袁伦渠、曹艳红）。

界经济的主流，对我国经济的发展影响很大，对经济的影响必将引起就业的变化，因此加入世贸组织对我国的劳动就业市场也将产生深远的影响。

一、加入世贸组织对就业的影响

加入世贸组织后我国的劳动力就业市场将发生重大变化，劳动力就业数量会有所增长，但就业结构将会发生较大的调整，对高素质劳动力的需求会增大。过去较多地受国家保护、不具有竞争力的国有企业和竞争力弱、受冲击大的部门从业人员失业率将会上升，一些企业富余人员、低技能人员和年老体弱者面临失业或下岗的威胁；从农业中分离出来的富余劳动力进一步增加，就业人口将更多地向第二、三产业转移；沿海地区劳动密集型、出口导向型的三资企业、乡镇企业和私营企业有可能容纳大量的就业。加入世贸组织意味着中国经济体制的进一步改革，打破国家垄断和金融业的改革会有利于私营中小型企业的发展，而中小企业应是主要的就业渠道。

（一）在就业总量上，加入世贸组织将缓解我国目前的就业压力

世界贸易组织通过贸易自由化和贸易的扩大促进经济增长，有利于创造更多的就业机会。与贸易保护主义消极保护就业的做法相反，世贸组织更多的是通过促进经济发展和产业结构的调整解决失业问题，因为技术进步、劳动生产率的提高及就业间的替代性始终是影响就业水平的重要因素。

加入世贸组织前，受国际壁垒的影响，我国的经济增长速度趋缓，劳动力需求量呈下降趋势，即使按“十五”期间我国经济增长速度为 7%，就业弹性系数为 0.13 的假设，2005 年我国的城镇剩余劳动力仍将达 2 167 万人；而加入世贸组织后，据一些国际组织预测，中国每年国内生产总值（GDP）的增长率可望提高 2.94 个百分点，相当于 300 多亿美元，而每个百分点的提升又可带来 400 万个就业机会，即中国每年可增加将近 1 200 万个就业岗位，这近 1 200 万个就业机会将会大量消化掉我国的剩余劳动力，从而大大缓解目前我国严峻的就业形势。

当然，加入世贸组织也会使部分国有企业出现职工失业下岗现象，这是正常的，并不可怕，因为加入世贸组织同样会进一步拓宽下岗职工的再就业门路。加入世贸组织后，由于放宽了国外资本进入中国市场的准入限制，将直接刺激国外资本在中国的投资。国外资本在中国投资的扩大，一方面可以直接增加就

业，另一方面也会带动国内投资，从而进一步提供就业机会。改革开放20年来，外商投资企业为我国劳动者提供了1 000多万个就业机会，直接或间接培训了许多管理人才与技术人才，尤其是20世纪90年代以来，我国城镇70%以上的劳动就业与外资有关。此外，加入世贸组织后除了日益增长的外商投资企业和外国企业为我国劳动者提供就业机会外，我国企业也将享受世贸组织其他成员国提供的最惠国待遇和国民待遇，这无疑将有利于我国进一步扩大产品出口和劳务输出，进而可以提高我国国内企业对劳动力的吸纳程度。

（二）在就业结构上，加入世贸组织将使我国的就业结构发生较大的变化

加入世贸组织后，我国三大产业将参与国际社会竞争，这就意味着较大的经济结构调整，经济结构调整必然带来就业结构的调整，就业结构调整孕育着大量的劳动力重新配置。

从国民经济结构看，加入世贸组织将导致第一产业占国民经济的比重以更快的速度下降。由于我国农业受资源缺乏、规模经济和组织化程度的约束，农产品在国际市场上不具备竞争力，再加上恩格尔效应的作用，农业部门特别是种植业部门在总产出中的比重将会有较大程度的下降，在农业内部受到高度保护的农业部门会有所收缩。由于我国农业就业人数占总就业人数近一半，农业生产的收缩将会产生更多的剩余劳动力，这些农业中的剩余劳动力将大量转向制造业和服务业，从而加剧流动人口的增加，带来更多的社会问题。关于就业机构变化的模拟结构表明，大约有960万农业劳动力需要转移到制造业和服务业。

加入世贸组织将给纺织业、服装制造业、制鞋业、玩具制造业等劳动密集型企业带来新的发展机遇。“多纤维协定”的逐步废除，极大地提高了中国纺织品和服装工业的出口竞争力，其中纺织品出口将增长63.8%，纺织品和服装部门的产出将分别提高25.5%和74%，由于这些行业的劳动密集型特征，它们的增长有利于解决大量非熟练劳动力的就业问题，可以吸收大量农村失业人口，促进我国的城市化进程。

加入世贸组织对于尚处于幼稚期的技术密集型、资本密集型企业以及金融、商业等服务业来说，会受到一定的冲击。诸如汽车、计算机、通信设备、机床、医药化工等行业，其产品虽然在国内仍有潜在需求，但在质量、价格、技术等方面与进口商品存在一定的差距，因此一旦进口商品开始涌入，势必使这些行业处于不利的境地，从而引起企业的破产或重组，迫使许多行业进行更大幅度的裁员，

导致劳动力更加富余。允许资金实力雄厚的外国企业在中国介入金融、商业等服务业，也将加剧服务业的竞争，加大金融市场的风险，短期内可能会出现国有企业亏损面扩大，破产企业增多，下岗或失业人员增加的状况，从而对社会保障、再就业等工程造成更大的压力。但这未尝是一件坏事，从长远来看，加入世贸组织能加速我国国有企业改革的进程，将国有企业真正推向市场，增强其竞争力，这些行业的从业人员在经过技能培训、深造之后，可能会适应更激烈的竞争。在这一过程中，有些素质低、接受能力差的人被淘汰也是正常现象。

（三）劳动力流动尤其是高素质人才的流动更加频繁

国际分工和产业结构调整必然导致劳动力的流动。加入世贸组织后，世界500强中的其他200多家可望尽快进驻中国，大量的跨国公司进来后，会逐步实现人才的本地化，以降低成本，获得更大效益。由于外企的薪酬水平高、用人制度灵活、发展机会多，对国有企事业单位的核心人才将产生较强的吸引力。而在与市场经济接轨的情况下，人才的合理流动又是一种必然规律。因此大批的业务骨干将从国企流向外企，造成国企由于人才流失而效率低下。而国企由于多方面的原因，其待遇是不可能大幅提高的，这就决定了在人才竞争方面我国将长期处于不利地位。如何在激烈的竞争中留住并吸引高素质人才，成为我国企业人才资源管理部门面临的重要课题。

还有可能出现的人才流向就是海外军团的“回归热”。前些年出国学习和工作的一些人才由于既没有语言障碍和文化差异，又了解中国的商业习惯和国外的竞争环境，并具有一定的国内外关系，在加入世贸组织后的国内人才市场上将大有用武之地。香港地区的管理人才与技术人才也有深入内地发展的趋势。

（四）加入世贸组织对劳动力素质提出了更高的要求

加入世贸组织之后随着竞争的加剧，企业对员工技术水平、文化水平的要求不断提高，员工们将不再满足于现有的知识水平和结构，学习将贯穿于人的一生。实用型人才、高科技人才将更加抢手，有更多的发展机会。新兴产业有巨大的就业需求，如IT产业和IT相关服务产业，这对年纪轻、学历高、技能熟练、竞争力强的人才将是一个巨大的机遇。富有经验的市场或行业管理者、成熟的专业和技术人才将供不应求，薪金水涨船高。一般来讲，掌握一门外语、懂计算机知识，同时又有一门专业知识的人才将如鱼得水，懂技术、善管理、了解国际市场运作规律的人才最受欢迎。

（五）劳务输出结构发生变化

劳务输出是我国的一大强项，加入世贸组织后这一强项将更具优势。据专家介绍，目前国际劳动力市场需求潜力巨大，不仅亚非拉各国，就是在欧洲、北美也有机会等待我们挖掘。发达国家仍需要输入普通劳动力且绝对数在增长，发展中国家对技术型劳动力的需求也在增长。但随着科技进步，普通劳动力的需求相对减少，技术型劳动力的流动将会增加，单一的劳务结构在向多层次发展，这是国际产业结构调整对国际劳动力市场、劳动力结构产生的影响。

（六）加入世贸组织后人才市场将更加活跃

加入世贸组织必将大量地增加中国与外界的多种交往，如投资、贸易、教育活动。这将直接导致对律师、会计师、医师、保险精算师等人才的迫切需求。因此这些职业将更加火爆；加入世贸组织将会使我国的外贸管理体制发生很大的变化，外贸经营权将从审批制过渡到登记制，因此拥有进出口经营权的企业会大大增加，对外贸专业人员的需求会更大，需求会更高；加入世贸组织后境外人员将大量进入我国旅游观光考察，因此熟悉计算机操作、旅游专业毕业的管理人才和导游人才将是企业争夺的对象；市场竞争将使人才竞争愈演愈烈，生活节奏加快，心理疾病增加，心理医生也迎来自己的发展机遇；还有外语人才、谈判人才、信息业人才等也将在人才市场中走俏。

二、加快改革步伐，适应加入世贸组织后劳动就业的新形势

由上述分析可知，加入世贸组织对我国劳动就业的影响是多方面的，虽然有很多问题尚待深入研究，但就目前而言必须加快以下几个方面的改革步伐。

（一）加快社会保障制度改革

加入世贸组织后，由于经济体制改革的深化及就业结构的调整，我国劳动力的流动将更加频繁，社会保障体系更显重要，社会保障范围更广、层次更深。因此必须加快养老保险、失业保险、医疗保险等社会保障制度改革，把国有企业承担的社会职能分离出来，建立起独立于企业的、并能切实为职工提供基本生活保障的社会保障制度，为劳动力的竞争和流动解除后顾之忧，为市场运行提供一个较稳定的社会环境。

（二）加强对劳动者的培训和各类专业人才的培养

加入世贸组织后我国将面对激烈的国际竞争环境，国际市场的竞争要求参

与者具有较强的综合开发和实际应用能力，具有灵活的应变能力和果断的决策能力，具有熟练的外语会话、公关和谈判能力，具有运用现代技术进行信息处理、分析、设计等能力。然而我国现有的人才状况却很难适应这一要求，因此必须加快教育体制改革，建立知识转化为生产力的激励机制，通过培训把学校教育变成终身教育，真正把人力资源开发放在国民经济管理的重要地位，时刻加强对各类专门人才的培养，造就一大批熟悉现代市场经济和国际通行规则的经济管理和法律人才。

（三）加强劳动立法，规范劳动力市场运行秩序

中国加入世贸组织后，目前用来规范劳动力市场和调处劳动关系的法律、法规不仅在数量上不足，而且在相关内容上也难以适应新形势的要求。为此，必须加快劳动立法步伐，在《劳动法》的基础上，通过制定《就业促进法》《社会保障法》《劳动合同法》等法规，有计划、有步骤地建立包括规范市场主体行为和维护市场秩序以及政府宏观调控、保护劳动者和用人单位合法权利等一整套法律制度，为劳动力市场的健康运行提供法律保障，促进我国劳动力市场的发育和完善。

（四）提高劳动力市场执法监察人员素质，加大执法力度，改进监管办法

我国加入世贸组织后，由于外资企业的大量进入，执法监察的对象将更加广泛；执法监察的内容更广，涉及诸如知识产权、技术秘密等一系列新情况、新问题；执法监察使用的法律法规会更多，执法监察方式既要考察国内的执法习惯，还要考虑国际间通行的执法方式。这就需要我们加强对执法人员的培训，改善劳动力市场的监管方式和方法，增加透明度，保证劳动力市场在公平、公正、公开的环境中规范地运行。

中小企业就业质量分析[①]

一、就业质量的基本内涵

就业是劳动者与生产资料结合从事社会劳动并获得报酬或经营收入的经

① 本文发表在2010年第5期的《中国国情国力》上（作者徐平国、袁伦渠）。

济活动。它包括数量和质量两个方面：有多少劳动者能够与生产资料结合并获得相应收入，这反映的是就业数量；而劳动者与生产资料结合得好坏，如工资高低、工作稳定性如何、工作环境是否安全健康、是否享有社会保障等，体现的就是就业质量。

就业质量是就业活动不可或缺的重要组成部分。就业质量不仅关系到劳动者的权益保护，它的优劣还会直接影响到就业数量。当前，在我国劳动就业领域中，劳动力数量供大于求、结构不适应需要与就业质量不高的矛盾同时存在，二者相互作用，加剧了就业形势的严峻。因此，解决我国的就业问题，就要在促进经济增长，不断扩大就业规模的同时，把提升就业质量作为一项长期而紧迫的任务来抓，以扩大就业规模为提高就业质量创造条件，以提高就业质量促进就业数量的增加，双管齐下，推动就业工作快速、健康、可持续发展。

2010 年中央经济工作会议提出着力优化经济结构和提高经济增长质量。这是贯彻落实科学发展观、转变经济发展方式的重要内容，是解决我国发展面临的突出矛盾和问题的有效途径。不断改善就业质量，是提高经济增长质量，构建民主法治、公平正义、诚信友爱、安全有序、充满活力的和谐社会的必然要求。

二、我国中小企业就业质量问题的现状及分析

我国中小企业数已超过 4 000 多万户，占全国企业总数的 99%以上，中小企业创造的国内生产总值占 60%，上缴税收占 50%，就业人数占 75%，进出口总额占 69%，开发新产品占 82%以上。中小企业在繁荣经济、促进增长、扩大就业、推动创新等方面发挥着越来越重要的作用，已经成为推动中国经济社会持续发展的关键因素之一。在我国，中小企业对社会的最大贡献是就业，它们不仅安置了大量的城市下岗职工，吸收了大批农村剩余劳动力，还有效解决了许多大学生的就业问题。

然而，另一方面，与其显著的就业创造功能相伴，中小企业的就业质量问题也一直比较突出。由于中小企业普遍受到资金和技术条件的限制，为了规避用工成本，企业的生产条件及劳动用工行为不可避免地存在许多不规范之处，加上外部监管力度有限，中小企业的从业者劳动权益受损情况相对比较严重，可以说，在中小企业范围内存在着严重的就业质量的赤字。主要表现在以下四

个方面。

第一，就业岗位不稳定，劳动者合法权益缺乏保障。据湖南省一份劳动力抽样调查显示，这种现象主要表现在：一是劳动合同签订率低，未签订合同的雇员所占比重达到 56.7%，集中在制造业、建筑业、批发和零售业，所占比重分别是 40.0%、15.2%和 9.6%。二是劳动合同普遍呈现短期化，用人单位劳动合同一年一签的做法成主流。雇员签订固定期合同的期限在一年及以下的占 71%，两年以上的仅占 10%。其中农民工绝大多数没有签订劳动合同，即使签订了合同，也大多为“霸王合同”，劳动关系缺乏法律的有效约束。二是职业稳定性差，就业人员每周工作时间在 20 小时以下的占 5.3%，就业人员时常处于就业和失业的交替中。

第二，劳动报酬偏低，拖欠工资的现象比较普遍。不少非公有制中小企业，往往以最低工资标准为参考来确定职工的劳动报酬。广东省总工会公布的农民工基本状况调查结果显示，在广东的农民工中有近一半人的工资在 800 元以下，达到全省职工平均工资水平的仅占一成。800 元还是临界数，更有很多农民工拿着三四百元的月薪，仅能维持最基本的生活。大学毕业生的就业质量也不容乐观，一份国家教育部发展研究中心的调查报告显示，大学生在毕业后最初的 5 年里，有 1/3 的人更换过工作岗位。部分私营、个体就业人员和农民工不仅劳动报酬低且难以兑现，企业拖欠、克扣、压低职工工资的现象普遍存在，拖欠农民工工资的案例屡见不鲜。资料显示：高达 65%的农民工工资被拖欠。

第三，劳动环境差，超时劳动现象严重。一是体力劳动者的工作环境差，健康得不到保障，特别是农民工更显突出。最近几年，全国每年各类安全生产事故平均 100 多万起，死亡 14 万多人。平均每 3 天，就有一次死亡 10～29 人的特大事故发生。而这些恶性事故中的死亡者，绝大多数都是农民工。二是就业者超时劳动现象普遍。中国青少年研究中心公布的《城镇青年就业失业状况与分析（2009）》显示城镇就业人员周平均工作时间约为 44.6 小时，加班已成为大多数城镇就业者的一种工作常态。

第四，个体、私营企业劳动保障程度低。由于我国目前非公有制单位就业存在着社会保障体系难以覆盖、劳动合同签订率低、劳资关系极为松散等问题，致使非公有制经济就业的增加，从一定程度上对社会整体就业质量提出了更高要求。资料显示：非公企业寿命一般只有四五年的时间，每年有 20 万个非公企业破产倒闭，企业生存生态恶化，拿不出更多的钱提高工人工资、改善工人待遇。

就业岗位不稳，就业质量不高，带来了方方面面的社会问题，影响了政府和社会扶持下岗失业人员再就业资金的使用效果，加大了政府对职业介绍、职业培训的开支。反复的求职和失业还严重影响了人们的就业信心，增加了社会救济的负担。这种状况也进一步拉大了行业间、企业内外的收入差距，有失社会公正与公平。由此产生的劳动争议增多，又影响了社会的和谐与稳定。

造成上述中小企业就业质量问题的原因，可归结于政府责任缺失，企业管理不规范以及劳动者自我保护意识薄弱三个方面。

（一）政府制度环境缺陷和责任的缺失

（1）制度环境的缺陷使得大部分中小企业的经营成本过高，难以发挥出本应具有的更大的促进经济增长和解决就业的作用。准入限制依然存在，制约了就业渠道的扩大；融资渠道不畅，抑制了就业机会的创造；税费负担过重，阻碍了就业规模的扩大。

（2）政府责任的缺失。政府没有强制要求建立稳定的工资增长机制，只是规定了各地有权根据当地实际情况制定当地的最低工资，但缺乏对这一制度的监督和审核。政府的基础管理薄弱，对私营企业社会保险信息不能及时掌握，直接影响到私企的参保缴费。法制不健全，《社会保险费征缴暂行条例》对非公有经济没有强制要求。

（二）企业自身条件所限和用工管理不规范

（1）中小企业自身的管理水平、技术水平和服务水平低制约了其自身的发展。缺少经营管理经验和科学的管理方法，对内部管理和发挥激励机制作用的认识也较肤浅；技术水平低，产品同质性严重，市场竞争激烈；盲目扩大生产经营规模和追求多元化发展道路，从而使企业出现资金短缺、产品质量不高，服务跟不上等困难。

（2）劳动用工管理不规范，职工的权益无法保障。用人单位不与劳动者签订劳动合同、不建立职工健康档案、不参加工伤社会保险的问题普遍存在，一些劳动者合法权益都没有建立，而当劳动者在权益受到损害后，由于没有明确的劳动关系，私营企业逃避本应由其承担的保险责任和义务。

（三）劳动者的就业能力和自我保护意识差

（1）就业能力的缺失是导致中小企业从业者缺乏就业稳定性、恐惧企业倒闭或裁员的根本原因。多数中小企业从业者由于缺乏核心技能或专业能力，对自己未来的职业发展方向没有明确掌握，导致每一次就业岗位的转换都处于退步或原地踏步的状态。

（2）职工维护自身权益的意识薄弱。自身素质不高导致对一些相关的法律规定不了解，不了解工作场所职业病危害真相；参保意识薄弱，谁给钱就给谁干，参不参保无所谓。

三、提高我国中小企业就业质量的建议

中小企业的生存和发展、中小企业从业者的就业保障需要各方综合努力来实现。政府首当其冲，其主要责任是加大当前对中小企业的支持力度，为中小企业提供良好的政策环境；企业作为生产经营主体，应从自主创新和科技研发入手，提高企业的市场竞争能力；劳动者则应注重自身素质和技能的提升，凭借出色的就业能力来获得高质量的就业。

（一）政府部门

（1）政府应切实解决中小企业融资难问题，为中小企业提供危机贷款，放宽贷款门槛、健全政策性担保机构，扩大中小企业贷款规模。同时，大范围减免或缓收停收中小企业各项税收和行政事业性收费，增加对中小企业的财政补贴额度，提供支持中小企业战胜困境的贴息资金，以帮助中小企业开源节流。从长期看，政府还要破除中小企业行业进入的管制壁垒，拓展中小企业的国内发展空间，帮助企业扩大内销；支持中小企业实行产业转型和结构优化。扩展中小企业引进国外创新成果的合理渠道，加大企业自主科技创新的扶持力度。

（2）各级政府部门要高度重视有关就业质量的各项工作，完善就业领域中主要的法律缺陷，并且要扩大对就业质量的宣传。完善社会保障立法，将主要职业病纳入工伤保险范畴，既可保障劳动者权益，又分散了用人单位的经营风险。要规范参保单位缴费行为，强化企业参保缴费的法律意识，查处违纪行为，堵塞各种漏洞，保证基金的按时足额征收，对无故晚缴的单位要一并征收滞纳金。

（二）中小企业

（1）中小企业要逐步建立现代企业制度，以减少决策失误、提高企业经营稳定性，为提高企业的核心竞争能力奠定基础。在技术方面，重视技术创新，加强研发投入，培育企业核心技术。在人才方面，重视人才的培养和使用，特别是对于企业的核心人才，更要注重从招聘、考核、晋升等多个环节、使用多种手段来进行培养和激励。在品牌方面，要找准市场定位，强化品牌管理，打造具有核心价值的企业品牌，通过品牌获得更大的市场份额和经济利益。

（2）中小企业要在最低工资制度的基础上建立合适的工资增长机制，根据经济效益、工资指导线和劳动力市场价位适时合理调整工资，要确保企业利润增长与职工工资增长同步。企业要规范用人制度，切实保护劳动者合法权益，一旦招聘人员就必须按照《劳动合同法》的相关规定与劳动者签订合同及参加相关的社会保险项目。企业要全面落实劳动卫生规程，减少职业危害。

（三）劳动者个人

（1）中小企业从业者一般具有较多的从业经验，实践能力较强，但知识陈旧，技术落后，不能从容应对快速的市场变化。因此，一要注意在工作中提升自己的技能水平和业务能力，在干中学；二要注意在业余时间有针对性地参加社会学习或自学，加快知识更新速度，扩张知识积累。三要做好职业发展规划，避免随波逐流，实现成功转型。

（2）中小企业从业者要加强自我保护意识，主动要求与用人单位签订劳动合同，在劳动过程中要求单位提供基本的安全劳动环境。

加强科技创新对就业促进作用的建议[①]

内容提要：本文是作者参与国务院参事室“科技创新驱动”调研组工作的一部分。本文研究了科技创新驱动和就业优先政策，分析了科学技术是第一生产力的观点和技术进步作为双刃剑对就业数量和就业结构的影响，提出了科技

① 本文系袁伦渠、刘盾撰写，摘自2015年8月浙江出版联合集团出版的《科技资源优化配置与中国发展》一书。

创新促进就业的如下建议：强化企业原始创新动力；有选择地对有吸纳就业作用的生产性服务业、中小企业和劳动密集型企业采取先进技术；发展现代职业教育，解决好科技创新带来的结构性失业；机器代人要因地制宜。

党的十八大做出实施创新驱动发展战略的重大部署，强调科技创新是提高社会生产力和综合国力的战略支撑，必须放在国家发展全局的核心位置。李克强总理在政府报告中又强调："就业是民生之本，坚持实施就业优先战略和更加积极的就业政策，以创业带动就业。"

可见科技创新和就业优先都是国家的重要发展战略。因此如何处理科技创新和就业优先战略的关系是一个值得深刻探讨的问题。

自从 1978 年邓小平提出"科学技术是第一生产力"的观点以来，随着科技进步对我国经济增长贡献率的上升，科技创新对就业的影响就一直被探讨。科技进步与就业的作用究竟是正相关还是负相关成为一个争论不休的问题。一部分学者认为科技进步造成了失业率增加，主张限制高新技术产业的发展，大力发展劳动密集型、技术含量低的产业，从而扩大就业；另一部分学者持相反观点，认为科技进步有助于解决就业问题，主张全面发展高新技术产业，淘汰劳动密集型、技术含量低的产业。

的确，科技创新对就业的数量和结构都有影响。早在 1817 年，古典经济学家大卫·李嘉图就指出，技术进步是一把"双刃剑"，它在促进就业增加的同时也会造成结构性失业。对这一现象，有人称之为"李嘉图之谜"。科技创新对就业数量的影响表现为替代效应和补偿效应两种相反的效应。一方面，科技创新导致资本对劳动的替代，造成就业减少；另一方面，科技创新带来的生产成本低、产品需求增加、市场规模扩大又增加对就业的需求。科技创新对就业结构的影响则表现为"技能退化型"创新和"技能偏向型"两种创新。所谓技能退化型创新，是指科技创新引起的劳动分工专业化、工艺流程标准化会降低部分行业对劳动技能的要求；所谓技能偏向型创新，是指生产过程技术含量的提高和高新技术产业的迅速发展又会提高部分行业对劳动技能的要求。这就是科技创新对就业数量和就业结构变化的双重效应。

经济社会的发展离不开科技创新，社会的和谐离不开充分就业。科技创新对就业既有积极作用也有消极影响，而它们的综合效应取决于两者之间的互动和协调程度。因此，客观分析科技创新在我国就业领域所扮演的角色，选择适当的科技进步方式，充分发挥科技创新对就业的促进作用，实现就业数量的增长和供求结构的匹配，是我们研究的初衷。

一、关于北京市科技创新与就业关系的研究成果[①]

为了深入地研究科技创新与就业的关系，我们曾经对近十几年北京的科技创新与就业之间的关系进行过4年的研究，从宏观研究和微观调研得出的结论是：从短期和局部来看，科技进步替代的就业岗位大于补偿的就业岗位，但从长期全局来看，科技进步的补偿岗位大于替代岗位。北京市科技创新促进了就业数量的增长、就业质量的提高和就业结构的优化。

（一）北京市科技创新与就业关系的宏观分析

在宏观方面，我们通过对1999—2012年北京统计年鉴的公开数据进行综合分析，得到了如下结论：

从就业数量的角度而言，尽管在一定时期内就业的替代效应比较明显，但是创新活动提高了地区生产总值和劳动生产率，以更大的经济规模创造了对劳动力的更多需求，从而产生了更大的就业补偿效应，其综合效应促进了就业的增长。同时，科技创新催生了对更多科研人员和专业技术人员的需求以及产业升级和更多新产业的产生，这对促进就业数量和质量的提高都产生了积极影响。

从就业结构的角度来看，一方面，科技创新提高了地区从业人员整体的学历水平，优化了就业者队伍。北京市就业人口中拥有大专以上学历从业人员的比例从2003的26.2%上升到了2012年的53.6%，其中本科以上学历就业人员的比例增长最为明显，由13.8%增加到了34.3%；另一方面，科技创新促进了北京市劳动力向第三产业的转移，优化了就业的产业结构，使第三产业就业人数比例从2003年的59%增加到了2012年的75.6%，尤其是交通运输、信息传输、科学研究、计算机服务等高科技行业近几年的就业数量上升较快。由此可以看出北京市科技创新对就业结构升级产生了积极的作用。

（二）北京市科技创新与就业关系的微观分析

在微观分析中我们对北京市130家企业从2008—2010年的企业科技创新

---

① 袁伦渠主持的北京市科学技术委员会项目“北京市科技创新促进就业的分析及对策研究”成果，项目编号：Z101110001810013。

和就业情况进行了问卷调查，并将企业的科技创新活动分为产品创新、过程创新和组织创新三大类，分别分析了企业创新对就业的影响状况及影响路径。从调查结果可以了解到，近几年来，大多数被调查企业都曾实施过各种不同形式的创新活动，并且这些创新活动对企业的就业无论在数量上还是结构上都有显著的正面影响。

在就业数量方面，大部分被调查企业的员工数量都有所增长，其中约有一半的企业员工数量增长幅度在50%以上。为了进一步研究就业数量的增长是否源于企业的创新活动以及哪种类型的创新对就业的影响最大，我们采用了统计模型进行分析，结果表明：企业产品的原始创新可以明显地促进员工数量增长；组织创新通过改善企业的运营效率与竞争力，导致市场份额扩大进而促进员工数量增长，并且组织创新往往与其他类型的科技创新相伴而生，其就业弹性系数最大；过程创新通过提高企业销售额显著促进了员工增长。

在就业结构方面，科技创新的影响主要表现在以下三方面：在员工的技能结构上，企业内部的专业技术人员和管理人员比重在增加，一线工作人员和操作工人的比重在降低，在被调查企业中，管理人员和技术人员的平均总比例从2008年的38.03%增加到了2010年的48.6%，这也反映了企业的科技创新活动更表现出技能偏向型的特征；在年龄结构上，企业员工逐步年轻化，30岁以下员工比例从2008年的45.92%上升到了2010年的52.51%，而40岁以上人员比例明显减少；在学历结构的变化上呈现出高学历发展趋势，被调查企业中拥有硕士及以上学历的人员比例从2008年的15.85%快速上升到了2010年的20.64%，而高中及以下学历人员比例从28.2%降低到了24.5%，从而彰显了科技创新对就业结构的优化。

从对北京市的研究中我们可以得到的启发是：尽管科技创新对就业的影响是一个同时具有替代效应和补偿效应的“双刃剑”，但我们可以通过科技政策和产业政策的选择、调整，将科技创新引向有利于就业的方向。

二、加强科技创新对就业促进作用的建议

我国有13亿人口、9.2亿劳动力，长期面临着劳动力供给大于需求的严重就业压力。当前就业压力主要集中在三大群体，一是庞大的农民工群体，2013年农民工有2.69亿人，其中外出者1.66亿人，本地就业者1.03亿人；二是以

高校毕业生为主体的青年就业难问题，2013年应届毕业生699万，2014年727万；三是大量失业人员再就业和帮助就业困难群体实现就业难度仍然很大。

总的来说，当前我国劳动力市场面临着总量上供大于求和结构上供需不协调的双重压力。如何妥善安排这三大群体的就业问题是我国长期的社会经济任务。因此，为了加强科技创新对就业的促进作用，建议的思路是：坚持实施就业优先的宏观经济战略为指导，扩大就业数量，提升就业质量，协调就业结构，尽量采取各种措施减少科技创新对就业带来的替代效应，增加科技创新带来的补偿效应，最大限度地提升科技创新对就业的促进作用，实现科技创新与就业二者的双赢。我们根据对北京市科技创新与就业关系的研究成果，同时系统梳理了科技创新对就业影响研究的相关文献，谨提出如下建议：

（一）在坚持“就业优先战略”的前提下，科技创新优先支持有利于促进就业的生产性服务业

“十二五”规划纲要指出“坚持把促进就业放在经济社会发展的优先位置”，要求科技创新要以促进就业和改善民生为首要目标，而非片面地追求产业技术的“高精尖”。优先支持发展生产性服务业，既符合倡导科技创新、促进产业结构升级的方针政策，又能最大限度地发挥科技创新对就业的拉动作用。

据估算，我国就业弹性高的前十名的行业中大部分为生产性服务行业，其中包括：信息传输，网络，计算机服务和软件业，租赁和商务服务业，水利、环境和公共设施管理业，科学研究和技术服务业，金融业等。

生产性服务业是指为满足供应链的中间需求，给生产制造过程的各环节或阶段提供服务产品的行业。实践证明，生产性服务业是人力资本和知识资本密集的行业。这些高技术服务业既体现科技创新支持生产力发展的方向，又是具有较高就业弹性的行业，因此对就业的拉动作用较强。

（二）确立企业科技创新的主体地位，强化企业原始创新动力，促进就业

从微观层面对北京市企业创新与就业关系的研究中发现，引进吸收再创新对就业的促进作用不大，企业的原始创新对就业的促进作用非常明显。而我国企业的科技创新整体上恰恰表现出技术引进较多，原始创新较少的特点。在调查中发现，企业原始创新动力不足的根源是创新利益不足，因为原始创新是一项高投入、高风险、长周期的活动，大量的资金、人员投入很难在短期内获得回报。而创新主体所获得的创新成果却往往通过模仿、学习等途径被其他企业

所利用，导致企业在创新投入方面存在着天然的激励不足。因此，在发挥企业创新市场主导的同时，还应当发挥政府的引导作用，以利于科技创新促进就业。

为此，政府应该通过有针对性的政策制定和制度优化，形成一个完整的企业原始创新支持体系，使之发挥对就业的促进作用，具体包括：

（1）政府通过财政拨款资助、贷款贴息和资金投入等方式扶持和引导企业进行创新活动，以降低企业创新成本，引导企业选择创新方向。

（2）加快培育创新服务体系促进企业产学研合作原始创新。产学研合作原始创新系统可以优化企业的资源获取方式，有效降低企业原始创新成本，分散创新风险，提高企业原始创新动力，优化劳动力技能结构的匹配程度，促进就业。

（3）加强对国内企业原始创新产品的政府采购力度，有效扩大科技创新企业的市场份额，提高创新企业的利润，进而促进创新企业对劳动力的吸纳。

（4）加强对原始创新科研成果的知识产权保护，包括：加大对侵权行为的打击力度，提高仿冒产品被查处的概率，加大侵权企业赔款和罚款力度，使企业可以从创新中得到回报。

（三）处理好科技创新与发展现代职业教育体系的关系，解决科技创新导致的结构性失业问题

科技创新势必带来企业的技术装备升级乃至产业结构调整，从而有可能造成结构性失业。与此相适应，必须对教育结构进行战略性调整，以劳动力市场需求为导向，建立健全一套紧贴劳动力市场需求、紧随技术进步的现代职业技能教育体系，培养和造就大批不同类型的科技人才和技能人才，及时有效地满足快速变化的产业升级需求，解决科技创新导致的结构性失业。另外，一支高素质的技术人才队伍也是有利推动科技创新的生力军。有学者指出，一些发达国家（尤其德国、日本最为典型）之所以成为创新强国，不仅仅是依赖研究机构少数精英的智慧，更重要的是依赖标准化的生产体系和与之相适应的高质量的劳动力队伍，尤其是研发人员与处于生产一线的技术工人的互动与共同努力，对产品、流程的持续改进与数据积累。

（四）有选择地应用先进技术，采取积极的就业政策

科技创新对就业的影响既然是一把双刃剑，政府就应当通过引导，选择适当的产业政策和科技政策，注意发展对就业有积极作用的中小企业，推动与劳动密集型产业协同发展，尽量规避技术进步对就业的不利影响。

政府在选择产业政策和科技政策时，要考虑发挥我国劳动力资源丰富的优势。要尽量采用对就业负面影响小的技术，技术的进步和推广使用不应导致先进技术严重排挤劳动力的现象。

第一，要让企业尤其是具备较强就业拉动作用的中小企业和劳动密集型企业发挥科技创新的主体作用。这不仅有利于唤醒全社会的科技创新活力，提升科技创新的经济效率，还能借助要素价格机制，充分发挥当前我国劳动力资源丰富的比较优势，提升创新的就业促进作用。在存在富余劳动力、用工成本低廉的情况下，企业可能会更倾向于使用劳动密集的生产技术，甚至采取节约资本型的科技创新。例如：比亚迪公司在自主研发制造锂电池的过程中，就走了一条“人工代替机器”的路子。它们把日本厂商昂贵的全自动生产线分解成 7 个车间，每个车间又分解成若干简单、易操作的工序。一条日产 10 万只锂电池的生产线，比亚迪使用 2 000 个工人，设备投资仅 5 000 万元人民币，而日本虽然只要 200 个工人，设备却需要 1 亿美元，结果比亚迪每块电池的成本只有 1 元人民币左右，日本则达到 5～6 元人民币。

就农业部门而言，我国农业劳动力资源丰富，目前尚不能普遍采用欧美国家机械化农耕模式，而应采用生物技术、信息技术等高新技术发展高效农业，取得既促进农业进步又增加劳动就业的效果。

第二，机器换人要因地制宜。据人民日报刊载的一条消息：在工业基础薄弱，大量富余劳动力急待转移的西部地区（2014 年政府工作报告提出，将有一亿人口到西部城镇落户）竟然也有地方领导片面强调产业升级，主张机器换人。在西部地区的某山区县一个企业引进了一套高科技设备，结果 50 多名职工被裁减，一次性将职工人数减少了 1/3。被裁减职工群情激愤，采取了不合作态度，将车间的钥匙、工具箱、保管物品藏起来不肯交出，甚至将企业的电闸关掉……

因此我们主张，不发达地区不要与发达地区攀比，我们国家不要与发达国家攀比，有条件的地区适当地推行机器换人，不具备条件的地区应多考虑就业岗位。尤其地方领导不能盲目跟风，应当通盘考虑、妥善处理机器和人的关系。

转型升级、机器换人是一项长期复杂的系统工程，不可一蹴而就。既要大胆实践，又要稳妥把握，要充分考虑我国国情和各地实际，统筹新兴产业和传统产业、科技创新与扩大就业的关系，循序渐进，努力实现转型升级与经济发展、扩大就业协同共进。

收入分配问题

旧中国产业工人的工资水平之衡量[①]

某个时期工资水平的高低，必须有衡量之标准。近代产业在中国的产生和发展，一极是财富的积累，而对立的一极则是贫困和劳动折磨的积累。丰富的劳动力资源，以其极为低廉的价格，为中国近代的剥削者们提供了丰厚的利润，而为自己留下的却是“一片浸满了泪水和汗水的黑面包”。[②]本文试图从两个方面对旧中国产业工人的工资水平做出分析和评价。

（一）劳动力价格偏离价值的程度

工资（劳动力的价格）是劳动力价值的货币表现，劳动力的价值是由再生产劳动力所必需的生活资料的价值决定的，因而，在一定时期内，劳动力价格背离其价值的程度可以用来衡量同期工资水平的高低程度。

在劳动力的价值标准一定的情况下，劳动力这种特殊商品的价格不仅诸如其他商品一样受其供求关系的影响，“依购买劳动的资本家和出卖劳动的工人之间的竞争情形为转移”[③]，而且还受到特定社会的道德标准的影响。伴随着近代产业在中国的产生和发展，机器的使用，大批的儿童、妇女和小生产者被抛入生产过程；并且，在浓厚的封建气息的土壤中滋长出来的资本主义生产关系夹带着愚昧和野蛮，因为如此，中国近代劳动力的出售经常处于十分被动的地位，工资标准一直是低于劳动力的价值标准。下面引用了工资标准较高的1928年上海工人的工资情况和生活费用的对比来说明这一问题，如表1所示。

① 潘功胜、袁伦渠，1983年。

②《公有法典》商务印书馆59年版P41。

③《马克思恩格斯选集》第1卷P336。

表 1　1928 年上海工人的工资和生活费用　　单位：元

业别（1）	工资（2）	生活费用（3）	（4）=（2）/（3）×100%	业别（1）	工资（2）	生活费用（3）	（4）=（2）/（3）×100%
棉纺	15.50	27.20	57	漂染	20.78	27.20	76
丝纺	24.88	27.20	91	机器	30.34	27.20	112
棉织	22.05	27.20	81	电机	21.13	27.20	78
针织	17.87	27.20	66	造船	32.13	27.20	118
毛织	14.31	27.20	53	面粉	16.95	27.20	62
造纸	21.55	27.20	79	榨油	15.42	27.20	57
皂烛	17.64	27.20	65	制蛋	21.11	27.20	78
火柴	19.30	27.20	71	烟草	22.62	27.20	83
制革	18.29	27.20	67	自来水	25.24	27.20	93
搪瓷	17.49	27.20	64	电气	25.45	27.20	94
				印刷	40.20	27.20	148

说明：（2）栏摘自《旧中国的资本主义生产关系》P127；（3）栏来自 1931 年国民党工商部对全国 30 个城市的调查资料，仅包括衣食住等最低生活费用；（4）栏依据（2）、（3）栏整理而得，计算时尾数经过取舍。

通过表 1 可以看到：21 个行业中只有机器、造船、印刷 3 个行业的工人工资超过了最低生活标准，其他 18 个行业却都在 27.20 元的水平之下，其中一半之多的行业（13 个行业）在最低生活标准的 80%之下，有的竟只有 50%。如果将医药费、子女教育费等算进去，这个比例还会低得多。从中可见旧中国的工资水平之一斑，工人收入微薄，工资水平低下。

如果我们从动态的角度——时间序列的角度去做一番考察，呈现的情形为之更糟。1927 年大革命失败后，物价上涨，而工人的名义工资却呈现下降的趋势，致使不仅劳动力的价格和其价值的背离程度未得以缓和，而是差距越拉越大，这从上海工人的工资实际收入指数和工人生活费指数下降幅度的对比中可以得到解释，如表 2 所示。

表 2　上海工人的工资实际收入指数和工人生活费指数

年份	1931	1932	1933	1934	1935	1936	1937	总平均
工人工资实际收入指数	−4.36	−3.16	−4.77	−10.45	−15	−20.7	−22.6	−13.5
工人生活费指数	−2.5	−7.5	−16.8	−16.6	−15.5	−10.1	+7	−10.31

资料来源：《上海劳工统计》国际劳工局中国分局编

从表 2 可以看出：1931—1937 年的 6 年间，工人的年平均实际收入呈直线下降，同期的生活费指数也虽有下降，1937 年以后开始回升，工资指数的下降幅度快于生活费指数，其必然的结果是工人生活更加恶化，劳动力价格和其价值的差距扩大了。

（二）消费构成的优势

收入水平的高低决定着生活水平的好坏，而生活水平的优劣又反映着收入的多少。由于消费构成是反映人民生活水平的一项重要指标，所以可以通过对消费构成的分析来衡量收入水平的高低。

人们的消费需要服从一定的层次，首先是生理的需要——肉体的需要，除此以外的一切需要都是这一需要得以满足以后的事。因而，人们在获得一定数量的消费品之后（不论其是实物形式，还是货币形式），首先是解决生存的问题，而在生存的条件中，又主要解决吃、穿、住的问题，其中对食物的需求又居于首位。只有在这种基本的生存资料得以满足之后，才能谈得上享受和发展的问题。这种消费的层次制约着收入分配的层次，而收入分配的层次及其在各层次间的分配比例取决于收入的多少。这正如德国著名经济学家恩格尔所提出的那样，他认为，一个家庭的收入越少，其总支出中用于购买食物的费用所占的比重就越大；反之，一个家庭的收入越多，其总支出中用于购买食物的费用所占的比重就越小。借以反映食物费占总支出比例的指标，谓之恩格尔系数。依赖于上述原理，下面引用了两组资料分析一下旧中国劳动人民的消费构成（如表 3、表 4 所示），借以反映其收入水平的高低。

表 3　1918 年清华学校校役生活费用支出情况

项目	食物	衣服	其他必需品	杂项
比重/%	84.7	13.2	1.4	0.7

资料来源：《中国劳动年鉴》 P174

表 4　1943 年昆明中央机器厂 127 厂工人家庭消费支出情况

项目	食物	衣服	燃料	杂项
比重/%	64.0	4.0	10.4	21.7

资料来源：《劳动经济学》，北京经济学院劳动经济系编

从上面的两个调查资料可以看到，工人收入的绝大比重（60%以上）用于购买食物，在表 3 中，食物及衣服两项所占的比重竟高达总支出的 98%，表 4 中的食物、衣服、燃料 3 项也高达 80%，这种消费结构仅能维持最低限度的生存，是一种极低水平的消费结构，它是旧中国工人的工资水平异常之低的客观反映，微薄的工资使他们只能吃最粗劣的饮食，住茅棚土屋，穿褴褛的衣服，经常处于饥寒交迫之中，“资本来到人间，从头到脚，每个毛孔都滴着血和肮脏的东西”[①]。

综上所述，无论从劳动力的价格偏离其价值的角度，还是从消费构成的角度都反映了旧中国的劳动力资源之廉价，工资水平之低下。

社会主义初级阶段必须坚持以按劳分配为主体的多种分配形式[②]

内容提要：本文是在党中央提出我国尚处于社会主义初级阶段理论以后撰写的，本文突破了按劳分配是唯一分配制度的理论，提出分配应实行以按劳分配为主和按资金、按经营成果、按资本和劳动力价值为补充的多元分配形式，突破了国家统一分配的形式，实行国家对企业按劳分配，企业对职工按劳分配的二级按劳分配，提出了解决社会分配不公问题的措施。

① 《资本论》第一卷第 829 页

② 本文发表在 1989 年 11 月的《经济与管理研究》上。

中央领导同志在国庆四十周年讲话中指出："发展以公有制为主体的多种经济成分，必然在分配体制上实行以按劳分配为主体的多种分配形式。"这是对我国社会主义初级阶段个人消费品分配制度最完整、最科学的概括。要贯彻这一精神，我认为应当注意以下几点。

一、明确按劳分配为主体，其他分配形式为补充的观点

社会主义初级阶段经济成分以公有制经济为主，以个体经济、私营经济，以及中外合资、中外合作和外资企业为辅，此外，在公有制经济内部还出现了承包、租赁等所有权与经营权分离的形式以及股份制等。与此相适应，在分配体制上，除了按劳分配这种主要形式外，还有按资金分配、按经营成果分配、按资本和劳动力价值分配等补充分配形式。但应看到，社会主义初级阶段毕竟是社会主义社会，决不能不适当地任意限制按劳分配原则实行的范围，我国广大人民根据按劳分配原则获得的收入应成为生活的主要来源。其他分配形式虽然在当前是合法的，但应看到其中有非劳收入甚至剥削的一面，况且占的比重很小，仅处于从属的地位，不应当喧宾夺主过分夸大其作用。

二、贯彻按劳分配原则应坚持两级按劳分配的观点

过去在公有制内部实行的按劳分配，主要是产品经济条件下的一级分配，即按人头确定企业的工资总额，依照统一的工资标准在全国范围内实行同步增长工资的制度，企业工资总额同其经济效益脱节，职工工资同其劳动成果脱节，形成企业吃国家"大锅饭"，职工吃企业"大锅饭"这两个平均主义，挫伤了企业经营管理和职工劳动的积极性。十年改革中随着对按劳分配认识的深化，在当前有计划商品经济的条件下，实行了两级按劳分配的原则，即国家对企业实行按劳分配，企业的工资总额和奖金随其经济效益好坏上下浮动；企业对其职工进行按劳分配，即在自己工资总额的范围内，根据每个职工的劳动贡献，支付相应的劳动报酬。两级按劳分配有助于解决分配上两个平均主义和"大锅饭"问题，调动企业和职工两个积极性。两级按劳分配是十年改革的重要成果，应当坚持，不应产生怀疑。

三、认真解决社会分配不公问题

社会分配不公主要表现在两个方面，一是平均主义，二是收入过分悬殊。平均主义主要发生于工资劳动者之间。平均主义也是一种分配不公，因为它意味着多劳不多得，贡献小的侵吞贡献大的人的劳动果实，在这个意义上可以说平均主义也是一种剥削，它成了培养懒汉的温床，因此必须解决。

收入过分悬殊是一种新的社会分配不公。当前主要表现在以下几个方面：（1）不同产业间职工的平均收入差距过大；（2）某些行业如涉外服务单位及部分文艺工作者收入偏高；（3）租赁企业承租人收入过高；（4）部分合资企业职工收入偏高；（5）部分个体户和私营企业主收入过高；（6）部分职工第二职业收入过高，部分离退人员再就业收入过高等。这种新的分配不公不仅严重干扰了按劳分配原则的贯彻执行，而且引起广大群体的不满，成了严重的社会和政治问题。

我认为，解决社会分配不公，特别是解决一部分人收入过高的问题，应本着“保护合法收入，调节过高收入，取缔非法收入”的原则，采取以下几条措施：（1）清理整顿各类公司，打击“官倒”及形形色色的非法经营活动，严格控制公司各类人员的工资、津贴和奖金。（2）进一步完善经营承包责任制，对提取奖金过高的企业，要降低奖金提取比例，对企业承包、租赁、经营者个人收入和晋级升资采取必要的监督和审批制度。（3）加强税收管理，建立个人收入申报制度，打击偷漏税行为，严重者要绳之以法。（4）加强对职工从事第二职业的研究和管理。（5）加强思想政治工作，企业党委和职代会要参与并监督企业工资的分配。

关于社会主义市场经济收入分配体制改革的几个问题[①]

一、关于社会主义市场经济收入分配体制框架

社会主义市场经济体制的基本框架既然是独立自主的企业、平等竞争的市场和宏观调控的政府的有机结合，那么，社会主义市场经济收入分配体制作为

① 本文发表在 1995 年 1–2 合刊的《中央电大经济》上。

社会主义市场经济体制的一个组成部分，其构筑的框架应当是：企业的自主分配，劳动力市场上的平等竞争，政府的宏观调控。

要做到企业自主分配，首先贯彻《全民所有制工业企业转换经营机制条例》，将工资分配权交给企业，使工资分配的主体由国家转为企业。为防止企业追求收入最大化的倾向，约束企业的分配行为，必须探索一条既能从外部对企业的工资分配进行调控，又能促使企业从自我发展的需要出发，自觉地对工资分配进行自我约束的有效途径，建立起内外结合的企业分配约束机制。

其次是劳动者在市场上平等竞争。在市场经济中，劳动力作为一种生产要素必然也要进入市场。在劳动力市场上，社会主义劳动者以平等的权利参与竞争。劳动者的工资，一是取决于劳动者本身的素质，二是取决于劳动力的供求情况。

政府的宏观调控，主要指运用法律、经济手段的间接调控解决地区间、产业间和社会各类人员间的分配不公。例如：制定最低工资法，保障劳动者的基本生活；加强税收，征收个人调节税等。

社会主义市场经济收入分配体制的建立还要兼顾效率与公平，既要促进效率，拉开差距，又要防止两极分化，逐步实现共同富裕。当前，不同行业之间、不同产业之间、不同地区之间以及社会各类人员之间收入上的高低悬殊，都是极不正常的现象。笔者认为，正常的现象应当是，在发育完善的市场条件下，劳动力平等竞争和合理流动的结果，必然能消除产业之间、行业之间、企业之间收入的过分悬殊。相反，在企业内部，由于劳动者素质高低不同，在企业自主分配的情况下，必然是有所差别、拉开档次，不应当是平均主义的。解决分配不公问题：一是国家宏观调控，以解决地区之间、产业间和社会各类人员之间的高低悬殊，反对不平等竞争和以非法手段暴富；二是要加强对个人高收入的税收。

应当看到，我国向社会主义市场经济体制过渡刚刚起步，国有企业经营机制的转换和政府职能的转变尚需时日，劳动力市场尚未发育成熟。在这种情况下，社会主义市场经济收入分配体制自然很难形成。在此之前，作为一种过渡，仍不能否定两级按劳分配理论和工效挂钩的作用。两级按劳分配理论是由计划（产品）经济条件下的一级（全社会用一把尺子衡量劳动，一竿子插到底）按劳分配转变为两级（或说多级）按劳分配，即由按人头分配工资总额，按照统一的工资标准在全国范围内实行同步增长的工资制度，转变为国家对企业实行按劳分配，即国家根据企业的经济效益确定企业工资总额，也就是企业的工资总额与其经济效益挂钩，然后企业在其内部，在自己工资总额的范围内，根据劳动者劳动的数量和质量，通过一定的工资制度和工资形式进行分配。两级按劳分配理论和工效挂钩的做法，尽管没有突破计划经济体制的框框，是计划经济体制内部的改革，其第一级按劳分配比较复杂，确定的指标、基数、比例也难免带有主观性，但是，它由对企业下达指令性绝对额工资指标改为按经济效益指标规定企业工资增减，在某种意义上已体现出市场经济的因素。

两级按劳分配理论，是党的十一届三中全会以来，广大理论工作者和实际工作者经过长期的理论探讨和反复实践，对马克思主义按劳分配理论认识的深化和发展，曾对我国1985年开始的企业工资改革提供了理论根据。在由计划经济向社会主义市场经济体制过渡的过程中仍有自己的积极作用。它和以按劳分配为主体、多种分配形式为补充的理论，以及企业分配与机关事业单位分配脱钩的理论一样，是我国对马克思主义按劳分配理论认识的突破和发展。

二、关于社会主义市场经济条件下按劳分配的特点

研究这个问题，首先要对按劳分配这一概念作一个界定。我们所说的按劳分配，是马克思主义经典作家论述的按劳分配，即对社会总产品做了六项扣除后，按照劳动的三种形态（流动的、凝结的和潜在的），或按劳动的数量和质量，对个人消费品的分配。

我国目前正处于社会主义的初级阶段。这就使在社会主义市场经济条件下的按劳分配规律不能不打上社会主义的初级阶段的烙印。在社会主义初级阶段，由于实行以按劳分配为主体，多种分配形式为补充的分配制度，决定了社会主义市场经济条件下按劳分配的特点是：以按劳分配为主体，其他分配形式为补充。不能不看到，按劳分配实行的范围相对缩小，实行的程度相对较低。或者说，在社会主义初级阶段，按劳分配实行的广度和深度都受到了一定程度的限制，带有不充分性。

先看按劳分配的广度受到一定程度的限制。在社会主义初级阶段，由于生产力水平低，各地区经济发展水平不平衡，存在以公有制经济为主体，包括个体经济、私营经济、三资经济（企业）为补充的多种经济成分，与此相应，在

分配体制上，除了按劳分配这种主要形式外，还有按资金（或生产资料）分配、按经营成果分配、按资本和劳动力价值分配等补充分配形式。由此可见，社会主义初级阶段的按劳分配，较之于马克思主义经典作家所设想的社会主义高级阶段的分配，即在全社会实行公有制，生产由国家统一计划、产品由国家统一调拨，工资实行统一的标准，全社会同工同酬的按劳分配来说，在范围上要狭窄得多，也就是说，分配的广度受到了限制。当然，应说明的是，社会主义初级阶段毕竟是社会主义社会，我国广大劳动人民根据按劳分配获得的收入应成为主要的生活来源。其他分配形式在当前虽然是合法的、允许的，但应看到，其中有非劳动收入甚至剥削的一面，不应喧宾夺主，过分夸大其作用。

再看按劳分配的深度受到一定程度的限制。在社会主义初级阶段的公有制内部，存在全民所有制和集体所有制等形式，在全民所有制与集体所有制之间，还不能实行统一标准的按劳分配，在集体所有制之间，由于它们占有的生产资料数量和质量不同，也不能实行统一标准的按劳分配。即使在全民所有制内部，也不可能完全的、彻底的按劳分配。国营企业改称国有企业，这一字之差，反映了所有权与经营权的分离。当前不少国有企业实行了承包制、租赁制、股份制等。与此相适应，在国有企业中，除了实行按劳分配以外，还出现了承包人和承租人的风险收入，股息、红利等非劳因素的分配形式。可见，在公有制内部，较之马克思主义经典作家所设想的社会主义高级阶段的一竿子插到底的完全彻底的按劳分配来说，在深度上也受到一定程度的影响。

初级阶段下的按劳分配的实行在深度上受到的限制，还表现在它的实现本身带有复杂性。原因是，在社会主义市场经济条件下，由于市场规律的作用，劳动者报酬的多少，不仅取决于他为社会提供了社会必要劳动及其创造的价值，而且还取决于这些价值是否实现和实现的程度。所以，劳动者报酬不仅受按劳分配规律的支配，还要受到价值规律、市场价格、供求关系等一系列非劳因素的影响。它必须经过一系列经济机制的作用才能最终实现。在劳动者的收入中，由企业经营管理水平提高带来的收入是按劳分配规律作用的结果，由技术设备先进带来的收入是级差收益，由产品适销对路带来的收入是价值规律作用的结果。所以说，社会主义初级阶段下的按劳分配带有不完全性、不彻底性。

铁路人工成本与职工总量控制研究①

内容提要：本文是作者主持的铁道部课题"'九五'期间铁路职工总量控制和用工制度研究"的核心内容。本课题首次将人工成本理论引入铁路企业管理，用人工成本直接控制职工总量，提出了"九五"期间铁路职工总量由行政手段控制转向以经济手段控制的思路和措施。此研究成果得到铁道部的肯定，并在成都铁路局实施。

人工成本是一个企业为劳动者花费的全部费用，是企业在生产经营和提供劳务过程中，直接或间接支付或投资于劳动者的全部费用。在1996年10月召开的第11次国际劳工统计学家会议上，来自世界各国的劳工统计学家们就人工成本的统计达成了一致的意见，形成了《关于人工成本统计的决议》。在该决议中，人工成本定义为：雇主因雇佣劳动力而发生的所有费用。根据国际劳工局的解释和我国具体情况，我们认为，可给人工成本下这样一个定义：企业在生产经营活动中，根据国家的劳动人事政策、法令和管理制度规定所负担的全部人事费用。它包括：生产工人、企业管理人员、销售人员及生产服务人员的工资及其税前列支的各种奖金、津贴；工资性的物价补贴；按工资总额一定比例提取福利费；职工培训费；按职工工资总额缴纳的各种保险费，包括由企业负担的离退休人员的保险费和活动费；按工资总额提取的工会经费；劳动保护费；企业负担的职工住房津贴；企业代缴的个人收入调节税；劳动力及各类人员的招聘费。

由于人工成本直接关系到一个国家的宏观经济政策及其在国际市场上的竞争力，因而世界许多国家对人工成本统计十分重视。据统计，到目前为止，全世界已有近50个国家或地区进行着人工成本的调查和统计，其中包括美国、日本、英国、法国、德国、意大利、新加坡等。鉴于制造业的重要性，各国对人工成本的抽样统计以及国际间的比较也都以制造业为重点，日本的人工成本计算比较详细，有关机构对劳动分配率和人事费用率等指标进行了统计分析，为各国人工成本的研究开了先河。

---

① 本文发表在1997年第4期的《铁道劳动》上。

我国长期习惯于对工资和各项保险福利进行分项统计，从未对人工成本进行专门的研究。值得欣慰的是，我国劳动部门已开始重视人工成本的问题，于1994年年底分别在北京、上海、天津、河北等省市进行深入的抽样统计工作，1996年上半年得出了抽样调查分析报告，取得了较好的效果，劳动经济研究人员认为，我国应建立人工成本统计制度，加强对人工成本的研究和控制，为国民经济的发展和提高企业的经济效益服务。

一、人工成本研究的重要意义

1. 增加利润和增加职工收入

我国习惯于用 $C+V+M$ 来表示企业总产值的结构。$C+V$ 为成本，M 为剩余价值或利润。在 $C+V$ 中，C 是物耗成本，V 是人工成本。传统的管理方式把 $C+V$ 和 M 对立起来，认为要想增加 M，就应尽量压低 $C+V$。由于技术进步较慢，在 C 和 V 两者之间，V 又成为压低的对象。

在现代管理模式中，虽然获取利润仍是企业最关心的事情，但是管理的观念和方法已发生了很大的变化。现代企业更加注重 $V+M$ 的扩充和增大，$V+M$ 是企业的附加价值，是劳动者通过劳动过程新创造的价值，是社会财富增加的源泉。用附加价值经营的观点来看，V 和 M 两者是同一源泉的，也可以同方向变化。其意义是：把蛋糕做大，利润和劳动者工资可以一起增加。关键是如何扩大附加价值，动态地保持好人工成本和利润互相协调的关系。

在市场经济中，企业在商品市场谋求价格优势的竞争能力取决于成本水平的高低；在劳动力市场上吸引高素质的劳动者的竞争能力取决于向员工支付的工资和保险福利水平的高低。企业要保持市场竞争的优势，不完全取决于低成本和高利润率，还取决于所支付的工资和人工成本的高低，并通过附加价值的经营和劳动效率的提高不断扩大人工成本的支付能力。我国目前存在的三资企业就有这样的优势，它们有高素质的劳动者，提供高效率的劳动，增加更多的附加价值，同时带来了低成本、高利润率和职工的高收入。

2. 有利于企业进行成本核算，加强管理

在企业的生产和经营中，会发生多种多样的费用，如生产资料的耗费，活劳动的耗费，土地、资源的占用等。用最少的投资换取最大的产出，是所有企业一致的努力目标。

通过对本单位人工成本当年与往年水平（或若干年的平均水平，历史最高、最低水平）的对比，可以发现人工成本是增加了还是减少了，增加或减少的原因是国家宏观政策的变化还是自己管理中的不足。通过对人工成本各构成部分的比例合理性分析，各部分的发展趋势及其增减的合理性分析，以及与同类企业人工成本的比较，可以发现本单位产品竞争能力的强弱，找到自己的不足，从而改变人工成本的投入方向和水平，使人工成本使用更加合理。

3. 有利于国际交流与合作

人工成本是企业人力资源管理统计的指标，也是进行国际交流可比性较强的指标，因为它能反映出劳动力费用支出的全貌，反映劳动力市场的价格，这在世界各国基本上都是一致的。通过人工成本主要指标的国际比较，企业可以看出在哪个国家或哪个地区投资效果比较好，甚至可以判断出生产哪些产品创利更大，从而决定投资方向和数量。目前我国劳动力价格较低，人工成本相对廉价有利于提高我国产品在国际上的竞争力，也是吸引外资的有利因素。

二、反映人工成本的指标

由于不同企业职工人数不同，工资总额不同，人工成本总额不同。人工成本总额不能直接衡量企业之间的成本高低，必须设计出反映人工成本的指标。人工成本的指标可以分为进行人工成本横向比较的绝对数指标和反映经济效益的相对数指标。

（一）相对数指标

相对数指标包括劳动分配率、人事费用率和总成本人工成本含量三种。

1. 劳动分配率

企业劳动分配率有两种表达方式，一是附加价值工资率，二是附加价值人工成本率。

$$\text{附加价值工资率}=\frac{\text{工资总额}}{\text{附加价值}}\times 100\%$$

$$\text{附加价值人工成本率}=\frac{\text{人工成本总额}}{\text{附加价值}}\times 100\%$$

以上两式中“附加价值”是指企业投入劳动力和资本所赚到的金额，即V+M，是企业经营由生产销售后新创造出来的价值。劳动分配率指标不但可以反映工资总额在新价值中的比例，而且可以反映人工成本总额在新价值中的比例，它的意义很大。显然，劳动分配率越低，企业利润越高，它可以进行企业之间、产业之间、地区之间甚至国际之间的比较。

一般制造业的附加价值计算公式为：

附加价值=销售收入-制成品和在制品库存金额-外购原材料、燃料和动力费用-管理费和销售费用中的物质消耗费用

铁路运输企业的附加值计算与一般企业有所不同，因为运输业的产品不具有实物形态，没有制成品和在制品。因此：

铁路运输企业的附加价值=营业收入-外购原材料、燃料和动力费-管理和销售费中的物质消耗费用

附加价值产生后的分配为：

附加价值=折旧额+人工成本总额+运输利润

2. 人事费用率

企业人事费用率就是人工成本在企业销售额或总产值中所占的比例，其公式为：

$$人事费用率=\frac{人工成本总额}{销售额（或总产值）}\times 100\%$$

该指标反映人工成本在销售收入中的比例，越小越好。

3. 总成本人工成本含量

$$总成本人工成本含量=\frac{人工成本总额}{总成本}\times 100\%$$

$$=\frac{人工成本总额}{物资消耗+人工成本总额+其他费用}\times 100\%$$

如果企业生产同规格的单一产品，其单位产品成本的人工成本的含量只要用总成本人工成本除以产品数量即可求出。如果企业生产的是不同类型的产品，则要分别核算不同产品的总成本和人工成本。

这一指标只是成本与成本比较，不能仅就它的数据变动就断定企业人工成本控制效果的好坏，但是在企业成本管理上有用，如在企业销售收入总成本含量发生变动时，具体分析物耗成本和人工成本各自对总成本数值变动的影响程度。

（二）绝对数指标

绝对数指标包括职工平均工资和职工平均人工成本这两个指标。它们表示：第一，企业职工收入的高低；第二，企业使用一名职工大致需要支出多少人工费用；第三，企业在劳动市场上的竞争能力有多大。

劳动分配率和人事费用率这两个相对数指标可以显示投入的人工成本和效益状况，但是却不能表示企业职工的工资水平和保险福利水平的高低，也就不能作为企业向劳动力市场提供劳动力价格的信号。在劳动力市场上，劳动者择业中非常重视各企业所能提供的工资和保险福利水平。企业要吸引高素质的劳动力到企业工作并提高企业职工的劳动积极性，也需要将人均工资水平与人均人工成本的水平稳步提高作为目标。

（三）适度的人工成本控制标准

企业在制定利润计划并测量适度的人工成本控制线时，考虑市场竞争因素，尽可能满足下面两个条件：

第一，企业每人平均人工成本≥竞争对手；

第二，企业人事费用率和劳动分配率≤竞争对手。

企业在国内市场竞争对手中最好同时满足这两个条件。在国际市场竞争中，由于我国现在是一个发展中国家，劳动生产率水平还大大低于多数竞争对手，工资水平也低，因此根本无法满足第一个条件。我国企业要创造在国际市场的竞争优势，关键是满足第二个条件的要求。为此应制定出适度的人工成本控制线。可采取节约用人、提高劳动效率等控制人工成本的手段满足第二个条件。

三、铁路运输业人工成本的计算

表 1 是铁路运输业 1994—1995 年度收入、支出及劳资状况。

表 1　铁路运输业 1994—1995 年度收入、支出及劳资状况

项目	1994 年	1995 年	增幅
职工总数/人	2 010 589	2 008 580	−0.1%
工资总额/千元	14 929 061	18 935 115	26.8%
人均工资/元	7 425	9 427	27.0%

续表

项目	1994 年	1995 年	增幅
劳保福利费总额/千元	3 892 046	1 406 159	−63.9%
人均社会保险福利费/元	1 936	692	−64.3%
运输总收入/万元	5 828 239	6 320 686	8.5%
营业支出/万元	5 708 620	6 405 619	12.2%
其中：折旧/万元	658 049		
运输总支出/万元	5 998 499	6 740 015	12.4%
运输利润/万元	−291 071	−641 276	
劳动生产率/（万换算吨公里/人年）	80.70	82.4	2.1%
总产量/百万换算吨公里	1 623 337	1 655 786	2.0%

资料来源：《全国铁路统计资料汇编（1994）》《全国铁路统计资料汇编（1995）》

根据表 1 中铁路运输业在 1994、1995 年度收入、支出及劳资状况数据可以计算出 1994—1995 年的人工成本水平指标。计算公式如下：

$$劳动分配率=\frac{工资总额+劳动保险福利费总额}{附加价值}\times 100\%$$

铁路企业职工人工成本的住房补贴和职工教育经费目前还难以统计，但可以用工资总额与劳动保险福利费总额之和来近似地代替人工成本总额计算。附加价值由下式确定：

$$附加值=折旧额+人工成本总额+运输利润$$

$$人事费用率=\frac{人工成本总额}{总收入}\times 100\%$$

$$总成本人工成本含量=\frac{人工成本总额}{总支出}\times 100\%$$

根据上面的公式和表 1 资料的计算可得出统计表 2。

表 2　1994—1995 年度铁路运输业人工成本状况表

项目	1994 年	1995 年	增幅
劳动分配率	83.7%	95.5%	14.1%

续表

项目	1994 年	1995 年	增幅
人事费用率	32.2%	32.2%	—
总成本人工成本含量	31.4%	30.2%	−3.8%
人均工资/元	7 425	9 427	27.0%
人均人工成本/元	9 361	10 127	8.2%
人工成本中工资比重	79.3%	93.1%	−17.4%
人工成本总额/千元	18 821 107	20 341 274	8.1%

从表 1 和表 2 可以看出，铁路运输业 1995 年劳动生产率比 1994 年增长 2.1%，人均工资增长 27.0%，是不合理的。根据工资理论，工资水平增长幅度应小于劳动生产率增长幅度。如果 1995 年人均工资支出增长幅度不超过劳动生产率增长 2.1%的幅度，假设二者增长幅度持平，可节约工资支出为：

$$[9\,427-7\,425\times(1+2.1\%)]\times2\,008\,580=37.08（亿元）$$

式中：9 427——铁路运输业职工 1995 年人均工资；

7 425——铁路运输业职工 1994 年人均工资；

2.1%——1995 年劳动生产率增加率；

2 008 580——1995 年铁路运输业职工总人数。

1995 年运输总支出与运输收入的差额为：

6 740 015−6 320 686=41.93 亿元（见表 1）

如舍掉其他因素不计，可以认为是新增加的工资支出 37.08 亿元侵蚀了利润，占据了运输企业亏损的绝大部分。这说明节约工资、控制人工成本是铁路企业减少亏损的重要途径。但由于人均工资和人均人工成本具有刚性特点而不能减少，因此只能控制和减少人工成本总量，为此就需要减少职工总量。

将铁路运输业的人工成本水平指标与其他行业企业做一个大概的比较就可以初步认清目前所处的状况。

铁路运输业的总成本人工成本含量在 1994 年、1995 年两年中均超过 30%，而同期邯郸钢铁公司的总成本人工成本含量为 10.86%，上海宝钢为 8.86%，中国民航为 4.95%～7.3%。而同期这些企业均盈利，而铁路两年均亏损，所以铁路的人事费用率更高，这些企业的人事费用率更低。在人均人工成本方面，上海宝钢 1994 年为 3.67 万元，邯郸钢铁公司为 1 万元左右，中国民航职工仅人均年收入就超过了 1 万元（1994 年为 11 500 元，1995 年为 15 100 元），而铁路运输业 1995 年为 10 127 元。这些企业的人均人工成本支出均高于铁路运输业，具有更大的竞争优势。铁路行业发达的日本，铁路运输部门的人事费用率多年来稳定维持在 11%左右的水平上，也远低于我国铁路运输业人事费用率 30%以上的水平。我国铁路运输业人工成本水平偏高，这是明显的事实。

我国铁路运输业的人均人工成本明显低于邯郸钢铁公司和上海宝钢，而人均人工成本在总成本中的含量又高于邯郸钢铁公司和上海宝钢，其原因十分清楚，铁路职工队伍太庞大了，已不符合市场经济的要求，不利于企业的长远发展。全行业过高的人工成本总量吞噬了企业的利润，降低了企业的劳动生产率，影响了铁路运输业摆脱困境目标的实现，使铁路运输业陷入不断亏损的恶性循环。而且铁路运输业至今没有自己的人工成本核算体系，经营管理落后，不符合市场经济的要求，即价格=成本+利润总是由既定成本水平出发制定其他相关指标，而不是市场竞争环境决定成本水平。与铁路运输业相比，很多企业已经认识到了这一点，树立了正确的成本观念，努力使企业去适应市场要求。在这场竞争中，邯郸钢铁公司和上海宝钢都走在了铁路运输业的前面。对铁路运输业来讲，必须尽快确立铁路人工成本水平指标的计算，核算适当的人工成本水平和职工总量以帮助铁路运输计划的制定，摆脱人工成本管理不力的情况。

四、铁路运输业人工成本总量及职工总量的控制方法

铁路运输业一个时期以来面临全行业亏损的原因固然很多，但其中的一个主要原因，正如朱镕基副总理所说，就是人员过多。铁路运输业要解困、扭转亏损局面，只有背水一战，走减员增效的路子，把主业多余的人员减下来，分流到其他行业中去。

铁路运输业职工总量的控制方法可以用人工成本指标计算来取得。

根据人工成本指标上限计算公式，可以求出铁路运输业人工成本指标的上限。运输支出及运输成本构成表见表 3。

表 3　运输支出及运输成本构成表

项目	1994 年	1995 年
营运成本/万元	5 279 566	5 821 993
管理费用、财务费用/万元	429 054	583 626
营业支出/万元	5 708 620	6 405 619
其中：人均人工成本/万元	1 157 807	1 395 596
折旧/万元	658 049	737 290
材料、燃料、电力/万元	1 977 812	2 187 883
其他/万元	1 914 952	2 084 850
营业外净支出/万元	289 879	334 396
运输总支出/万元	5 998 499	6 740 015

资料来源：《全国铁路统计资料汇编（1994）》《全国铁路统计资料汇编（1995）》。

假定：

（1）管理费用、财务费用、营业支出中的折旧及其他、营业外净支出均记为固定成本，而人工成本和营业支出中的材料、燃料、电力支出记为变动支出，单位收入取当年收入率，1994 年为 359 元/万换算吨公里，1995 年为 381 元/万换算吨公里。

（2）职工人均工资福利、人均人工成本并不下降。

（3）铁路运输业在运输市场的份额不受其职工总量变化的影响。

根据以上假设条件和表 3 的数据，利用人工成本指标公式可为职工总量控制提供具体方法。

计算过程如下（根据 1995 年资料数据计算）：

变动成本总额=人工成本+材料、燃料、电力支出=2 034 127.4+2 187 883=4 222 010.4（万元）

$$单位变动成本=\frac{变动成本总额}{总产量}=\frac{4\,222\,010.4\times10^4}{1\,655\,786\times10^2}\times100\%=255$$（元/万换算吨公里）

固定成本=运输总支出−变动成本=6 740 015−4 222 010.4=2 518 004.6（万元）

$$盈亏平衡点收入=\frac{固定成本}{1-\frac{单位变动成本}{单位收入}}=\frac{2\,518\,004.6}{1-255/381}=760.7（亿元）$$

使用人事费用率为企业人工成本控制的主指标，则人工成本支付的最高限度公式为：

$$人事费用率最高支付限度=\frac{人工成本}{盈亏平衡点销售收入}\times100\%$$

$$=\frac{2\,034\,127.4}{760.7\times10^4}\times100\%=26.7\%$$

当人事费用率为26.7%时，铁路运输业职工人数上限为：

$$职工人数上限=\frac{1995年收入\times人事费用率最高支付限度}{平均人工成本}$$

$$=\frac{6\,320\,686\times26.7\%\times10^4}{10\,127}=1\,666\,459（人）$$

过剩就业人数=实际职工人数－职工人数上限=2 008 580－1 666 459

=342 121（人）

过剩人工成本支出=10 127×342 121=34.65（亿元）

将以上计算结果列入表4。

表4　职工总量控制决策表

项目	1994年	1995年
固定成本/万元	213.9	251.8
单位变动成本/（元/万换算吨公里）	237.8	255.0
平衡点收入/亿元	633.6	760.7
人事费用率最高支付限度	29.7%	26.7%
职工人数上限	1 849 148	1 666 459
过剩就业人数	161 441	342 121
过剩人工成本支出/亿元	15.1	34.65

从表4可以看出，1995年铁路运输业只需用人1 666 459人，过剩就业人数达到342 121人。显然减少铁路运输业人员是对铁路发展前景具有重大影

响的举措。

铁路运输业困难的重要原因就是富余人员过多，人浮于事，只有切实把富余人员减下去，人工总成本降下来，效率提上去，铁路运输业才有生存和发展的希望。人工成本的水平反映了职工总量控制的好坏和劳动生产率的高低，铁路运输业可以通过对人工成本的控制间接控制职工总量。当前，压缩职工队伍，降低人工成本总量，从而降低企业总成本是当务之急。

参考文献：

[1] 翁天真. 最新工资管理实务全书[M]. 北京：红旗出版社，1996.

[2] 狄煌. 企业人工成本分析方法和控制策略. 中国劳动科学研究院劳动工资研究所.

发达国家缩小收入差距的策略①

编者按：国外发达国家在调整收入分配格局、约束垄断行业收入和规范收入分配秩序方面采取了一系列缩小居民收入差距的措施，对我国改革收入分配制度具有一定的借鉴作用。其主要做法是：加大劳动收入在初次收入分配中的比重；增加个人所得税的边际税率、开征高额的遗产税、赠与税和消费税调节再分配中的收入差距；通过制定法律、加大财政转移支付、建立安全的社会保障体系，平衡地区间、行业间的收入差距；通过慈善公益组织完善社会救助体系构建弱势群体的安全网；国家通过立法，引入竞争机制约束垄断行业的收入；利用法律与经济的手段，严格财产稽查制度限制高管收入，规范收入秩序。

一、国外发达国家通过制定收入分配格局的政策缩小收入差距

（一）初次分配：加大劳动收入在初次收入分配中的比重

初次分配中重点确保中等收入人群占多数，培育中产阶级。欧美国家通过工资、福利和税收调节等来巩固和扩大中产阶级的比重。美国、加拿大政府通过实施有关最低工资、工资支付、同工同酬、加班工资、休假权益等法律法规规范初次分配。

① 本文发表在 2010 年第 4 期的《中国劳动》上，作者张影强、袁伦渠。

加大劳动收入在收入分配中的比重，是美国和英国缩小收入差距的一个重要政策。有学者统计，美国在1870—1984年间的114年中，劳动收入在国民收入中所占比重由50%增至74.3%，资本要素收入所占比重由24.5%下降到16.6%。英国在1860—1984年的124年中，劳动收入所占比重由45.2%增加到68.8%，资本要素所占比重由36.5%降为21.9%。这表明，在美国英国的国民收入分配格局中，资本要素收入始终占小头，而劳动收入始终占大头。由此，从普遍意义上避免了收入分配中的严重两极分化。

（二）再次分配：严格税收制度，完善社会保障体系，缩小收入差距

1. 严格个人税收制度

第一，实行个人所得税是缩小收入差距最直接和有效的方法。1973年英国加入欧洲经济共同体之后，开始实行累进税率，税收制度进一步完善。年薪在4 800英镑以下的低收入者不用纳税，超过的部分分三个等级按不同比例纳税，最高收入的所得税税率为40%，这个标准随着每年的通货膨胀率调整。20世纪90年代，英国税后基尼系数由税前近0.5降至0.37。目前，美国个人所得税采用六级超额累进税率结构，税率分别为10%、15%、25%、28%、33%和35%。仅累进所得税一项，就使最低和最高收入群体的差距大幅度缩小。据统计，瑞典的中等收入者要缴纳的个人所得税税率为31%，大公司经理则为60%～70%，最高达到85%。1971—1992年，加拿大个人收入的基尼系数，在征收个人所得税之前为0.491，在征收个人所得税之后下降至0.359。在芬兰，低收入者和高收入者的所得税税率差别很大。在20世纪90年代，高收入者的最高税率（包括国家所得税和地方所得税）曾达到65%，目前最高税率仍高达60%。就是说，高收入者真正拿到手的收入只有40%。而芬兰360万纳税人中的近100万低收入者则无须向国家缴纳所得税，仅需缴纳地方税。

第二，巨额遗产税也是缩小收入差距一个重要的手段。美国遗产税的起征点较高，并按物价指数浮动。1999年的起征点为65万美元，税率实行超额累进制，最高税率达55%。日本现行遗产税税率共分13个档次，从10%到70%。按英国税法规定，遗产税和赠与税合并一起征收。为防止富人通过提前转移财产逃避遗产税，税法规定，继承人除了要对死者遗留的财产缴纳遗产税外，还要对死者7年内赠与的财产，根据赠与及死亡的年限，按不同的税率缴纳赠与

税。此外，以消费税间接调节社会成员之间的贫富差距。在发达国家，购置豪华住宅、名牌轿车、奢侈品、化妆品，享用高档宴会、高档休闲娱乐以及饲养宠物等都算作高消费，要征收高额的特别消费税。

2. 健全的社会保障体系

第一，再分配中注重完善社会保障制度，构建弱势群体的“安全网”。社会保障体系逐步扩大覆盖面。西方各国的社会保障覆盖面达 95%以上，很多国家接近 100%。

全力推动社会保障制度法制化。英国早在 1572 年就开始征收“济贫税”；美国于 1933 年颁布《联邦紧急救济法》，1935 年制定了《社会保障法案》。到 20 世纪 50 年代，几乎所有西方国家均完成了有关社会保障制度的立法，设立了相应的管理机构。法国的家庭补助金明显向最贫困者和仅能维持最低生活水准的家庭倾斜。墨西哥的《全国团结计划》、秘鲁的《社会救助计划》等都规定具体目标、救助对象人数以及投入的资金数目。

第二，高比例的社会保障财政转移支付构建完善的社会保障体系。以 1960 年到 1975 年间公共养老金支出增长为例，德国增长了 6.1 倍，英国增长了 8.9 倍，比利时增长了 9.6 倍，瑞典增长了 12.4 倍，法国增长了 18.5 倍。再从社会保障等福利支出占 GDP 的比例看，澳大利亚从 1960 年的 7.4%上升到 1980 年的 12.8%，日本从 4.1%上升到 12.9%，瑞典从 10.8%上升到 25.9%，瑞士从 4.9%上升到 14.5%。到 1980 年，社会保障和卫生支出占财政支出的比重在瑞典达到 56.4%，在法国达到 57.5%，在荷兰为 54.2%，在英国为 47.6%。如果加上教育支出的话，所占比重在瑞典、法国、荷兰、英国更是分别高达 71.4%、68.3%、67.8%和 60.6%。美国社会保障支出快速增长的趋势也非常明显，卫生和社会保障等福利支出占财政支出的比重从 1965 年的 24%提高到 1975 年的 42%。

第三，完善的社会福利体系也是高社会保障体系的重要组成部分。欧美等国家目前实行的福利财政政策，几乎涵盖了人们的生老病死、失业、退休、住房等社会生活中的方方面面，内容广泛，项目繁杂。目前，英国的福利制度大致可分为 7 类：儿童和孕妇福利、伤残或疾病福利、退休福利、寡妇福利、失业福利、低收入福利和社会基金等。美国政府还通过建立一套较完善的社会保障体系来关怀社会弱势群体，向他们提供基本的收入、医疗、住房等方面的福利，以确保他们能过上体面的温饱生活。美国的社会安全福利制度创建于1935年，通过70年的不断修改和完善，已经建成为一个由社会保险、社会救济和社会福利三部分组成的完善的社会保障体系。主要包括提供医疗服务、残疾保险、住房补贴、失业救助、社会安全福利金、退休金、低收入家庭子女津贴和学童营养补助等，涉及生、老、病、死、伤、残、退休、教育、就业等。这些福利尤其对退休的老年人和残疾人提供了有力的生活保障。

（三）第三次分配：通过慈善公益组织，完善社会救助体系

慈善公益事业是较为发达国家，通过多种途径和方式的捐助活动，将一些人的财产直接或间接转移到另一些人手中，客观上起到了国民收入再分配的作用，因而称为第三次分配。第三次分配犹如一只“温柔的手”，其主体不是传统意义上的市场与政府，而是慈善公益组织（民间组织、非营利组织）。第三次分配是建立在自愿性的基础上，它奉行“道德原则”，以募集、自愿捐赠和资助等慈善公益方式对社会资源和社会财富进行的分配，以让社会分配更趋公平。

在西方发达国家，第三次分配已普遍发展得比较成熟，渐趋理性。如美国的富裕阶层——企业和个人，每年通过各类基金会做出的慈善公益捐助有6 700多亿美元，通过第三次分配的财富，占到美国GDP的9%。在美国，富人捐助慈善事业已经成为一种社会风气，政府不再需要进行这方面的劝诫。而在香港，政府则会给予那些为社会做出贡献的慈善家以很高的荣誉。

国外政府还通过减税等手段，鼓励富人捐助公益事业，从而避免财富因世代相传而过度集中。美国规定，如果一个企业向社会捐出善款的数额超过应缴税收的10%，那么应该减免10%的税款，如果不到10%，则可以在缴税时扣除已经捐出的善款。

在德国，对普通民众来说，不仅募捐额可以凭收据在个人所得税中扣除，而且德国红十字会等公益机构还会为其提供诸如免费急救等相应的优惠服务，捐赠者可谓名利双收。

所以，第三次分配在救助社会弱势群体方面起到了对政府救济的补充作用。对救济贫困人口和稳定社会也起到一定作用。在西方发达国家，慈善事业已是稳定社会，完善分配，缩小贫富差距，弥补政府职能缺失的一项重要手段。

二、国外发达国家通过立法和竞争约束垄断行业的收入

西方发达国家针对垄断的改革，首先就是立法，同时通过立法实行竞争。例如：英国于20世纪80年代初相继制定了《电信法》《电力法》《自来水法》等。政府对这些行业立法的目标是建立有效的竞争机制，促使企业提高效率，增进社会福利，并且明确政府规制机构的权限和规制程序等，使政府规制机构的运作有法可依。

在欧洲国家，铁路行业一直是一个垄断行业，存在很多垄断问题，政府针对这一情况开始把竞争机制引入铁路行业，像瑞典和英国的铁路部门都已经开始逐渐利用竞争机制，以此来提高其运行效率。

电力系统在各个国家历来也是垄断行业。俄罗斯电力体制改革始于1992年，政府决定用10年的时间进行非垄断化改革。俄电力系统“一夜之间”由国家所有制转变成股份制，成立了俄罗斯统一电力公司，规定职工工资高于最低标准1.9倍。

20世纪80年代后，美国联邦和各州政府开始逐步放松对电力行业的管制，通过有效的竞争使电价下降，为消费者带来福利，员工的收入与公司绩效直接挂钩。

日本一直实行各电力公司分地区发输配售垂直一体化体制，电力公司全部为私有（民营）企业。1995年，日本开始引入独立发电企业，2000年开始分三级逐级开放大用户，到目前为止，除家庭用户以外，所有大用户都可自由选择供电商。通过改革，电力企业的收益率也有所提高。而电力行业职工的收入也在从垄断走向竞争的过程中逐渐与日本平均工资水平持平。

三、国外发达国家规范收入秩序的措施

1. 限制高管收入

面对上市公司高管薪酬过高的问题，美国已经采取了多项措施进行限制。1992年，美国证券监管机构要求上市公司披露高管的薪酬；1993年美国国会再次制定法律，规定公司高管如果没有很好的业绩，不能享受薪酬100万美元以上部分的税收减免。2004年要求上市公司将期权成本算作公司开支。后来，又通过一项法案，努力将上市公司高管最高年薪限制在100万美元之内，或是5

年税后收入的平均值之内。美国总统奥巴马 2009 年 2 月 4 日颁布限薪令，规定接受政府注资的银行和其他企业高管，年薪上限为 50 万美元，为美国普通家庭收入的 12 倍。

2. 设立薪酬委员会

企业设立薪酬委员制约高管人员过高薪酬，在英国、美国等发达国家的企业董事会内部，普遍设立薪酬委员会（compensation committee），该委员会是一个主要由外部董事和独立董事组成的机构，专门负责评估包括 CEO、其他执行董事在内的高级管理人员的绩效、制定和核定董事会成员以及高级管理人员的一揽子补偿方案。

3. 采取年薪制

国外经营者年薪收入包括两部分，一部分是基薪和奖金等短期激励部分，另一部分是股票和股票期权等长期激励部分。此外，还有预支年休金、福利津贴和在职消费等。由于发达国家企业管理模式不尽相同，经营者收入中各部分的权重也有所不同。美国企业经理报酬中股票期权收入高，日本企业经理报酬总奖金和在职消费数额高，德国企业经理报酬中几乎没有股票期权。西方国家企业经营者享受优厚的职位消费待遇。这些费用一般计入成本，属于税前分享部分。

4. 严格财产稽查制度

法国早在 1998 年就制定了《政治家生活资金透明度法》，这是规范公职人员财产申报的一项专门法律。根据该法规，总统候选人、参议院和国民议会的议员及地方官员在上任后的 15 天内和离职的时候，必须向各自所属的议院办公厅提交一份以其名誉作保的准确、真实的财产状况申报单。

美国的财产申报制度始于 1978 年颁布的《政府官员行为道德法》。根据这项法律，包括总统、副总统、国会议员、联邦法官以及行政、立法和司法三大机构的工作人员，必须在任职前报告自己的财产状况，上任后还须按月申报。同时，财产申报不只限于申报者本人，还须包括其配偶和抚养子女的有关情况。除在国家安全部门工作或其他不宜暴露身份的官员外，各受理申报的机关均须将财产申报资料公开，供大众查阅复印，以便接受社会监督。

美国实行严格的财产稽查制度。美国人一出生就获得一个社会安全号码，他一生所有经济活动和个人财务资料都与此挂钩，美税务部门就利用该号码查证个人的财务收入状况，核实其纳税情况。在强大的计算机系统支持下，通过这个高效的信息稽核系统，税收部门可以通过对纳税人的各种信息进行交叉审核，有效打击偷漏税的非法收入。

早在 1993 年，日本国会议员财产申报制度就已开始。根据 1992 年通过的《为确立政治伦理的国会议员资产公开法》（简称《资产公开法》）规定，新当选议员有义务公布所持有的资产，具体包括建筑、土地、高尔夫俱乐部会员权、定期存款、车、证券等。

社会保障问题

健全社会保障制度促进企业经营机制的转换①

内容提要：本文是党的十三大提出建立社会主义市场经济体制和现代企业制度的决定后，作者论证的健全社会保障制度是企业由政府附属物转变为现代企业制度的重要保证。

社会主义市场经济要求企业必须转换经营机制，使之由政府的附属物变成自主经营、自负盈亏、自我发展、自我约束的商品生产者和经营者。为此，1993年国务院颁布了《全民所有制工业企业转换经营机制条例》（下称《条例》）。贯彻《条例》是建立社会主义市场经济体制系统工程中的"主体工程"，是目前各项工作的重中之重。

但是，贯彻《条例》，转换企业经营机制，要为企业创造一个良好的社会环境，其中重要内容之一是《条例》第45条所规定的，要建立和健全社会保障制度。

建立和健全社会保障制度之所以能促进企业经营机制的转换。因为：

第一，建立和健全社会保障制度有利于落实企业的劳动用工权。企业要成为独立的商品生产者和经营者，应有权根据自身的任务和经营特点，对劳动力的数量和质量提出要求，有权根据法律、法规等有关规定解聘、辞退、开除职工，也就是说，有劳动用工权。但是，有一个前提条件，就是对这些被解聘、辞退、开除而失去生活来源的人，国家和社会有责任提供失业保险，使之在失

① 本文发表在1994年3月31日的《中国劳动报》上。

业期间能够得到一定数量和一定期限的失业保险金，保证其基本生活。这样，企业辞退（解雇）职工的后顾之忧解除了，职工担心失业后无保障的后顾之忧也解除了，企业要用的人进得来，不要的人出得去，企业才能有真正的用工自主权。如果不是这样，企业劳动用工权就是一句空话。目前，我国企业隐性失业严重，企业多余人员强调以内部消化为主，难以推向社会，很重要的一个原因就是社会保障制度不健全。我国1986年所建立的失业保险制度，运行7年来，发挥了积极作用。但它有一个根本缺陷就是实施范围窄，仅限于全民所有制企业的几种人，不适用其他经济成分的职工。这种规定不利于鼓励各种经济成分长期共同发展，也不利于企业用工自主权的发挥。

第二，建立和完善社会保障制度可以为企业之间的平等竞争创造条件。在社会主义市场经济条件下，企业必须进入市场，并在市场中进行平等竞争。但是，多年来我国的社会保障制度不健全，影响了企业的竞争。以养老保险为例：由于各企业职工的年龄构成不同，有些企业老职工多，退休费负担重，有些企业青年职工多，退休费负担轻。企业之间退休费用这种畸重畸轻的现象严重影响了它们在同一起跑线上的平等竞争。只有健全养老保险制度，实行退休费用统筹，由目前的县、地（市）统筹发展到省级统筹，才可以在更大范围内分担企业的风险。统筹的范围越大，企业之间的竞争就越平等。将来实行全国一体化社会养老保险制度时，企业就可以在全国范围内平等竞争了。养老保险是如此，其他如失业保险、工伤保险、医疗保险、生育和疾病保险业亦如此。这是一方面。

另一方面，社会保障制度还可以通过保护弱者、向低收入者倾斜而有利于企业的竞争。我们知道，市场经济是鼓励强者的。企业在市场竞争中，由于各种原因会出现有兴有衰的情况，有的企业兴旺发达，有的企业甚至会倒闭、破产。如果没有社会保障制度，破产、倒闭的企业的职工就会失去生活来源，从而导致社会的不安定，影响社会主义市场经济的运行。如果我们能建立和完善独立于企业之外的不受企业经济效益影响的、切实保障职工生活的失业保险，给失去工作机会的劳动者提供基本生活保险等，就可以保护在市场竞争中的弱者和低收入者，安定社会，促进社会主义市场经济的稳定运行。

第三，建立和健全社会保障制度有助于人才流动，有助于劳动者选择企业和工作。劳动者作为国家和企业的主人，有权根据自己的专长和爱好选择企业和工作。但是，我国20世纪50年代建立的社会保险制度在“文化大革命”中遭到破坏，各项社会保险制度的实施和管理基本由企业包揽，成为“企业行为”，社会保险变成“企业保险”。这样，由于各企业经济效益不同，职工的保险待遇也不相同，在不同所有制企业之间差别更大，个体和私营企业则没有保险待遇。因此，全民所有制企业职工和其他所有制企业职工的互相流动就很难做到。从事个体经营更是顾虑重重。只有实行社会保险的社会统筹，时机成熟时，再推行不分所有制，不分用工形式，统一项目、统一标准的一体化的社会保险制度，才能从根本上消除这一弊端，为职工的全方位流动创造条件。

从以上分析可以看出，建立和健全社会保障制度，将社会保险由过去的企业行为变成社会行为、政府行为，让企业从烦琐的事务中解脱出来，在市场中奋力搏击，这是企业转换经营机制的重要前提也是社会主义市场经济顺利运行的基础。

还是“失业救济金”的提法好①

内容提要：1995年底，《中国劳动报》编者向我征求失业保险的物质保障应如何表达，我查阅英汉双解词典的英文解释，斟酌再三认为“失业救济金”的提法好，《中国劳动报》接受了这一建议并刊登此文，有关政府部门也在公文中采用了这一概念。

失业保险是劳动者由于失业中断生活来源时由国家或社会为其提供物质保障的一种社会保险制度。对于这种“物质保障”，究竟用什么词语来表达，目前报纸杂志、教材著作甚至政府文件中的用法都很不一致。可以看到的用法大致有这样几个：失业保险金、失业津贴、失业补助金、失业补偿金、失业救济金等。这些混乱提法，容易引起歧义。

翻开《英汉双解字典》，可知以上几种提法可能源于对“unemployment benefit”这个英文词组中“benefit”一词的诸多中文解释：（以公民或保险会社社员身份而有资格领取之）救济金、保险金、金钱给付、津贴等。它的英文解释是：allowance of money to which a person is entitled as a citizen or as a member

① 本文发表在1996年1月9日的《中国劳动报》上。

of an insurance society，etc ……可直接译为：支付给公民或有保险会成员身份者的特别经费。而“unemployment benefit”这个词组的英文解释则是：money paid from insurance funds to a worker who cannot get employment，可直译为：从保险基金中支付给失业工人之特别款项。我想，我们应当从“unemployment benefit”的英文解释的本意中来寻求一个恰当的、不易引起歧义的提法。那么，用一个什么词才能确切地表达“从保险基金中支付给失业工人之特别款项”这个意思呢？首先，用“失业保险金”不妥。那会像用养老保险金、工伤保险金、医疗保险金、生育保险金分别表示养老、工伤、医疗、生育保险的各项待遇一样过于笼统。其次，用“失业津贴”也不恰当。因为“津贴”的“津”字意思是“润泽”，“贴”是补助，“津贴”即另外给些贴补使之生活更好之意。就经济学意义来说，“津贴”应理解为原有收入基础上的贴补。新中国成立前的革命战争时期实行供给制，部队和机关工作人员除由公家供应吃穿外，还可按级别领到一定数额的零用钱，这种零用钱叫“津贴”。新中国成立后我国实行的诸如野外津贴、保健津贴、伙食津贴等都是指工资以外的收入。失业工人中断工作没有收入，根本谈不上原有收入基础上的补贴。因此，“失业津贴”的用法也不恰当。“失业救助金”也同样不恰当。至于“失业补偿金”的说法也不可取，因为失业保障是对失业工人的物质帮助，不是补助和偿还。我认为，恰当确切的用法应当是“失业救济金”。“救济”的含义是“用财物帮助有困难的人”。失业工人中断生活来源，需要以物质帮助渡过难关。1986 年 7 月国务院颁布的《国营企业待业保险暂行规定》中就采用了“待业（失业）救济金”的提法。

失业保险制度是当前社会保险改革的重点之一。为避免各级干部和广大职工对失业保险的物质保障和待遇产生歧义和误解，建议有关部门对上述混乱的概念加以澄清和规范，统一采用“失业救济金”的提法。

莫忘离退休老职工的历史贡献①

内容提要：这是作者作为北京市人大代表，1997 年在北京市第十届人民代表大会第五次会议上的发言，同年 11 月 20 日在《经济学消息报》上发表。该

① 本文发表在 1997 年 11 月 20 日的《经济学消息报》上。

文引用经典作家的论述并列举大量数据，提出养老保险基金的不足应由国有企业资产划拨充实的观点，这在当时虽然得到离退休老同志的欢迎，但还是一个敏感的话题，并未得到官方和公众的承认。事隔18年后，财政部部长楼继伟才在2015年举行的“中国发展高层论坛”上指出“降低社保缴费率的前提是划拨国资补充社保基金”。2015年5月21日《光明日报》刊登李思辉的“划转国有资产充实社保资金是正道”的文章，划拨国有资产来充实养老基金的政策，有的地方已经落了地[①]。至此作者18年前提出的观点才得到了迟到的肯定。写作此文曾参考有关专家的观点和提供的资料，特此感谢。

据统计，截至1995年底，我国离退休老职工已达2 241万人。如何看待这样一个庞大的社会群体，当今社会上不少人把他们当成了包袱，甚至一些媒介也常常说，某企业在职职工与离退休职工的比例是多少，几个在职职工养活一个离退休人员等。对此，离退休老职工自然十分委屈和不服气：工作了一辈子，到头来还让年轻人养活？！

在这里，很有必要为这些离退休老职工说几句公道话。首先，应当看到离退休老职工的不可磨灭的历史贡献。大家知道，新中国成立初期以至以后的一个相当长的时期内，我国实行的是低工资制，广大职工在“三个人的饭五个人吃”的情况下艰苦卓绝地进行了156项重点工程为中心的社会主义建设。有专家统计，从新中国成立初期到1978年，职工的实际平均工资每年只递增0.38%，到1978年全国职工的年货币平均工资才仅仅615元，居民人均储蓄只有21.88元，而国家的积累率却由1952年的21.4%上升到1978年的36.5%，有的年份竟高达43.8%，工资总额占国民收入的比重仅为18.9%。国有资产的总量，新中国成立初期只有200亿元，1993年却上升到34 950亿元，增长了173倍。由此可以看出，我国的国有资产，是过去长期实行低工资、低消费、高积累的政策所造成的，这当中除了广大农民作出的巨大贡献外，主要是目前离退休老职

① 可参考2015年3月23日《新京报》社论“弥补养老保险不足需国有资产补充”；2015年5月21日《光明日报》李思辉文章“划转国有资产充实社保资金是正道”。又参见2017年11月19日《北京青年报》第8版：“避免将基本养老保险基金缺口转移给下一代人，国企国有资本10%划转社保”，指出国务院印发《划拨部分国有资本充实社保基金实施方案》是全面贯彻落实党的十九大精神，深入贯彻习近平新时代中国特色社会主义思想，加强社会保险体系建设的重要举措。

工过去劳动的积累，他们的功劳不可磨灭。

其次，离退休老职工有权利要求对过去被扣除的养老保险进行补偿。大家都知道，已离退休老职工大多是在高度集中统一的计划经济体制工作的。当时的社会保险包括养老保险是以马克思《哥达纲领批判》一书中提出的6项扣除和列宁提出的“最好的工人保险是国家保险”“一切保险费都由企业和国家负担”的理论为根据的。在这一理论指导下，劳动者的工资并不包括养老保险费，因为他们的工资在分配前已作了6项扣除，其中包括职工养老费用的扣除。但是，被扣除的养老保险费用并没有形成养老基金，而是一部分以税利形式上交国家，形成国有资产或挪作他用，一部分留作企业，扩大再生产，存在于企业现有的资产中。这两部分形成的国有资产，在产权制度改革后，都统一归并在国有资产管理部门。因此，离退休老职工有权要求对自己的养老金进行补偿。

通过以上分析可以看出，离退休人员不是包袱，而有历史贡献；不应被嫌弃，而应受到尊敬。在人类社会中，一切物质财富和精神财富都是不断继承的，不存在什么年轻人养活老年人，下一代养活上一代人的问题。

当前，我国正由计划经济体制向市场经济体制转变，在建立与之相适应的养老保险制度的过程中，应在承认离退休职工的历史贡献，承认他们的养老金来自他们过去所创造的利润，应当给他们的历史贡献给予补偿。解决这部分人的养老待遇问题，是国家和社会应尽的职责和义务。

如何偿还已被扣除的变为国有资产的离退休职工的养老保险费，是个值得研究的问题。现在让企业用在职职工创造的利润来偿还，这不仅不公平，而且会加重企业的负担，影响现代企业制度的建立和参与市场竞争。解决的办法，不少专家学者和经济工作者已提出了一些设想和建议，可供有关政府部门参考，主要有：

（1）由政府每年拿出财政收入的一定比例偿还，或由政府财政负担离退休老职工的养老费用；

（2）从国有资产中划出一块给养老保险金，以其收益充当养老保险待遇；

（3）进行股份制改造的企业，可以划拨一定的股份并将其红利作为养老保险金；

（4）在破产、撤销和解散企业的清偿过程中，应首先从原有资产和出让土地使用权的收费中拿出足够的养老保险专项基金，解决离退休老职工的养老保险待遇问题；

（5）建立养老保险金的定期调整增长机制，保证养老金不因物价上涨而贬值，并使离退休职工分享经济社会发展的成果。

关于建立企业补充养老保险制度的几点看法①

内容提要：这是1996年国家劳动社会保障部主持的国际合作项目“中国企业养老保险改革与立法研究”（已用中英两种文字出版）研究中的子课题，我承担的该子课题经过对劳动部门和企业的调研，提出了企业补充养老保险的实施条件、资金来源、鼓励政策、基金分担、待遇水平和发展对策，为我国企业补充养老保险制度的制定提供了理论依据和操作措施，推动了该制度的试点工作，得到了国家劳动部的肯定和上海市等政府部门的好评。

1997年7月国务院就建立统一的企业职工基本养老保险制度作出了决定。目前各省、自治区和直辖市正按照这一决定精神，制定或已经制定了统一企业职工基本保险制度实施办法。随着统一的企业职工基本养老保险制度的实施，研究并制定企业补充养老保险的工作已提到了议事日程。

早在20世纪80年代，我国就有少数企业举办了补充养老保险。1995年12月劳动部制定了《关于建立企业补充养老保险制度的决定》，对发展企业补充养老保险提出了一些政策性规定。一些地方、行业还出台了具体规定和办法，在关于缴费比例、优惠政策、资金的来源渠道，以及待遇水平等方面采取了各自不同的做法。

当前，企业补充养老保险存在的问题是：第一，国家对发展企业补充养老保险虽然提出了原则，但尚未有统一的具体政策，缺乏必要的政策支持，例如，缺乏明确的税收优惠政策，影响了企业补充养老保险的发展。第二，各地区各行业和某些大型企业对企业补充养老保险虽然作了相应的规定，但制度不健全、办法不规范、制度不统一。第三，一些地区和部分企业的领导存在短期行为和

① 本文发表在1998年第5期上的《市场与人口分析》，该文曾转载在1998年第10期的《上海劳动》，引起上海劳动部门的重视并作为重要参考。企业补充养老保险即企业年金。

认识上的误区，对实行企业补充养老保险的积极性不高，探索的步子太慢。目前基本养老保险覆盖的职工1.2亿人，而企业补充养老保险覆盖的职工不到300万，覆盖面显然太小。这反过来又制约了基本养老保险制度的改革，使基本养老保险的工资替代率难以降下来。

鉴于以上企业补充养老保险的现状和存在的问题，本文试图对该制度试行的必要性、特征、原则和政策等作一些探讨。

一、实行企业补充养老保险的必要性

（一）具有法律、政策依据，符合国际惯例

企业补充养老保险是多层次养老保险制度的一个重要组成部分。所谓多层次养老保险制度，就是国家基本养老保险、企业补充养老保险和职工个人储蓄养老保险相结合的养老保险制度。世界上不少国家都实行多层次的养老保险制度。我国是一个发展中国家，人口众多，地区之间经济发展不平衡。实行多层次的养老保险制度，可以较好地体现国家、企业和个人的责任和利益，既能起到保障生活和安定社会的作用，又能适应不同经济条件企业的需要，有利于养老保险机制的建立和社会保障事业的发展。

企业补充养老保险是指在国家法定的基本养老保险的基础上，企业根据自身的经济能力从本企业自有资金中另外为职工增加一部分养老金，为提高养老待遇水平，改善退休生活而建立的一种辅助性的养老保险制度。在我国，建立企业补充养老保险制度是有法律和政策为依据的。《中华人民共和国劳动法》第75条规定："国家鼓励用人单位根据本单位实际情况为劳动者建立补充保险。国家倡导劳动者个人进行储蓄性保险。"1991年《国务院关于企业职工养老保险制度改革的决定》指出，随着经济的发展，我国要逐步建立起基本养老保险、企业补充养老保险和职工个人储蓄性养老保险相结合的制度，即多层次的养老保险制度。1993年《中共中央关于建立社会主义市场经济体制若干问题的决定》《中华人民共和国国民经济和社会发展"九五"计划和2010年远景目标纲要》（下称《纲要》）都明确在我国建立市场经济体制时，要建立多层次的社会保险体系。《纲要》指出："要大力发展企业补充养老保险和个人储蓄养老保险。"

我国实行企业补充养老保险不仅有法律政策依据，而且符合国际惯例。在国外，一般把企业自主为职工举办的养老保险称为职业养老金计划或私人养老

金计划。在美国，职业养老金计划（企业补充退休金）是多层次养老保险的一个组成部分，其基金主要来自企业主向社会保险机构的投保，并加存款利息，由国家滚存而成。其目的是弥补国家统一实行的基本养老金的不足，保证退休者的基本生活，巩固雇员队伍。英国的退休年金一般包括基本年金和补充年金两部分，企业雇员除基本年金外，还可以享受额外的补充退休年金。瑞士的社会保险由所谓“三根支柱”支撑。这“三根支柱”是联邦社会保险、职业互助金和个人保险储金。第二根支柱职业互助金是联邦社会保险的补充，其功能是保证雇员退休后获得更高一些生活水平。

（二）减轻基本养老保险的压力，适应人口老龄化迅速到来的需要

我国的基本国情是：人口多、底子薄、生产力水平低。在这种经济条件下，只有通过实行企业补充养老保险建立起多层次的养老保险体系才能使养老保险与各方面的经济承受能力相适应，缓解日益尖锐的退休费用供求矛盾，为退休人员提供足够的收入保障。

我国在计划经济体制下，实行单一的养老保险制度，养老保险的责任高度集中于政府，企业和职工没有直接责任，待遇标准由国家规定，并且全国统一。这一特点必然要求较高的工资替代率。但是这种单一层次的养老保险制度已不能适应人口老龄化迅速到来的形势。我国第四次人口普查表明，中国大陆人口已达 11.3 亿（目前实际已达 12 亿），其中 60 岁及 60 岁以上的老年人口占总人口的比重为 8.95%，65 岁及 65 岁以上的老年人口的比重为 5.58%。到 20 世纪末，这两个比重将分别达到 10%和 7%。按照联合国关于人口老龄化标准的规定，届时我国将进入老龄型国家的行列。到 2020 年，我国老年人口的比重将达到 18%，绝对数为 2.5 亿人。到 2040 年，将达到 25%，绝对数为 3.4 亿人。在今后 40 年内，我国老年人口将以年平均 3%的速度增长，这是世界上少有的人口老龄化高速度。发达国家 60 岁及 60 岁以上的老年人口的比重由 7%上升到 10%，一般需要 50 年到 100 年的时间，而我国仅经历了 10 年的时间。人口老龄化过程呈现出时间短、速度快的特点，这势必使国家养老保险的费用负担越来越重，与国民经济增长速度越来越不协调，以致超过国家和企业的经济负担能力。据有关方面预测，到 2000 年我国进入老龄型国家行列时，退休费用占职工工资总额的比重将达到或超过国际通常认为的 30%的极限。这表明，我国养老保险费用的供给与需求之间存在越来越尖锐的矛盾，指望用提高企业缴费比

例的办法，来解决由于人口老龄化带来的沉重财政负担是行不通的，必须寻找新的途径。

针对计划经济体制下养老保险制度的弊端，缓解养老保险费用供求矛盾的可行途径是：从我国经济发展的现实出发，实行多层次的养老保险制度，分散养老保险责任，将统一的较高的工资替代率降下来，国家只为退休人员提供基本生活保障。进一步提高养老保险待遇水平，则要依靠企业和职工的努力，通过建立企业补充养老保险制度来解决。由此可见，企业补充养老保险正是在我国迎接人口老龄化挑战，寻求养老保险新对策的情势下应运而生的。

(三) 增强养老保险制度的灵活性，与企业不同的经济效益相适应

计划经济体制下的养老保险制度的特点是：决策集中、制度僵化、适应性差。其弊端很多。首先，政府制定和调整养老保险政策的难度都很大。因为全国实行单一的养老保险制度，要提高养老保险待遇，就意味着全国都要提高，从而普遍加重企业的经济负担。由于各个企业的经济承受能力不同，所有企业都提高养老保险待遇很难行得通；若要减少企业负担，又意味着普遍降低养老水平，这又不能反映不同企业的经济能力，显然也是不可取的。凡此种种，就使我们在制定和调整养老保险政策时，往往陷入进退两难的境地。其次，在全国实行等齐划一的养老待遇标准的条件下，不论企业经营好坏，一律执行同一的养老待遇标准，这就割断了养老待遇水平与企业经济效益之间的联系。企业经济效益好时，不能提高企业职工的养老待遇；企业经济效益差，甚至亏损时也不能降低养老待遇。这既不能体现公平分配原则，也不利于鼓励企业提高经济效益。

企业补充养老保险制度的建立，有助于克服旧体制下养老保险的弊端，能够将我国养老保险制度改造成为既具有统一性又具有灵活性的制度。这是因为，基本养老保险可以保障退休人员的基本生活，企业补充养老保险可以根据各个企业的不同经营状况，在补充养老待遇上拉开差距，便于国家有区别地确定养老保险水平和适时调整养老待遇，从而使我国的养老保险做到与经济发展水平和企业的经济承受能力相适应。

(四) 增强企业的凝聚力和吸引力，适应市场竞争的需要

在市场经济体制下，企业之间必然要展开竞争。竞争和优胜劣汰的结果必然使一部分企业兴旺发达，一部分企业衰败甚至破产。实行企业补充养老保险，

可以采取激励原则，对那些工龄长、表现好、工作在艰苦岗位上的职工给予更多的补充养老保险金，有助于增强企业的凝聚力和吸引力，留住和吸引优秀的科技人才与熟练的生产骨干，以便增强企业的竞争力，使强者更强，弱者由弱变强。

（五）减少现期消费需求，引导合理消费

企业补充保险基金来自企业的自有基金，是自由基金中用于消费基金的一个构成部分。在一定时期内，企业自有资金是一个定量，用于补充保险的部分多了，用于其他消费的部分就会减少；反之亦然，此消彼长。补充养老保险是通过长期储蓄积累实现的，形成一种延期消费需求。因此实行企业补充养老保险可以将一部分现期消费转化为延期消费，从而能够减少现期消费需求，减轻市场压力。特别是在经济体制转轨的现阶段，由于企业收入分配越来越不合理地向个人倾斜，职工不规范收入所占比重不断增加，而规范性收入则不断减少，导致企业职工收入的增长远远超过了国民收入的增长速度。职工个人收入的急剧扩张，必然要推动消费猛烈膨胀，加速脱离实际的消费升级。实行企业补充养老保险能够将企业的相当一部分消费基金，引导到用于解决养老这一紧迫的社会问题上来，从而有助于抑制消费膨胀，形成合理的消费结构。

二、实行企业补充养老保险的可行性

在我国，实行企业补充养老保险不仅是必要的，也是完全可行的。首先，理论上是可行的。诚然，社会保险的性质是“互助互济、共担风险”。实行企业补充养老保险之后，就会相对减少可供统一调剂的养老保险基金，在一定程度上可能会削弱互济互助的功能，承担风险的能力有下降。但是，由于基本养老保险仍占主导地位，对整个养老保险制度互济互助功能的削弱并不太大。况且，在社会主义初级阶段，我国生产力水平比较低，各地区经济发展水平差别比较大，各行业各企业经济利益不尽一致，经济效益存在差别。将如此众多的行业和企业集合成为一个利益共同体，完全实现养老保险的互助互济、共担风险的功能是相当困难的。实行企业补充养老保险可以反映我国各地区的不同生产力水平和各企业的不同经济利益和经济效益，有利于我国养老保险事业的发展和社会主义市场经济体制的建立。

其次，在经济上是可行的。企业自有资金是实行补充养老保险的物质基础。

近几年虽然有相当一部分企业亏损，经济效益不好，但总有一部分企业经济效益较好，自有资金比较充裕，有能力为本企业职工提供补充养老保险。今后，随着国民经济的发展和经济效益的不断提高，还会有更多的企业拥有自有资金，为实行补充养老保险提供较雄厚的物质基础。

最后，在实际操作上也具有可行性。早在1991年国务院在《企业职工养老保险制度改革的决定》中就提出了建立包括企业补充养老保险在内的多层次的养老保险制度。此后，不少省、自治区和直辖市都先后制定了一些实施办法，并在一些企业试行。其他一些地区和行业的少数企业也按照《决定》的精神，自行实施了企业补充养老保险。所有这些积极做法，都为企业补充养老保险的推行取得了宝贵的经验，打下一定的基础。同时，新的养老金计发办法的逐步推行，也使许多地区的领导、企业和职工逐步认识到建立补充养老保险的必要性，增强了推行补充养老保险的积极性。此外，国家税制改革取消了奖金税，为企业自主使用自有资金实行补充养老保险提供了宽松的外部环境。

三、企业补充养老保险的特征

企业补充养老保险同国家基本养老保险相比，具有如下特征：

（一）半强制性

企业补充养老保险的半强制性表现在，国家只规定实施补充保险的条件，并采取适当的鼓励政策予以引导，而不直接规定待遇标准，具体标准由企业依据自身经济条件自主决定。经济效益好的企业多补充，效益差的少补充，没有效益的不补充。允许企业之间存在一定差别，不强求统一。

企业补充养老保险之所以要有一定的强制性，是因为一些企业不愿意提供补充养老保险。这种情况在公有制企业和私营企业都存在。公有制企业存在短期行为，不进行长远考虑，宁肯多发奖金多发工资而不愿意为职工提供补充养老保险。一部分职工也有类似的短期心态，认为补充保险是几十年以后的事，毕竟不如现在多增加收入，看得见、摸得着。在私营企业，由于追求利润最大化，企业主想方设法拒绝为职工提供补充养老保险。鉴于以上情况就有必要由国家以立法形式，通过规定实施补充条件，强制符合条件的企业为其职工提供补充养老金，以保证在企业的短期行为与养老保险的长期目标发生矛盾时，制约企业服从长期目标，实行补充养老保险制度。

（二）无互济性

与国家制定的基本养老金不同的是，企业补充养老保险基金不是以社会统筹形式建立的，而是由企业从自有资金中直接为职工提供的。企业补充养老保险基金的这种来源，决定了它不能在各个企业之间进行调剂，不具有互助互济功能，所以也不会普遍加重企业负担。

（三）完全积累性

企业补充养老保险基金的构成，也不同于国家基本养老保险基金，它不包括现付基金和调剂基金两部分，仅有积累基金构成。其基金模式是完全积累式，企业向职工提供的补充养老金记入职工个人养老保险账户，累计储存，到职工退休时据此支付补充养老金。由于分配的透明度较高，有利于职工参与的积极性，并起到对社会保险工作的监督作用。

四、企业补充养老保险的实施条件和分配原则

（一）实施条件

我们认为，实施企业补充养老保险至少应具备三个条件：第一，企业盈利达到一定水平，经济效益较好。如果企业只有微利，扣除生产性投入之后所剩无几，就不可能提供补充保险。第二，依法履行纳税义务。企业纳税体现着国家与企业之间的分配关系。国家征税、企业纳税所形成的税收关系，是以国家为主体的分配关系，税收代表着国家的整体利益，而企业补充保险主要体现企业与职工之间的分配关系，代表着局部利益。整体利益制约着局部利益，是获得局部利益的前提条件。企业只有在依法履行了纳税义务，确保国家整体利益实现的前提下，才能进行内部分配，为职工提供补充保险。第三，按时足额缴纳基本养老保险费。在多层次养老保险制度中，基本养老保险起着主导的作用。因此，确保基本养老保险基金的形成是实施补充保险的先决条件。按时足额缴纳基本养老保险费，就是满足这一先决条件的具体措施。此外，基本养老保险还制约着补充保险弹性幅度的最大量限，基本养老保险的最低量界定之后，才能确定补充保险的最高补充量。

（二）基金的分配原则

企业补充养老保险的基金分配应遵循公平与效率相结合的原则。在企业经

济效益允许的情况下，一方面，应使全体职工都能从补充保险中受益，因为他们都为企业盈利做出了贡献，理应具有平等地享受补充养老保险的权力；另一方面，又要根据职工的工作年限、贡献大小、表现好坏、岗位类别等条件划分若干档次，适当拉开差距，鼓励他们为提高企业盈利水平多做贡献。只有把两方面正确结合起来，才有利于发挥补充养老保险提高生产效率的作用。

企业补充养老保险基金的分配还应当遵循权利与义务相统一的原则。实行补充养老保险的企业，每个职工都有享受补充养老保险的权利，同时也应当履行自己的劳动义务，才能享受补充养老保险待遇；如在法定工作时间内，有违纪或违法行为，则不能享受补充养老保险。职工在劳动合同期满或经批准转入其他企业工作时，应允许其已记账的补充养老保险金随之转移，以保障劳动者享受社会保险的合法权利，促进劳动力在社会范围的合理流动。

五、企业补充养老保险的资金来源和鼓励政策

（一）资金来源

就实行企业补充养老保险的目的及其所发挥的功能而言，其资金来源的最终渠道应是企业自有资金。补充保险费用只有从自有资金开支，才能分散养老保险的责任，从而达到建立多层次养老保险体系的目的。

但是，当前相当多的企业面临着经济困难，市场规范又未完全建立起来，企业盈利水平并不确切反映其经营状况，养老待遇结构还不可能完全按照多层次养老保险目标模式加以规范。因此，当前补充养老保险资金完全限定在自有资金，实行起来还很困难。有鉴于此，作为过渡措施，企业补充养老保险资金的来源应以多渠道相结合为宜。首先是企业自有资金。目前，各地在试行企业补充养老保险中所规定的资金来源渠道，如自有资金、职工奖励基金和福利基金、企业风险准备金、企业工资准备金等，皆属于企业自有资金范围，作为补充保险资金来源是可行的。其次，国家让利形成的企业补充养老保险资金。国家让利的形式较多，为推动企业补充养老保险的发展国家所采取的各种鼓励或优惠政策，例如允许部分补充保险费用进入成本、对用于补充保险的费用免征企业所得税等，均可视为国家让利，起着减轻企业的经济负担、增加补充保险资金来源的作用。

对上述资金来源渠道，应按照“企业负担为主、国家让利为辅”的原则确

定各方的适当比例。既要体现"企业补充"的性质，又要兼顾各方利益，以保证补充养老保险资金的来源，使这一制度顺利推行。

（二）鼓励优惠政策

1. 免税政策

首先，应当对企业补充保险费用免征企业所得税。其次，对运用储存的企业补充养老保险基金进行投资所得，也应免征企业所得税。此外，根据我国个人收入调节税的有关规定，已经将干部、职工的退职费、退休金、离休工资、离休生活补助费列入免税范围，因此，职工所得企业补充养老金也应免征个人所得税。

2. 补偿政策

为了减轻企业的经济负担，可以允许企业补充养老保险费用的一部分进入成本，使原来由企业负担的这部分费用，从产品销售收入中得到补偿。其目的是减少企业的计税基数。

3. 实行特优利率和补贴率

企业补充养老保险基金储存的时间长，一般要 30～35 年，且积累数额庞大。为了保值增值，国家必须对储存银行的补充养老保险基金实行特优利率和保值贴补率。

上述优惠政策，虽然使国家当前利益受到一定的损失，但是却能够改善职工的退休生活，有利于国家的长治久安。

退休双轨制的历史背景和解决建议①

编者按：为充分发挥国务院参事参政议政的重要作用，2012 年两会期间，人民网与国务院参事室合作，就社会热点问题请各位参事发表意见建议，进行

① 此文发表在国务院参事室、中央文史馆主办的《国是咨询》2012 年第二期上。此文系 2012 年两会期间，作者在国务院参事室与人民网联合主办的"两会深阅读"栏目上 3 月 4 日接受的访谈。访谈中作者分析了实行市场经济前国家机关人员和企业职工实行不同退休制度的历史背景，以及实行市场经济和现代企业制度后二者差别的原因及不合理性，指出破除机关事业单位和企业退休制度的双重标准，实现二者并轨和统一的必要性。此文发布在人民网上，受到社会各界的热议，有 160 多条留言，被 177 人分享，最高点击量突破 3 万。

深度解读。人民网两会专题特开设“两会深阅读”栏目，集中发表各位参事的真知灼见。以下是国务院参事袁伦渠特为人民网撰写的署名文章《退休双轨制的历史背景和解决建议》。

社会经济发展犹如一列火车，一方面要有动力机制，促使其飞奔向前，另一方面要有稳定机制保障其平稳前进不至颠覆。社会经济正是在动力机制和稳定机制的交互作用下向前发展的，稳定机制包括法律制度等国家机器，而社会保障就是其中一个重要的稳定机制。因此，我们说，社会保障是社会经济发展的“安全网”“减震器”。社会保障主要包括社会保险、社会福利、社会救助、慈善事业等。它通过具有互助精神的社会救助和慈善事业无偿的援助弱势群体，通过社会互济的社会保险化解个人的生活风险，以及通过社会福利向社会成员免费提供公共服务等发挥社会“安全网”“减震器”的作用。

改革开放 30 多年来，社会保障以追求公平正义为基本原则，在调解社会收入分配方面具有其他制度不可替代的作用，当前我国社会保障存在的问题是：城乡之间、地区之间、机关事业单位和企业之间、不同群体之间社会保障待遇的差距很大，甚至一部分人没有任何保障。因此“十二五”规划，提出社会保障发展的总体目标是：坚持广覆盖、保基本、多层次、可持续方针，加快推进覆盖城乡居民的社会保障体系建设，实现新型农村社会养老保险全覆盖，完善实施城镇居民养老保险制度，实现基础养老金全国统筹。推动机关事业单位养老保险制度改革，进一步做实养老保险个人账户，实现跨省可接续。从长远来看，社会保障发展的趋势应当是，不应当仅仅将社会保障定性为维护社会的安全和稳定，而应当随着经济的发展和国家财富的增长，惠及全民，实现共享，实现基本保障制度普惠全民的目标。当前，应当侧重完善农村社会保障体系，逐步提高保障标准，加大扶贫投入，加快解决集中连片特殊困难地区的贫困问题。

下面是我对当前社会保障问题的粗浅看法。

一、目前由于退休制度实行双轨制，造成机关事业单位和企业单位退休金水平差别过大

造成这一问题是有历史背景的。企业职工的基本养老制度始建于 1951 年 2

月《中华人民共和国劳动保险条例》，机关事业单位养老保险制度始建于 1955 年 12 月《国务院关于国家机关工作人员退休处理暂行办法》，当时这两种养老保险制度享受条件大体相同，待遇标准互有高低。它们共同的理论根据是建立在苏联计划时期“最好的保险是国家保险”的理论基础上，国家机关、事业单位、企业退休金全由国家和企业负担，个人不交费，退休金根据本人工作年限长短和工资高低打一个折扣后就是个人的退休金，彼此差别不大。其后虽经修修补补的改进，但变化不大。这种制度一直持续到改革开放以后，社会主义市场经济建立之前。

改革开放后，随着市场经济的建立，企业成为自主经营、自负盈亏、自我发展、自我约束的商品生产者和经营者，企业职工退休基金不再由国家负担，实行社会统筹。即由个人、企业、国家补贴三方负担。养老金的计发办法实行社会统筹与个人账户相结合的模式，职工的养老金由统筹基金中的基础养老金和个人账户养老金组成，职工的退休金多少决定于企业的经济效益和职工的工资水平。在这种情况下，由于不同企业的经济效益不同或者同一企业不同时期经济效益不同，职工养老金水平就会不同。

与此同时，机关事业单位退休制度却没有进行相应的改革，退休金大多仍然由国家支付，计发办法也未改变，仍然保持着旱涝保收的局面，退休制度的双轨制就这样形成了。从而造成广大企业职工反映强烈的退休金水平的巨大差别。怎么解决呢？解决的办法不能够削高补低，降低机关事业单位人员的退休金水平向企业看齐，那样会引起机关事业单位的不满，影响稳定。当前比较现实的办法是逐渐增加国家对企业养老基金的投入，我国财政收入增长超过 GDP 和居民收入的增长速度，2011 年已经达到 10 万亿元，应当有能力做到。财政部部长谢旭人在全国财政工作会议上表示，我国已连续七年提高企业退休人员的基本养老金，2011 年月人均水平已达到 1 500 多元，2012 年将继续提高企业退休人员的养老金水平。但是，我认为根本的办法是进行机关公务员养老保险制度的改革。必须抛弃部门利益，痛下决心破除养老保险待遇的双重标准，实现机关事业单位与企业养老保险制度的并轨和统一，以实现社会公平正义。

二、关于引起广泛争议的“弹性退休制度”问题

我国现行退休年龄为男 60 岁，女 50 岁，女干部 55 岁，是新中国成立初

期规定的。那时人的平均寿命短，国家的社会经济发展水平低，劳动比较繁重、艰苦，女职工50岁，女干部55岁退休是对旧社会含辛茹苦、艰苦劳动的妇女的保护和照顾，使她们享受休息权，应当是合理的。现在国家经济社会情况好转，人的平均寿命长，身体健康，况且国外有些发达国家男女退休年龄已达65～67岁，因此适当提高退休年龄也是合理的。

我国退休年龄是否延长的争议问题，主要考虑的是延长退休年龄会挤占青年人的就业岗位，不利于就业。而按现行规定年龄过早退休，又会造成养老金的过多支出。我认为这是一个两难的问题，需要通过调研来权衡利弊。延长退休年龄主要涉及女职工，可以设计一个退休年龄的空间，女职工50～55岁，女干部55～60岁，让她们在这个年龄空间按自己的意愿自由选择。如果女职工想早退休享受生活，可在50岁退休，如果选择60岁退休是享受劳动参与的权利。

利用健康管理控制医疗费用：来自美国的经验与启示①

内容提要：本文是由作者撰写的国务院参事室课题《中美医疗保障比较研究》（2007—2012）中的一部分。美国的商业医保机构通过健康促进奖励计划、浮动费率、健康教育和健康咨询等健康管理手段，激励参保人员加强疾病防控，从源头上控制医疗费用。本文分析了健康管理的内容、作用及其对我国的启示，借鉴健康管理的经验对我国推进医疗体制改革、缓解“看病难，看病贵”问题有一定的现实意义，并为我国加强健康管理工作提出了若干政策建议。

一、健康管理的实施背景

在美国，商业医疗保险具有极其重要的地位。美国是唯一没有建立全民医疗保障制度的发达国家。全美56.7%的公民（约1.7亿人）购买商业医疗保险，

① 本文发表在2012年第11期的人力资源和社会保障部刊物《中国劳动》上，博士生张涛对此文有贡献。

43.5%的公民（约 1.2 亿人）享受社会医疗保险或医疗救助项目，另有近 15%的公民（约 4 700 万人）没有任何医疗保障[①]。商业医疗保险多为私营企业的雇主代为其雇员购买，并由雇主为雇员负担全部或部分保费。社会医疗保险项目包括医疗照顾计划（medicare）、医疗救助计划（medicaid）、儿童医疗保障计划（S-CHIP）、军队医疗保障计划（TRICARE & CHAMPVA）和联邦公务员医疗保险计划（FEHBP），分别覆盖 65 岁以上的老年人及晚期肾病患者、低收入家庭及残障人士、低收入或单亲家庭的儿童、军队现役人员及其家属、联邦与地方政府的公务员等。为了最大限度地节约财政支出，发挥市场机制的优势，美国的社会医疗保险也大多委托给商业医疗保险机构承办。政府只负责筹资与监管，承办商则负责日常经办管理工作，包括登记参保、理赔审核、费用报销、数据分析、咨询顾问，甚至遴选并管理定点医疗机构等。

自 20 世纪 50 年代以来，一系列原因促使美国的医疗保险费用支出迅速飙升，包括：（1）伴随着“战后黄金时代”的经济繁荣，人民收入水平大幅提高，医疗技术日新月异，人们的医疗消费期望大幅攀升。（2）随着人口老龄化和生活方式转变，慢性病与肥胖问题日益突出。尤其是 1965 年美国建立医疗照顾计划以来，65 岁以上老人被纳入社会医疗保障体系，社会医保费用支出更是呈井喷式增长。（3）垄断资本主义在医疗服务与医疗保险行业迅速扩张，历史悠久的行业垄断组织，如美国医学会（AMA）、美国医院协会（AHA）、美国医疗保险协会（AHIA）等组织的势力进一步增强，对医疗、医保费用的提高起到了推波助澜的作用。面对此形势，尼克松内阁于 1973 年开始了一系列医疗保险管理机制改革，业界称“管理式医疗”（managed care）。具体形式是：鼓励医保机构收购或自建医院，或者与各级定点医疗机构签订协议，组建“一体化医疗服务网络”（IDS）；在网络内，患者实现“社区首诊、分级诊疗、双向转诊”，严格控制就医流向；医保机构对医疗机构实行“按病种付费”“按人头付费”“总额预付”等新型付费方式；同时积极干预医疗行为，包括遵照“循证医学”，限定报销目录，推广最佳临床路径，加强费用与质量考核等。这些措施最初面向社会医保项目，由承办商负责实施，后来逐渐被商业医保机构借鉴，成为美国

① 文中有关美国健康管理的数据和实例均来自国务院参事室与美国蓝十字蓝盾医保集团合作开展的“中美医疗保障运行机制研究”项目的调研资料。

医保体系的普遍特征。

“管理式医疗”措施有效遏制了20世纪八九十年代美国的医疗费用的上涨势头。但是进入新世纪，传统的“管理式医疗”手段显得后继乏力。原因在于：一方面，慢性病和肥胖问题日益严重。据统计，将近一亿两千万美国人受某种慢性病困扰，如哮喘、糖尿病和心脑血管疾病，他们花费了全国75%的医疗费用；另据美国疾病防控中心统计，每年肥胖引致的医疗费用高达365亿美元。另一方面，医保机构对医疗机构的过度干预引起了医疗行业的强力反弹，后者通过市场权力、政治游说和舆论压力，对抗医保机构的干预。于是，“管理式医疗”的重点开始向一种新型的管理模式——健康管理转变。相比于传统的“管理式医疗”注重对医疗行为的事中干预和费用控制，健康管理旨在激励患者与医保机构、医疗机构的三方合作，加强疾病预防与控制，从源头上遏制医疗费用增长。在理念和方法上，注重从事中干预到事前预防、事中治疗、事后康复的全程管理转变，从“治标不治本”向“标本兼治”转变，从医保机构对医疗机构的干预向双方合作共赢转变。

二、健康管理的内容与效果

商业医保机构面向参保人员采取形式多样的健康管理措施，激励参保人员加强疾病防控，防患于未然。常见的健康管理措施包括：偏重预防保健服务的给付设计、健康促进奖励计划、浮动费率以及健康教育和健康咨询等。

（一）组建“以患者为中心的医疗服务之家”，实行全生命周期的健康管理

“以患者为中心的医疗服务之家”（patient centered medical home，PCMH）是一种新型的、由医保机构和各级医疗机构结成的一体化医疗服务网络。在PCMH中，负责各个专业领域、针对患者各个健康阶段的医务人员以契约形式被组织到一起，共同为患者提供涵盖预防保健、急症治疗、慢性病管理、病后康复的全程医疗服务。每个患者被指派给一名全科医生或注册护士，全程负责患者的病案管理与专科协调。各专科医生则在信息系统的支持下共享患者的病历信息，以便提供协调一致的专科服务（见图1）。这些医疗机构能够提供涵盖患者整个生命周期，或者患病前后各个阶段的医疗服务，真正达到了“记录一生、管理一生”的目的。

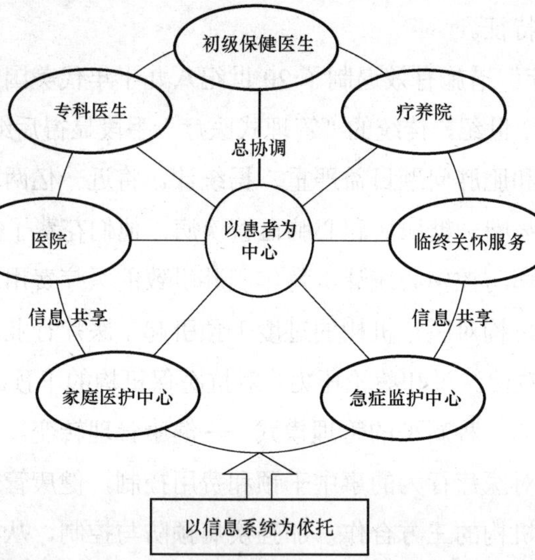

图1 以患者为中心的医疗服务之家

（二）采用形式多样的激励手段，鼓励患者主动采取疾病防控措施

美国的商业医保机构经常在保险产品的报销范围中包含丰富的预防保健服务，如疾病筛查、全面体检、牙科护理等，患者如果接受这些服务，费用可以部分甚至全额报销；或者推出不同形式的健康促进活动，鼓励参保人员采取定向的健康促进活动（如戒烟、健身、减压），并对达标人员提供物质奖励。有些医保机构还会同专业健康管理机构、健身俱乐部签约，对参保人员提供价格折扣。比如加州蓝十字蓝盾计划自2008年起推出了“职场健康促进活动”，鼓励参保人员参与健康状况评估、健康饮食规划、压力管理、戒烟与步行健身等一系列健康促进活动，对于完成任务指标的参与者，主办方会给予数额不同的奖励。两年后，参加者的总体健康风险降低了24%，每人每年潜在节约医疗费用277美元。

随着信息技术和健康统计学的发展，一种更富激励性的健康管理手段随之出现：基于大量的历史数据和完备的统计模型，医保机构根据参保人员的健康状况和疾病防控投入，预测该人员的健康发展趋势和患病风险，并据此调整保险费率。对健康管理活动的参与程度越高、健康指标表现越好，参保人员享受的保费减免就越多。比如科罗拉多州的凯撒医保计划推出了一项面向慢性病患者的试点项目。借助数字个人健康档案，公司定期跟踪参与者的病理相关健康指标及其接受例行检查与康复治疗的情况；基于这些历史数据，利用健康统计模型预测患者的病理发展趋势与预期医疗费用，据此调整下一期的医保费率。研究结果表明，参与者对例行检查与康复治疗的参与度大幅提高，健康指标明显改善。

（三）积极开展健康教育与健康咨询

除了上述激励性手段，医保机构通过各种媒体向参保人员开展健康教育，普及健康管理知识，强调健康管理的重要性；或者聘用健康顾问或病案管理人员，对潜在风险较大的参保人员（尤其是慢性病患者）进行跟踪管理，通过健康咨询服务，督导合理的求医用药日程及健康的生活方式。比如针对肥胖问题，马萨诸塞州蓝十字蓝盾计划启动了一个全方位的健康督导项目，整合了私人健身教练、营养学规划、健康教育与电话咨询等多项活动。每个参加者都被指定给一名健身教练和注册护士，负责全程指导其日常生活中与健康相关的活动。凯撒计划将每一名住院的冠状动脉患者指派给一名主管护士，督导患者经历一系列服务，包括心功能康复治疗、健身疗法、心理支持、健康风险纠正（如戒烟）等。出院后，主管药剂师负责跟踪指导药物治疗与例行检查。该项目让冠状动脉患者的死亡率骤降 75%，每年节省潜在费用 300 万美元。

三、对我国医保管理部门的启示与建议

（一）健康管理对我国医疗体制改革的现实意义

在当前的社会背景下，借鉴健康管理的有益经验，对于我国推进医疗体制改革，缓解“看病难，看病贵”问题有很强的现实意义。

首先，由于我国的全民基本医疗保险体系刚刚建立，群众的医疗保障水平大幅提高，参保人员对医疗服务的需求水平迅速攀升，医保费用支出随之迅速提高。从 2005—2009 年，我国的城镇基本医疗保险人均支出从 781.6 元上升到 1 864.9 元，新农合人均支出从 34.5 元增加到 110.8 元，年均增长率分别高达 24.3%和 33.9%[①]。照此趋势发展，如果不采取应对措施，医保基金的超支风险势难避免。

① 数据来源：《中国统计年鉴 2010》《中国卫生统计年鉴 2010》。

其次，经济转型带来了健康转型，尤其是工业化和社会变革改变了自然环境与生活方式，由此带来新的健康冲击；寿命延长和不良生活习惯带来的慢性病、生活水平提高带来的富贵病已成为日益突出的问题。这些问题会助推医保费用加速增长的趋势。

最后，当前无论是学术界还是业界，都把注意力集中于医保部门对医疗机构的管理，包括创新付费方式，优化临床路径等，但这些手段只能在医疗过程的事中或事后控制医疗费用，容易驱使医疗机构为了削减成本而忽视了质量，而且难以避免医、患、保之间的利益冲突。而健康管理能从根源上降低患病概率，或者帮助患者在病后尽快康复，既有利于控制潜在医疗费用，又有利于改善医疗服务效果、提高民众健康水平、促进医、患、保各方的和谐共赢，可谓一举多得。

（二）加强我国健康管理工作的政策建议

相比于美国，我国的健康管理尚处于探索阶段。新医改方案提出“建立健全包含疾病预防控制、健康教育、妇幼保健、精神卫生和卫生监督在内的公共卫生服务体系建设”，这些固然是做好健康管理的基础性工作，但与精细化、个性化的健康管理相距甚远。更重要的是，作为付费方的医保管理部门没有参与到健康管理实践中，也就无法利用经济杠杆激励医患双方积极参与健康管理活动。为此，笔者为加强我国的健康管理工作提出如下建议：

1. 加强医保信息系统建设与循证医学研究，为健康管理奠定技术基础

科学化、精细化、个性化的健康管理离不开个人数字健康档案的应用。相关部门加强互联互通、实用共享的医保信息系统建设，让参保人员本人、医保部门和各级医疗机构共享个人的健康与病历信息，让参保人员在生命周期的各个阶段接收到有针对性的预防保健或治疗康复服务，实现“记录一生、管理一生”的目的。与此同时，医保机构应与卫生部门密切合作，借鉴循证医学（evidence based medicine）研究的最新成果，健全联结特定疾病的预防、治疗、康复等各个阶段的临床路径，可以为健康管理提供科学依据，收到事半功倍的效果。

2. 构建一体化医疗服务网络，整合健康服务产业链

健康管理需要与一体化医疗服务网络（IDS）的建设结合起来。不妨借鉴发达国家新兴的“以患者为中心的医疗之家”（PCMH）的理念，将特定区域内

的各级医疗机构联系起来，并由社区医疗机构的全科医生全面负责片区内居民的健康事宜。让各专业领域、针对患者各个健康阶段的医务人员在全科医生的协调下，紧密合作，共同为患者提供涵盖预防保健、急症治疗、慢性病管理、病后康复的全程健康服务。医保部门通过设定限制性条款（比如规定到上一级医疗机构必须经全科医生转诊）、拉开报销额度差距等激励措施，引导患者在各级医疗机构间的合理流动。如此不仅能缓解患者过度向大医院集中的情况，还能促进整个健康产业的整合与升级，将行业重心从“治病救人”向预防保健转变，从传统意义上的“医疗服务”向更加全面的“健康服务”转变。

人力资源管理问题

中国劳动和社会保障立法对外国在华企业人力资源管理的影响[①]

内容提要：该中美合作项目全面系统地介绍了中国劳动社会保障立法的内容和外资在华企业的执行情况，此研究对外企熟悉和遵守中国劳动社会保险法律法规，正确处理外企雇主和中方员工的劳动关系，搞好人力资源属地管理，发挥了双方互利共赢重要作用，受到惠普、三星、壳牌、IBM 等跨国公司的欢迎。该书英文出版后，成了外企在华投资人力资源管理的重要指导书。本文系该项目的总结报告，发表在 2001 年第 5 期的《中国人力资源开发》上。

1979 年，中国颁布了第一部“中外合资企业经营法”，以此法律为依据，1980 年 5 月 1 日，港商伍沾德与中国民航北京管理局合资建立了北京航空食品有限公司，这是中国批准的全国第一家合资企业，在中国国家工商管理局的注册编号为 001 号。21 年后的今天，在中国的外商投资企业已多达 34 万家，累计投资总额接近 3 000 亿美元，外商投资企业进出口总额已占中国进出口总额的一半左右，在外商投资企业的就业人数约占全国非农业就业人口的 10%。可以预见，随着中国进一步的改革开放和即将加入 WTO，未来中国的外商投资企

① 本文系袁伦渠、林玳玳主持的中美合作项目“中国劳动和社会保障立法对外国在华企业人力资源管理的影响”课题（2001 年在美国纽约英文出版）的总结报告，发表在 2001 年第 5 期的《中国人力资源开发》上，英文版是 *Labor and Social Insurance Legislation in China: Trends and Developments for Operating in the New Economy*, Foreword by William H. Mobley, Edited by Jennifer Warren, PDI Global Research Consortia, LTD.

业将会更多。

面对为数众多的外商投资企业如何进行严格有效的管理，尤其是人力资源管理，以保障外商和中国员工双方的合法权益，处理好两者之间的劳动关系，吸引优秀人才到外企工作，这是中国政府和外商投资企业都十分关心的重大问题。市场经济是法制经济，因此，对外商企业及其员工依法管理，建立和完善劳动立法和社会保险立法便成为当务之急。

中国政府一直十分重视劳动立法和社会保险立法工作。1995 年 1 月 1 日《中华人民共和国劳动法》实施至今五年来，成效显著。但是中国劳动与社会保险的立法尚有许多不完善之处。在当前，为建立社会主义市场经济的需要和加入世贸组织的要求，中国政府一方面在加强劳动立法与社会保险立法，另外在根据国际惯例和国情修订原有的劳动法规和社会保险法规。在 2000 年召开的第九届全国人民代表大会第四次会议上，劳动合同法和社会保险立法工作被正式列入立法程序中。此外，中国劳动与社会保障部已提出今后五年内社会保险立法发展的整体方案。这些必将促进中国劳动法与社会保险法框架体系的进一步完善，也必将对外国在华企业的人力资源管理工作产生重大影响。

劳动立法的这些变化将影响外商投资企业在华人力资源管理。为此，我们对中国劳动立法与社会保险立法的现状与未来趋势及其对人力资源管理的影响进行了跟踪研究，其目的是使外商在华企业了解中国当前和未来的劳动与社会保险法律法规，更好地依法进行人力资源管理，维护外商和中国员工双方的合法权益，为外企吸收中国更多的最优秀人才，来华投资加盟，实现外商在华投资的长期发展和繁荣而做出努力。

一、外国在华企业执行中国劳动法与社会保险法的现状

中国实行改革开放政策以来，外资企业逐渐来到中国。中国也不断吸收了国外的劳动管理经验，劳动法制建设和管理日臻完善。特别是自 1995 年《劳动法》颁布以来，多数外国在华企业加强了对其内部员工的管理，严格执行中国劳动法律法规的各项规定，总体情况较好。各项主要劳动标准得以基本落实。一些高科技含量和现代化程度较高的外资企业，采用以人为本的先进经营管理理念，自觉遵守中国劳动法律法规，关心爱护职工，注重营造企业文化，保险福利待遇较法律规定的大部分国有企业更高，企业内部劳动关系和谐稳定。但

外资企业来自全世界各个地区，各国的社会经济发展水平不同，制度和文化迥异，在华企业的规模和现代化程度不一，企业经营管理理念也有很大差异，因此外国在华企业执行中国劳动法的情况差别很大，难以一概而论。总的来说，规模较大、现代化程度较高的企业，跨国公司企业管理的各方面都较为正规，劳动法执行情况也较好。而一些中小型企业，管理较为原始，执行劳动法情况也较差。

外商投资企业在执行中国社会保险立法方面目前存在以下一些情况：

第一，外国在华企业职工的保险福利待遇，一般都能按照当地有关部门的规定，由企业为职工办理养老保险、失业保险、医疗保险、提取住房公积金等等。多数企业还不同程度地为职工办理一些补充保险（意外伤害保险、补充养老保险等）。总的来说，保险福利要比国有企业好一些。

第二，各地区和各种不同的外资企业执行中国社会保险法律情况不同。大城市的跨国公司、大型外资企业比较守法，但在南方某些城市，执行情况较差。

第三，外地工（农民工、劳务工）被排除在社会保障之外。有些城市，外国在华企业招聘了相当数量的外地工（或劳务工、或离土不离乡的农民工），有的多达职工总数的一半，他们在工资上与正式合同制工人同工同酬，但不能享受养老保险、个人与家属的医疗保险等待遇。

第四，外资企业的参保率还不够高。一些地市级地方领导对在外资企业开展社会保险工作有畏难情绪，认为会把外商吓跑，搬到别的地区投资，因此对社会保险扩大覆盖面工作持观望态度，以致工作没有起色。

二、中国劳动立法和社会保险立法的趋势

中国劳动立法的发展趋势主要有以下八个方面：

第一，中国的《劳动法》已颁布六年了，但中国的劳动法律体系还不够完善。尽管有《劳动法》这样的基本法，但缺乏支持它的二级法律，只有大量的行政法规、规章和文件，立法层次较低。因此中国劳动立法的一个明显趋势是健全法规体系，补充二级法律，将现行的许多法规、规章和文件逐步提升为法律。

第二，中国的劳动和社会保障立法正在逐步取消外资企业与内资企业适用

不同法律的做法，给外资企业以国民待遇，同时撤销人才市场与劳动力市场的界限，建立统一的劳动力市场，让各个企业和求职者在平等的环境下竞争。

第三，由于中国现存大量的“隐性就业”和“隐性失业”，造成“劳动关系虚化”。为此，中国政府将会允许劳动者建立多重劳动关系，使隐性就业和隐性失业显性化。允许一个劳动者在与一个用人单位建立劳动关系时，也可与另一个用人单位建立正式的劳动关系，即一个雇员可以合法地同时受雇于两或三个雇主。用人单位无论以哪一种形式用工，只要发工资都必须按工资的一定比例缴纳社会保险费用，并按正式的劳动关系进行管理。

第四，中国将积极探索建立劳动用工许可制度，对不经劳动部门审核批准的企业，不得办理营业执照，确保“三同时”原则和各项劳动标准的落实。对重点行业、企业实行欠薪保障制度，对拖欠工资严重的企业要求按其工资总额的一定比例缴纳欠薪保障金，用于补发拖欠职工工资。

第五，正在修订的《工会法》和将要制定的《集体合同法》将扩大工会的权利，提高工会的地位，同时要求工会对集体合同承担法律责任，而不仅仅是道义上的责任。为使集体谈判能够真正开展起来，职工一方的集体谈判代表将得到有效的法律保护。

第六，法律发挥其效力的前提之一是公民要了解法律。为此，中国将深入开展劳动和社会保险法律法规宣传教育工作。

第七，劳动和社会保障部的高级官员多次重申要加强劳动监察工作，强调严格执法，因此在立法方面将会有如下动向：①制订详细的劳动法律实施细则，明确劳动执法部门的权利；②在法律规范中增加追究责任的条款，同时注意其可操作性；③增加劳动保障部门的执法强制手段，以增强对企业的威慑力；④增加劳动保障部门的执法权限，以便冲破地方某些机构对企业，尤其是对外商投资企业的不合理庇护。

第八，在中国当前供大于求的劳动力市场上，劳动者，尤其是女性劳动者处于弱者地位，法律将加强对他们的保护。

中国社会保险立法的发展趋势主要有以下八个方面：

第一，目前，养老保险费由企业自行申报，社会保险经办机构核定，这容易造成人为缩减养老保险缴费的问题。因此建议通过立法规定，由会计师事务所等社会中介机构来监督参保企业养老保险费的申报。

第二，由于城乡经济发展水平的差别，在一定历史阶段，城乡养老保险必须分别立法。但从长远趋势来看，必须建立农村养老保险制度。

第三，随着医疗保险制度改革的推进，医疗保险制度改革的配套文件相继出台，比较完善的医疗保险政策框架体系已基本形成。各地将从当地的实际情况出发，加快制定实施方案和各项配套政策。

第四，工伤、生育保险的立法还有待于进一步规范和完善。《工伤保险条例》已着手起草，建议研究制定《实施企业工伤保险行业差别费率指导办法》，着手进行《生育保险条例》的研究工作，逐步扩大工伤、生育保险覆盖范围。

第五，从 2001 年起，国有企业原则上不再建立新的再就业服务中心，企业新的减员原则上不再进入再就业服务中心，由企业依法与其解除劳动关系，按规定享受失业保险待遇。鉴于下岗保障和失业保障将逐步并轨，建议对老职工有所照顾，按工龄计算享受失业保险金的月份。

第六，虽然近几年失业保险的覆盖面逐年扩大，但对城镇从业的农民合同制工人尚未覆盖。《失业保险条例》中规定，城镇企事业单位招用的农民合同制工人，本人不缴纳失业保险费。因此，建议通过立法，明确按照劳动者皆有保险，谁用工谁投保、单位和个人共同承担保险费用的原则，真正实现由城镇职工向城镇从业人员过渡，只要实际发生用工行为，不论是正式录用还是试用期间，是短期还是长期聘用，也不论是否签订了劳动合同，都应缴费参保。

第七，随着社会保险覆盖范围的扩大和人口老龄化的到来，仅靠社会保险基金征缴单一渠道，已难以满足社会保险日益增长的支付需求。因此，国内有关专家建议应积极开拓新的稳定的社会保险筹资渠道，并经立法予以明确。此外，中国将通过立法建立社会保险基金的安全投资机制，在规范金融秩序的条件下，严格规定社会保险基金的投资方向和各项投资比例的上限，强化投资监管措施，保证社会保险基金的保值与增值。

第八，目前在社会保险方面发生争议纠纷进行仲裁或提起诉讼时，由于立法滞后，仲裁机构和人民法院无法根据有效的法律规定对社会保险争议、纠纷进行仲裁或判决，处于无法可依的状态。因此，中国将研究制定《社会保险争议处理办法》，明确社会保险行政争议处理机构，建立工作制度，积极探索和建立社会保险行政争议处理制度。

三、中国劳动和社会保障立法趋势对外企人力资源管理的影响

中国的劳动和社会保险法一直处于发展变化之中，逐步完善，向国际接轨，这些发展变化对外企主要有以下六个方面的影响。

第一，使人工成本上升，劳动法的贯彻和社会保障制度在外企的实行提高了员工的工资、福利和社会保险的待遇，缩短了工作时间，造成了企业人工成本上升。

第二，人才竞争平等化，《劳动法》颁布前，国企和外企的劳动用工制度差别较大。国企就业采用终身制，医疗费由全额负担。外企就业采用劳动合同制，没有养老和医疗保险，国企低工资，高福利，利于老年人，外企高工资，低福利，利于年轻人，现在，国企外企遵守同样的法规，在劳动力市场上平等竞争作为劳动力市场核心的高素质人才，成为各类企业争夺的重点。

第三，劳动法律体系建立后，劳动者和用人单位双方的行为都被规范，双方的合法权益都得到了保护。劳动争议相对减少，劳动关系趋于稳定，员工的权益得到保护，从而使劳动者工作更加努力，为用人单位创造出更多的财富，同时，劳动者又得到用人单位更多的回报，双方合作愉快，实现双赢。

第四，职业资格证书制度降低了选才成本和培训成本，中国劳动法律体系不断完善的一个明显成果是社会化的职业培训体系从无到有，逐步建立、发展起来了。职业资格证书制度大大降低了外企的选才成本和培训成本。这在一定程度上抵补了由于保险、福利的增加引起的人工成本的上扬。

第五，遵守劳动法有利于企业形象，企业遵守劳动法的程度则反映了企业对劳动者的尊重程度。《劳动法》颁布及其劳动法律体系建立完善后，遵守劳动法的程度成为企业人力资源管理的形象之一，也是企业间的又一竞争内容。

第六，促进管理民主化，管理民主化已成为世界趋势。中国境内的外企在这方面与世界水平尚有一定的差距。劳动法律体系逐步建立、完善后，中国境内的外企进行集体谈判，签订集体合同有了法律依据，大大促进了管理民主化的进程。

应关注煤炭行业高素质人才缺乏的问题[①]

应关注煤炭行业高素质人才的极度缺乏问题。劳动就业一方面是总量上的供大于求，另一方面也存在着结构失衡，即有人无事干，有事无人干的问题。这在煤炭行业极度缺乏高素质人才问题上十分明显。

近年来我国煤炭行业严重伤亡事故频出，2005年以来伤亡事故有所下降，但安全形势仍很严峻。原因固然很多，但其中一个重要原因是缺乏高素质人才和必要的技术支撑。国家机构改革和煤炭管理体制调整后，没有对艰苦行业，艰苦专业的人才培养做出安排。煤炭院校下放归地方后，15所煤炭院校的专业设置和专业方向基本上按地方发展的需要进行了调整，减少或干脆撤销了采矿地矿专业。煤炭企业在困难时期，受短期行为驱使，片面提出“减员增效”的口号，人为放大了企业人才饱和的信号，迫使高校做出办学方向和办学内容的调整，加之煤炭专业办学人才培养的成本高，国家又缺乏配套倾斜政策，使高校向办学效益高，就业好和社会需求量大的专业转移，不办或少办煤炭专业。加之煤炭行业是高危行业，环境艰苦，待遇又差，严重影响了原煤炭院校招生，人才培养和毕业生就业，致使绝大多数煤炭院校纷纷更名换姓，15所煤炭院校除中国矿业大学维持原名外，其余都分别改名为科技大学、工程技术大学、工商大学等，停招或少招了煤炭主体专业的学生。

煤炭高校招生的减少，造成煤炭企业人才严重短缺。如产煤大省河南，1998年至2005年全煤炭行业竟没有招进过一名采掘专业的本科生，而工程技术人员却流失2 200多人。再如宝鸡矿业集团1992年至2002年的10年时间里仅录用大专生1人，而同期却流失技术人员849人，国有重点煤炭企业铜川矿务局连续11年未新进大学生。阜新矿业集团6年未进采矿专业大学生，且流失了500多名中青年技术人员。人才的短缺严重影响了企业的发展和生产安全，部分企业的重要生产岗位和管理岗位如矿长、总工长期找不出合适人选，有的企业连区队管理岗位都只好找农民工顶替。结果煤矿行业技术人才难以接续，技术力量整体下降，安全事故频发，企业形象恶化，进一步加剧了人才流失。

---

① 2005年5月至9月袁伦渠参加国务院参事室赴煤矿安全调研后撰写，后应中国民盟中央主席张梅颖的邀请，2007年7月在中国民盟中央召开的座谈会上的发言，发表在2007年第9期的民盟中央机关刊物《群言》上。

鉴于当前煤炭管理体制和企业发展状况，短期内不可能靠市场调节实现煤炭人才的优化配置，需要政府采取强有力手段鼓励优秀人才在煤炭行业就业，充实技术力量，为此提出如下建议：

（1）加强煤矿安全科技创新基地和人才队伍建设，培养煤炭行业主体专业人才，鼓励高校尤其是煤炭院校培养安全技术人才，对紧缺专业加强奖励力度。

（2）尽快将煤炭行业一线人才的培训工作列入教育部“技能紧缺人才培养培训工程”，吸引有实践经验的职工和有志青年学习高职高专急需专业，实行合同培养，缩短学制，降低门槛，学费由国家和企业共同负担，学生免费入学，适当规范服务年限，毕业后到煤炭企业工作。

（3）为提高安全生产工作的地位和作用，应在《授予博士硕士学位和培养研究生的专业目录》中单设“安全科学与工程”为一级学科，以适应煤炭行业对高层次安全技术人才的需要。

（4）国家对艰苦行业、艰苦专业实行特殊保护，设置矿业人才专项奖金，鼓励高校相关毕业生到煤炭企业就业。

“人力资本”理论述评①

“人力资本”理论产生于20世纪50年代中期，诺贝尔奖金获得者，美国著名经济学家舒尔茨（T. W. Schultz）是这一理论的创始者和主要代表人物，他以“人力资本”理论为西方经济学开辟了一个全新的研究领域——教育投资与收益的研究领域。正确地认识、科学地分析和评价“人力资本”理论，吸取其合理的内核，对于开发我国的人力资源具有一定的参考价值。这是较早介绍和评价西方人力资本理论的尝试。

一、“人力资本”的概念

人力资本（human capital），是与物质资本（非人力资本）相对应的概念。舒尔茨认为，资本有两种表现形式，一种是人力资本，一种是物质资本，全面的资本概念应由上述两个方面组成。物质资本是体现于物质产品之上的，以生

① 摘自1988年12月袁伦渠、潘功胜、熊敏鹏所著的《现代劳动组织学——宏观论与微观论》第一章（中国财政经济出版社）。

产资料的数量和质量表示的资本；人力资本是体现于劳动者身上的，以劳动者的数量和质量表示的资本。此处的劳动者的数量是指一个社会中从事有用工作的人数及百分比，劳动时间在一定程度上代表着该社会的人力资本的多少；劳动者的质量是指技术、知识、熟练程度与其他类似可以影响人从事生产性工作能力的东西。每个劳动者在质的方面存在差异，就是同一个劳动者在其接受教育和训练的前后，其工作能力、技艺水平、熟练程度及劳动质量也会存在差异。

人力资本与物质资本具有相似性，如二者都具有生产性作用，二者的作用都能使国民收入增加，二者都需通过投资才能形成。但是，二者之间又有明显的区别，除表现的方式及对经济发展推动力的大小不同之外，还有其他诸多方面，如物质资本的所有权可以被继承或转让，而人力资本的所有权不具备继承或转让的属性。值得注意的是，人力资本与物质资本之间不仅具有相似性和区别，而且具有互补或替换性，用一定量的物质资本和一定量的人力资本可以产生一定量的收入，用较少量的物质资本和较多量的人力资本，或较多量的物质资本和较少量的人力资本，可以产生同量的国民收入。

二、“人力资本”理论兴起的历史背景

“人力资本”理论的兴起，有其深刻的社会历史根源，它既是科学技术进步和经济发展在理论上的反映，也是垄断资本追求利益的需要。

现代科学技术的飞跃，推动了劳动方式的推陈出新和劳动力结构的变化。近代劳动方式以劳动者操作机器进行生产为特征，现代劳动方式则呈现这样一种状态，一部分劳动者只起监护自动化设备运转的作用，另一部分劳动者则搬进了实验室，专门从事诸如编制运算程序、进行产品设计和工艺设计等方面的创造性劳动。劳动方式的变化推动了劳动力结构的变化，在企业内部，脑力劳动者的比重增加了，体力劳动者的比重相应减少；在主要从事体力劳动的雇员中，非熟练劳动者的比重趋于下降。可见，科学技术的迅速发展及其在生产过程中的物化，突出了劳动力质量在经济发展中的核心地位，而劳动力质量的提高又依赖于教育投资的增加，这是以舒尔茨为代表的“人力资本”理论兴起的经济条件。

现代科学技术革命也带来了资本剥削方式的变化以及竞争的加剧。资本家从对绝对剩余价值的榨取转向对相对剩余价值的榨取。由于高质量的劳动力能为资本家带来更多的剩余价值，因而现代垄断资本已经从对生产资料的垄断，

发展到对人力资本的垄断，可以认为，当前的经济竞争，主要的就是技术的竞争，技术的竞争就是人才的竞争，而人才的竞争则是教育的竞争。这就是“人力资本”理论兴起的主要社会背景。

三、“人力资本”理论概要

以舒尔茨为代表的“人力资本”理论包含下述主要内容和基本观点。

（一）“人力资本”是靠对人的投资形成的资本

人力资本的形成，在于对人的投资，人力资本的具体内容包括：

1. 用于教育和职工培训的支出

通过教育和在职培训，可以提高劳动力的质量，即提高劳动者的工作能力、技术水平和熟练程度。用于教育的支出包括进行正规的初等、中等及高等学校教育的支出。舒尔茨认为，要估计一般的教育成本，包括支付教师的薪金，图书管理员、行政人员的薪金，教育设备器材的费用，以及固定资产的折旧费用等，并不困难，但要估计学生在学习期间所放弃的收入则较难，而这项成本是必须计算在内的。用于职工培训的支出则是由厂商提供的，据美国学者克拉克估计，其支出大约和正规教育的支出差不多。

2. 用于卫生保健的支出

卫生保健事业的发展，一方面可以增加未来劳动者的数量（最明显的表现为婴儿死亡率的下降），另一方面保证现有劳动者的数量（减少疾病、死亡），提高劳动者的身体素质。无疑，保健支出是一种人力投资。

3. 用于劳动力国内流动的支出

劳动力的国内流动可以缓和各地劳动力的供需矛盾，并且为劳动者自身专长的发挥创造良好的条件。如果劳动力的供给大于需求，或者学非所用，用非所长，都将造成巨大的人力浪费和人力资本的损失。所以，用于劳动力国内流动的支出，是人力投资的一项内容。

4. 用于移民出入境的支出

移民是国际间人力的流动，它包括两个方面：一是国外人力迁移到本国，从而造成迁入国获得人力资本的增加；二是本国人力迁移到外国，从而造成本国人力资本的流失。如果出入境者是经过专业训练的人才，就使得人力迁入国免去了培养这些人力的投资，人力迁出国失去了培养这些人才所进行的投资；同样，也使他们省去或白白支付了劳动力从出生到出入境时的生育、抚养和保健费用。因此，在考虑人力资本时，须考虑移民的人力投资问题。

（二）在经济增长中，人力资本的作用大于物质资本的作用

舒尔茨认为，虽然人力资本和物质资本都是经济发展不可缺少的条件，但是，在现代经济条件下，人力资本的贡献远大于物质资本的贡献。当代劳动生产率的迅速提高，正是由于人力资本不断增加的结果。遭受战争重创的日本和西德之所以在战后能够得到迅速的恢复和发展，这与其过去长期的人力资本积累以及后来重视人力资本投资是分不开的。

（三）市场供求决定人力投资

舒尔茨认为，面对一个复杂多变的动态世界，一国试图通过计划来培养各级各类人才，往往难以奏效的。可行的办法，就是以劳动力的市场供求关系为依据，以人力价格的漂浮为衡量信号，对人力投资比例予以自发调节，即市场供求决定人力投资。

在资本有限的情况下，物质投资与人力资本的比例，取决于两种投资的收益率，哪种投资收益率高就增加哪种投资，哪种投资收益率低则减少哪种投资，当两者收益率相等时，就是最佳比例。

（四）人力投资收益率的计算

如同物质资本的投资具有收益一样，人力资本的投资也有收益问题，它以人力资本投资收益率来衡量。人力投资收益率即人力投资与其所带来的收益之间的比值。

如果不是计算全部教育过程的收益率，而是计算教育过程的某一阶段投资的收益率，则将某一级教育程度毕业生与前一级教育程度毕业生的收入差别，看成某一级教育投资的收益，然后与该级的教育投资之比，便是该阶段的教育投资收益率。

四、“人力资本”理论简评

“人力资本”理论反映了现代科学技术革命和社会化大生产的客观要求，因而有其合理的部分，这主要表现在，以人力资本积累为中心的人力投资理论，从理论上改变了以物质资本积累为中心的资产阶级传统经济增长理论；确认了人力投资是现代经济增长的重要因素，强调了提高人口质量对促进社会经济增长的重大作用；同时，这种理论重视教育投资的经济效益。

劳动关系问题

建立新时期和谐稳定的劳动关系①

劳动关系是雇主（或企业行政）与员工之间发生的经济利益关系。在新的历史时期，建立和谐稳定的劳动关系有助于维护企业和劳动者双方的合法权益，有助于我国社会主义市场经济体制和现代企业制度的建立，有助于以人为本、促进社会和人的全面发展的实现，有助于我国经济健康、持续、稳定的发展，有助于我国全面小康社会目标的实现。

一、新时期我国企业劳动关系的特点

随着我国经济体制改革的不断深入和市场经济的发展，人力资源配置的市场化已成为不可逆转的趋势，从而引起了企业劳动关系的深刻变化，出现了许多新的特点。

（1）政府在劳动关系中的主体地位逐渐弱化，劳动关系的确立主要通过市场机制来实现。由于用工主体由国家转变为企业和劳动者，加上企业法和劳动法的颁布和实施，企业和劳动者成为相对独立的利益主体，企业拥有用人自主权，劳动者可以自由选择职业，劳动关系双方的利益主体日益明显。

（2）劳动关系的表现形式多样化。在计划经济体制下，国有企业和集体企业都为公有，国家是劳动关系双方的主体，劳动关系单一、简单，矛盾冲突并不明显。在市场经济体制下，所有制形式变为以公有制为主体，多种经济成分并存，单一的劳动关系被打破，不同所有制性质的企业劳动关系表现形式也不同。

---

① 在中国劳动学会2004年度学会暨新时期劳动关系问题学术研讨会上的发言，后载于中国劳动学会主办《中国劳动学会通讯》2004年第5期（年会专刊）。

（3）劳动关系日益契约化。由于国家用工主体转变为企业用工主体，企业和劳动者各有自己的经济利益，因而需要利用劳动合同这种契约的形式来明确劳动关系双方的责任、权利和义务。

（4）劳动关系日趋复杂和不稳定。随着企业用人自主权和劳动者择业自主权的确立，企业越来越追求经济效益和实现利润最大化，劳动者为追求收入最大化与和谐的人际关系、宽松的劳动环境，也在不断地变更工作岗位和工作单位，劳动关系的这种动态发展一定程度上有利于劳动力的优化配置，另一方面也造成了劳动关系的不稳定，引发出一系列值得注意的问题。例如，用人单位法律意识淡薄，劳动合同内容不规范，管理不严，执行不全面，解除劳动合同不慎重，造成劳动关系的确立、变更、终止带有很大的随意性。劳动关系双方的利益摩擦日益增多。尤其值得注意的是，我国劳动力供大于求，劳动关系双方利益的摩擦多表现为企业侵犯职工的合法利益，使得劳动争议案件不断增加，成为社会不稳定的因素之一。

二、建立新时期和谐稳定的劳动关系

（1）进一步建立和健全具有中国特色的劳动关系法律体系，把劳动关系纳入法制化、规范化的轨道。

（2）加强劳动监察工作。一是强化劳动监察部门的职能，加大劳动监察工作的力度，运用法律手段纠正劳动关系主体的行为偏差，预防劳动纠纷，减少突发事件；二是健全劳动争议的调节与仲裁工作的机构；三是健全基层调节、劳动部门仲裁和人民法院裁决三者相互协调、齐抓共管处理劳动争议的组织网络，使劳动关系矛盾依法得到公正、及时的解决。

（3）大力培育、发展、完善劳动力市场，逐步建立起以职业介绍、就业培训、失业保险和生产自救为主要内容的劳动就业服务体系、社会保险体系、劳动关系协调体系，为建立和谐稳定的劳动关系创造条件。

（4）加强工会组织建设，推行集体协商谈判制度，保证职工的合法权益。党的十四大确定的建立社会主义市场经济体制后，所有制结构发生了巨大变化，除了公有制企业以外，外商投资企业、私营企业和混合所有制企业大量涌现，这些企业就业人数迅速增加，一些国有大中型企业也改为股份制企业，纯国有制企业逐渐减少，在外商投资企业、私营企业劳动关系日益复杂，用人单位违反劳动法、侵犯职工合法权益的现象时有发生，他们随意延长劳动时间、加强劳动强度、克扣工资、随意搜身甚至打骂工人致伤致死，他们不为职工创造安全的生产条件，让工人在有毒有害的环境中工作，重大伤亡事故屡屡发生，有的竟然签订生死合同，有的工人当天上工当天死亡，甚至出现了资本主义原始积累时期的血汗工资制度，旧中国半封建、半殖民地时期的封建把头制度和包身工制度也开始死灰复燃。这些侵犯职工合法权益的恶劣做法，加剧了劳动关系的紧张，引发多起职工群体事件。即使国有企业，为追求企业利润的最大化，也容易忽视以至侵犯职工群众的利益，引起社会的不安定。

在这种情况下，谁来维护劳动者的合法权益呢？其中一个重要的组织就是工会，由工会代表劳动关系中职工一方站出来维护职工的利益，工会为工人说话必须有法律依据，除了劳动法以外，还必须有工会法。2001 年 10 月颁布的《中华人民共和国工会法》第二十条明确规定："工会代表职工与企业以及实行企业化管理的事业单位进行平等协商，签订集体合同。"这一规定强化了工会在集体谈判中的核心地位，为集体谈判和集体协商制度的发展奠定了基础。但在实践中遇到了一些问题，正如人大教授陈延国同志指出的："工会的代表性和独立性问题；企业级别集体谈判的雇主角色不明，行业、区域集体谈判中的雇主组织缺位；谈判环节缺位，协商谈判机制尚未发挥作用，协议内容雷同，缺少针对性和可操作性"等问题。因此《中华人民共和国工会法》还应该进一步改进与完善，以便加强工会的维权力量，从而更好地保护工人的利益。

三、对劳动关系重要地位的几点认识

（1）劳动关系在政府工作中的重要地位。劳动保障工作应当包括就业、保障、劳动关系三个部分，缺乏劳动关系是不全面的，三位一体才是完整的。这就把劳动关系问题提高到相当的高度，也是对劳动经济学科研究的新发展。

（2）劳动关系在学术研究、学科建设中的重要地位。关于劳动经济学的研究对象，国内外学者有三种不同观点，国外有的学者认为是研究劳动组织，国内学者有的认为是研究人力资源的有效配置，还有的学者认为是研究劳动关系，日本劳动经济学和社会保障学的权威学者隅谷三喜男先生认为，劳动经济学按研究对象可分为两种：以劳动力市场为研究对象的称为劳动经济学；以劳资关系为研究对象的称为劳资关系经济学，他把劳动关系的研究提高到学科建设的高度，由此可见，劳动关系已成为劳动经济学的研究对象。最近，中国工运学院更名为中国劳动关系学院，显示出教育领域和工会系统对劳动关系的重视，其课程设置和学科建设将会做重大调整，重点也会转到劳动关系上来。

（3）劳动关系的研究领域应该扩大，对劳动关系的研究领域不能仅仅局限于企业雇主与雇员关系的研究上，应该扩大到全国、全社会范围的研究上面，全社会范围内的收入分配关系，尤其是收入差距问题应该是劳动关系研究的一个重要内容，收入差距可以包括四个方面：一是城乡收入差距，二是地区收入差距，三是城市内部收入差距，四是农村内部收入差距。目前我国收入差距越来越大，就全国来说基尼系数已达到 0.45（警戒线是 0.4），严重影响了社会的稳定。因此，缩小收入差距，协调利益关系应该是建立和谐稳定劳动关系的一部分。还有的学者提出了新三农的概念，即失地农民、无地农民、农民工。在城市化进程当中，失地农民越来越多，有的学者提出目前我国失地农民已达到 3 000 万，而且每年还以 100 万的速度增加。如何对失地农民进行合理的土地补偿，为他们解决就业和社会保障问题，也成为处理劳动关系的一项重要任务。

（4）政府应树立以和谐稳定的劳动关系为内容的科学的政绩观，科学的政绩观不应是宽马路、大广场、水泥森林，而应当是经济与社会的和谐、生态环境的保护、资源的低消耗，还应该破除对 GDP 的洋崇拜，应该使 GDP 的增加带来失业人员的减少，而不是相反。还有的学者认为衡量一个干部的政绩观应该包括五大指标：恩格尔系数、基尼系数、二元结构系数、人文发展系数、集约化系数；我认为除此之外还应该增加一项内容，那就是在宏观上协调、规范劳动关系，促进劳动关系的和谐稳定。

中国劳动关系的协调与和谐社会的构建①

一、新中国成立初期的劳动关系

新中国成立初期，即 1949—1953 年的国民经济恢复时期，此时遗留下来的

① 2011 年 11 月 3 日在韩国首尔中央劳动关系研究院研讨会上的讲演，2011 年 12 月 12 日发表于中国人力资源开发研究会劳动关系分会，第三届年会暨学术讨论会。

失业工人很多，约有480万人。国家一方面恢复和发展国民经济，为劳动者提供更多的就业岗位，另一方面则是积极地解决失业问题，采取的办法有：（1）对旧政权遗留下来的公教人员和企业职工采取“包下来”的政策，实行“原职原薪”；对私营工商业实行“公私兼顾、劳资两利”的政策，防止企业倒闭造成新的失业。（2）采取以工代赈、生产自救、技术培训、发放救济金等措施，以政府统一介绍就业和自行就业相结合的方式解决原有失业人员的就业问题。由于采用这样一些制度安排和实际操作措施，再加上努力恢复和发展国民经济为劳动者提供更多的就业岗位，使得这一时期的劳动关系得到缓和，社会比较稳定。

二、计划经济体制时期的劳动关系

中国1956年宣布进入社会主义建设时期，同时照搬苏联模式，实行单一的计划经济体制，劳动制度实行“统包统配”的终身固定工制，即“铁饭碗”制；分配制度上实行平均主义的“大锅饭”制；社会保险上实行国家保险制度。这种政策保护了劳动者的基本权利和平等的社会地位，避免了劳动关系的矛盾。但其弊端是：企业和劳动者都缺乏独立的身份，劳动者对企业、企业对国家高度依赖，企业无用人自主权，工人无就业选择权，不利于劳动力的正常流动和劳动资源的优化配置，劳动关系双方积极性无法发挥，导致企业的效率低下。

三、转轨时期的劳动关系

1978年党的十一届三中全会以后，中国开始由计划经济向市场经济体制转型。市场经济承认企业和劳动者双方的利益不同化，承认企业和劳动者双方追求利益的最大化。这一时期劳动关系的特点是：（1）劳动关系市场化。企业和劳动者可以相互选择，企业有用人自主权，劳动者有就业选择权，打破了“铁饭碗”制度。（2）劳动关系调解方式契约化。劳动者和企业平等协商签订劳动合同，约定各自的权利和义务。（3）工资实行企业自主经营、自主分配，劳动者实行按劳分配与按生产要素分配相结合的分配制度，打破了平均主义“大锅饭”。（4）社会保险实行企业、个人和政府三方负担，打破了国家保险制。

在市场经济条件下，与计划经济时期不同的是：劳动关系双方利益格局发生了重构和组合，矛盾摩擦不断加剧。我国正处于社会主义初级阶段，市场经济体制仍不够健全，劳动立法还不够完善，劳动者的充分就业权、劳动报酬权、平等合同权等权益尚未得到充分的保障；同时，由于中国正处于工业化和城镇化过程中，资本相对稀缺，劳动力供大于求，在生产要素中形成了强资本与弱劳动的态势，劳动关系紧张，劳动争议案件日益增多。

四、和谐社会的构建

中国转轨时期市场经济的实行在一定程度上提高了企业的效率，劳动者的积极性也得到一定程度的发挥。但是，收入分配的高低悬殊、劳动环境的恶化以及工作氛围的不民主也使得劳动争议案件日益增多，影响了社会的和谐和稳定。为此，中国政府正在采取一系列的政策和措施，缓和紧张的劳动关系，努力为劳动者创造较好的劳动条件和生活条件。

（1）完善三方协商机制。政府、代表劳动者的工会组织和代表雇主的企业联合会形成三方机制，共同参与劳动关系的协调，通过国家力量、资本力量和劳动者力量的有力结合，在制定法规、调整劳动关系、处理劳动争议等方面履行各自的义务，进行协商对话、弱化争议，建立规范有序、公正合理、互利共赢的新型劳动关系。

（2）建立和完善企业集体谈判机制。集体谈判是指企业的工会或职工代表与用人单位代表就职工的合法权益事项进行谈判并签订集体合同的行为。通过集体谈判签订集体合同，以弥补劳动立法和劳动合同的不足，维护劳动者的权益。

（3）加强工会在协调劳动关系中的作用。工会的基本职能是维护劳动者的合法权益，工会应当利用集体合同、职代会等重要环节加强劳资利益的协调、诉求的表达和权益保障机制的建设。

（4）改善劳动者的劳动环境和劳动条件。用人单位应当采用适当的技术和组织措施，消除生产环境中的不安全、不卫生因素，保护劳动者的人身安全和健康，防止工伤和职业病，遵守劳动法规定的工作时间和休息休假制度。

（5）构建和谐的企业文化、尊重劳动者的非经济需求。劳动是一种社会活动，企业不仅要实现经济目标也应当充分满足劳动者的非经济需求，包括劳动者自我实现和自我发展的需求，创造有希望的工作前景和发展空间，建立劳资双方的伙伴关系。

（6）实行产业民主化。劳动者在企业中应获得和发展参与权，在一定范围内参与资本的构成、管理决策和利润分配，实行分享权力、分享利润、人格受尊重的原则。

劳动关系涉及劳动者的生存和发展以及社会的和谐稳定。要使劳动关系真正促进产业的发展、社会文明的进步和共同富裕，就必须使劳动关系双方都得到公平的经济回报和可预期的利益增长。这就要求双方互相为本、互利共赢，企业将劳动者视为可创造财富的人力资本，劳动者通过企业利润的增长，实现自身价值进而得到更多的回报。企业与劳动者双方形成一个利益共同体，实现劳动关系的双赢局面。

劳动社会学问题

劳动社会学研究综述①

劳动社会学是一个年轻的社会学分支学科，第二次世界大战后在欧洲、苏联、东欧各国得到迅速发展，近年来我国学者也开始对劳动社会学给予很大的关注。本文综合各国学者的研究，将劳动社会学的主要研究内容与成果，综述如下。

一、劳动与人和社会的关系

民主德国学者主要从以下两个方面讨论劳动与人和社会的关系：（1）劳动对于社会和个人存在和发展的意义。（2）劳动的性质问题。民主德国学者认为，对于劳动的意义与作用的认识应该建立在马列主义如下四个基本原理的基础上，即劳动创造了人并决定着人的本质；劳动是人的本质力量的使用和表现；劳动是社会财富的源泉；劳动创造着人并服务于人的个性发展。个人最重要的社会联系，首先是个人与社会的联系，只有在劳动中才得以实现。关于劳动的性质，原民主德国学者认为，该问题反映了劳动作为一种社会现象的特征方面和本质两个方面，它是劳动社会学研究的出发点，对于劳动性质的研究是分析人的劳动态度以及与劳动领域有关的其他现象的必要前提。

中国学者对于劳动与人和社会的关系的研究包括：（1）劳动的基本含义。认为劳动是指人类创造自身生存和发展所必需的物质财富和精神财富的有目的的活动。（2）劳动的职能与分类，认为劳动的职能主要包括：劳动创造社会财

① 作者袁伦渠、周健，发表于中国社科院《社会学与社会调查》1990 年第 6 期。

富，劳动改造和完善社会，劳动满足着人的生存和发展需要。

二、劳动者的需要、动机和行为

民主德国学者主要研究的是社会主义制度下工人的劳动动机综合。内容包括：（1）依据经验研究和结果，将劳动动机以及构成劳动动机基础的需要分为四类：第一，社会动机（对有社会意义的活动的需要）；第二，成就动机（自我肯定的需要）；第三，接触动机（对协作和共同劳动的需要）；第四，物质报酬动机（对物质保证的需要）。（2）物质报酬动机的特点及其在动机综合中所处的地位。物质报酬动机的特点是：不同于其他动机，它不具有饱和性；工资是一种容易接受数量评价的因素；工资是最能使工人判断和评价自己工作岗位情况的最明显的因素；工资经常被看作是地位的象征。用差别对比方法研究的结果表明，物质报酬动机并不占首要地位，但也并非不重要。对于劳动社会学来说，更具有实践意义的是弄清哪些劳动者群体的首要劳动动机是物质报酬动机。

苏联学者侧重于研究人们的需要和利益以及他们同劳动活动的关系。他们认为，人之所以劳动，是因为他必须满足自身的不断发展着的需要。人的一切行动都可以用他的需要来解释。需要又分为初级需要（生理需要）和高级需要（社会需要）两类。利益是人的某种需要的表现形式。劳动者的个人物质利害关系对改善其劳动结果起着重要的作用。刺激劳动活动的因素分为精神因素和物质因素。如果一个人完成自己的工作是出于他喜欢自己的职业和劳动活动的内容，并能从工作中得到乐趣和尊敬，得到荣誉和自豪，此时他受到的是精神刺激因素的作用。当一个人完成工作的出发点既与劳动性质无关，也与劳动内容无关，而仅仅是为了经济上的需要时，激发他的工作的因素便是物质因素。在实践中，有效的和正确的做法应该是物质刺激和精神刺激相结合。

中国学者主要从以下四个方面进行一般性的探讨：（1）劳动者的需要，也分为物质需要和精神需要两种情况。（2）对需要结构的分析。（3）劳动者的动机，动机的分类，以及动机在行为中的作用。（4）劳动行为及其社会指导。认为劳动者的劳动行为主要受劳动环境、劳动者的性格、觉悟、道德观、劳动能力等诸因素的影响和制约。对劳动行为的社会指导包括启发引导需要、强化行为、奖励和惩罚等。

三、劳动者的劳动态度

苏联和民主德国学者把劳动态度作为一个需要研究的课题。

苏联学者重点研究的问题有：（1）决定劳动态度的有客观和主观因素。客观因素分为一般社会因素和特殊因素两种。一般社会因素包括整个社会政治制度和社会关系。特殊因素包括劳动性质和内容、劳动环境和条件、集体的社会心理气候、价值观体系等。主观因素包括工作人员的心理特点（性别、年龄、能力、爱好）、受制于社会的特点（文化发展水平、教育程度、专业技术水平）、个人价值观念。（2）劳动态度的测量指标，包括客观指标和主观指标。客观指标有：完成的工作量、遵守劳动纪律状况、生产积极性高低等。主观指标是指对工作和专业的满意程度。（3）改善劳动态度的措施研究。

民主德国学者的研究包括：（1）劳动态度的概念和劳动态度的评定。他们认为对劳动态度的研究仅限于职业工作范围。劳动态度首先表现为受生产关系所决定的劳动性质的一个特殊方面。劳动态度是一个人与人的劳动目标、劳动动机及价值定向相联系的概念。对于劳动态度的评定主要依据以下指标：劳动效率、参与的积极性、工作的主动精神、劳动纪律、集体中的关系等。（2）社会主义劳动态度的特点：在对异化劳动以及社会主义劳动特点讨论的基础上，对理想的社会主义劳动态度作出规定；高度的社会主义觉悟；责任心和义务感、高度的劳动生产率、工作地点的秩序和纪律；对劳动的热爱和需要；积极参与各种劳动的竞赛、生产革新运动等；互相支持、互相帮助的同志式关系；提高自己教育和技术水平的愿望。（3）社会主义劳动态度影响因素的分析。该项研究是一种实证研究，包括：确定检验劳动态度的指标体系；在调查的基础上从三个方面对影响因素进行相关分析。第一个方面：工作者个人的可变因素，包括性别、年龄、教育水平和技术水平、思想状况、家庭状况、居住地点、路途往返时间等。第二个方面：劳动环境的可变因素，包括工作者在生产活动中的整体化程度、参与程度、工作者对信息的了解情况，领导者的个性行为等。第三个方面：劳动内容和可变因素，主要是指工作的单调性、重要性、繁重程度、对技术和经验的要求等。

四、劳动集体的社会结构与劳动集体中的社会关系

苏联学者的研究包括：（1）劳动集体的概念、实质和种类。主要阐述劳动集体的定义。社会主义劳动集体的特征、劳动集体的分类以及各类群体的作用和特征。（2）劳动集体的职能及其评价标准。劳动集体的职能包括：目标职能、经济职能、协调职能、管理职能和教育职能。（3）劳动集体的社会结构包括集体成员和各种群体、社会规范以及在该集体和整个社会各个活动领域中产生的种种关系。社会结构可分为三级：高级集体，即独立的经济单位；中级集体，即车间、科室等单位；初级集体，即作业队、班组等单位。（4）完善劳动集体社会结构的措施。民主德国学者主要研究劳动群体中的社会主义集体关系的形成：第一，社会主义劳动集体的实质。认为社会主义劳动集体是一种特殊的，由历史决定的劳动群体形式。第二，劳动集体的结构。民主德国学者不同意西方学者将劳动组织的结构划分为正式结构和非正式结构，认为在劳动集体中主要包括职能结构或协作结构、政治思想结构、社会人口学结构和社会心理结构。第三，劳动集体的社会气氛以及决定劳动集体社会气氛的因素分析。

中国学者的研究包括：（1）劳动中的群体分类。分类的方法按照群体存在的状况，群体构成的原则、目的和方式，群体的规模以及群体成员联系的密切程度来划分。（2）劳动集体及其社会功能，包括劳动集体的定义、劳动集体的特征、劳动集体的组成和划分、劳动集体的社会功能等内容。（3）劳动集体的内部联系的方式。（4）集体意识及其培养。包括集体意识概念、作用以及培养和提高的途径。（5）劳动集体中的个人。主要研究个人与劳动集体的相互关系，以及劳动者之间的个体差异，包括利益的、心理的、生理的差异。（6）劳动者的社会身份与社会声望。论及劳动集体中社会身份的种类及特点、社会身份对人群关系的影响；社会声望的种类及其对劳动行为的影响。（7）劳动者之发生矛盾的原因。主要阐述劳动集体中劳动者之间矛盾的种类，包括从性质上、内容上、规模上的划分；劳动者之间矛盾的表现形式。（8）解决劳动者之间矛盾的方法。包括处理建设性矛盾和破坏性矛盾的方法。

五、劳动集体的领导

这是中国学者和苏联学者感兴趣的问题，主要内容包括：（1）劳动集体领

导过程的社会学实质，领导过程的职能和阶段。其中，领导过程的社会学实质主要论述领导者与执行者的关系；领导过程的职能，包括计划、组织、协调、鼓励、监督和教育；领导过程的阶段，实际指的是决策过程的阶段，包括确定目标、交代情况，分析情况、作出决策的四个阶段。（2）领导方法与领导作风。（3）领导者的素质、权威与评价。（4）领导班子的结构，是指年龄、知识、智能、专业、心理气质等方面的构成。（5）决定领导行为的因素。（6）劳动者参加生产管理的情况。

六、劳动集体的社会心理气氛与劳动的社会控制

这是一个受到普遍重视的研究课题。主要内容包括：（1）社会心理气氛及其对劳动集体的团结和发展的作用。（2）劳动集体中的冲突局面及其产生的原因和解决方法。（3）社会主义劳动纪律和加强纪律的社会学问题。（4）劳动秩序与劳动的社会控制等。

七、劳动的满意感与劳动的积极性

劳动的满意感是苏联学者关心的问题，内容包括：（1）劳动满意感的实质。劳动满意感是反映劳动者劳动的目标、生活态度、劳动动机及对工作的需要和愿望的心理状态。（2）影响劳动满意感的因素。研究内容有：生产工人对劳动环境因素的评价与领导者对这种评价的推测的差别；影响劳动满意感的最重要的因素系统及各个因素对整个满意感的影响程度；为了增加劳动满意感，企业领导者应该注意的问题；社会主义与资本主义条件下影响工人满意感因素的对比。

中国学者侧重对劳动的社会鼓励的研究，包括：（1）劳动积极性的含义，认为劳动积极性是指劳动者对待劳动的一种精神状态。（2）影响劳动积极性的物质和精神因素。（3）物质鼓励和实行物质鼓励必须具备的前提条件、形式。（4）精神鼓励的种类与形式。（5）对社会鼓励的调节，对鼓励手段的量的掌握。

八、职业指导与职业适应问题

这主要是苏联学者研究的题目。（1）职业指导的社会经济实质和内容，涉及的问题包括职业指导的目的、意义、必要性。职业指导是一个社会过程的组

成部分，包括职业信息、职业咨询、人员选拔及职业适应等问题。(2) 工作人员在生产部门的适应问题，包括社会适应与职业适应的含义与关系，社会角色冲突与职业适应的关系，适应过程的几个方面——专业适应（掌握新工种和熟悉工作岗位）和社会适应（融化于该生产集体之中）问题，反映职业适应开始和结束的基本指标及完全适应的标志，帮助青年人缩短适应期限措施以及企业应注意的问题。(3) 职业指导工作的形式与经验，涉及的问题包括现有职业指导系统的构成状况，学校教育、企业与学校的联合教育、大众传播媒介与职业指导的关系，各级职业指导委员会应该设置的职能部门，典型经验总结。

九、劳动者的八小时以外

这主要是中国学者讨论的题目。(1) 劳动时间与非劳动时间，内容包括：政治经济学意义上的劳动时间划分——必要劳动和剩余劳动时间，鼓励忠诚企业的措施，使工人增强对企业的依恋感，对打算离职人员做直接的劝说工作，在企业里创造工作者能充分发挥自己能力的含义与内容；非劳动时间在人类发展史的各个社会形态中数量、结构、性质的不同；非劳动时间中的自由支配时间与非自由支配时间比例及其决定因素。(2) 个人自由支配时间问题，包括个人自由支配时间由来，自由支配时间对于个人全面发展的意义和作用。(3) 单身职工的业余生活，包括单身职工的经济状况、消费构成、业余生活的主要内容和特点，以及帮助单身职工安排好自由支配时间的社会意义。(4) 劳动者的婚姻与家庭，包括婚姻与家庭对劳动者的含义，劳动者对家庭承担的义务，影响劳动者家庭幸福的因素，处理家庭成员关系的原则。(5) 家庭生活方式与家务劳动，包括物质生活条件、共同生活信念、生活情趣、消费水平对家庭生活方式的影响，家务劳动对劳动者的影响及其优化安排。(6) 劳动者生活消费的社会指导，论述的问题包括劳动者的生活消费构成——个人支配的消费与社会支配的消费，劳动者实际生活消费水平的构成——个人的和社会的消费水平总和，消费水平与消费结构的关系，对劳动者生活消费目的、方向和方式的社会指导。

总之，劳动社会学是一门年轻的学科，但各国学者对劳动社会学研究的学科体系是有较大差异的，并且还存在着以下两个共同的问题。(1) 在研究对象与内容上与其他学科有交叉重复之处，如劳动集体的领导问题，工业企业人员的使用问题，劳动者的需要、动机问题、劳动就业问题、劳动环境与劳动保护、劳动者的社会保险等。以上问题也是领导科学、劳动经济学、劳动心理学、行为科学等学科的研究题目。劳动社会学对以上问题的研究尚未在研究的内容与方法上与其他学科从本质上区别开来。（2）在研究的方法与风格上社会学的特性尚不明显，主要的表现：不是用社会学的语言和逻辑，而是用一般化的论述和简单的推理得出结论；对于问题的论述和分析缺乏实证资料的依托；对于某些问题的研究尚停留在对于概念和含义等基本范畴的理解和解说的水平上。

总体来说，民主德国学者的研究在内容和方法上更具有社会学的味道。

参考书目：

[1] 劳动社会学，R. 施托伯格. 劳动社会学. 袁伦渠，李步魁，译. 北京：劳动人事出版社，1985.

[2] 赵履宽，王子平. 劳动社会学概论. 上海：上海人民出版社，1984.

《劳动社会学》译者的话①

劳动社会学是从社会学分化出来的一门年青的科学学科，既是社会学的一个分支，又是劳动科学知识体系的组成部分。它的名字最初是由法国一家社会学杂志于1959年正式提出来的。几乎同时，苏联一些社会学家也开始使用这一名字。以后劳动社会学陆续在许多国家出现。进入20世纪70年代以来，苏联和东欧一些国家十分注意对劳动问题的社会学研究，发表了大量的文章和著作，并且引进了西方的调查研究方法，逐步建立了他们自己的劳动社会学。R. 施托伯格的这一著作就是确立劳动社会学地位的主要代表作之一（其他两本书是苏联1981年出版的马赫纳雷罗福的《劳动社会学》和南斯拉夫1982年出版的马尔科维奇的《劳动社会学》）。

劳动社会学是运用社会学的原理和方法研究人的劳动活动的学科。在这本书中，作者强调从社会学、心理学的角度去研究社会主义企业的劳动管理。作

① 选自R. 施托伯格著，袁伦渠、李步魁译的《劳动社会学》一书中“译者的话”（1985年由劳动人事出版社出版）。

者认为，企业是一个集体组织，工人不但有经济方面的要求，而且有社会心理方面的要求，因此，依靠对劳动过程进行自上而下的管理和运用物质刺激手段还不够，还必须注意人的因素，研究劳动者的政治觉悟，心理、生理状态和劳动者的愿望、动机、道德、价值观和目标等，从人的内心激发出动力，使之产生强力的工作愿望，以提高劳动效率。这就冲破了劳动经济管理中那种见物不见人的做法，指出了做好人的工作对调动工人劳动积极性的重要作用，从而丰富了企业劳动管理的内容。

本书主要研究了如下问题：劳动的性质和内容；人的劳动态度和劳动行为；劳动的满意感，其中包括劳动集体中的社会心理气氛，领导者的领导方法和领导作风；职业选择和人员流动；技术革命对劳动内容和劳动条件的影响；劳动社会学在企业中的应用等。

本书的特点是：第一，从社会总体的角度对劳动问题进行综合性整体性研究。在这一点上，劳动社会学与劳动经济学有很大的不同。劳动经济学主要从经济学角度研究劳动活动，即研究如何通过改善劳动组织和贯彻按劳分配原则等激发劳动者积极性，提高劳动效率。劳动社会学则把劳动活动作为一种受多种因素影响的综合性的社会现象来研究，着重探讨劳动活动产生的经济活动以外的社会学问题，研究社会、政治、心理、思想、人际关系、劳动条件等对调动劳动者的积极性、提高劳动效率的影响。

第二，研究方法的综合性。作者在本书中吸收和运用了经济学、社会学、心理学等学科的知识，对劳动问题进行多学科的综合研究。

第三，注重实地研究调查，坚持用事实和材料说话，这是本书的一个突出优点。作者在进行调查时，运用了抽样法、访问法、观察法、实验法等，并采用数理统计和电子计算机等现代技术手段对人的劳动态度和劳动行为加以测量。这是对劳动问题由单纯的定性分析到定量分析的有益尝试。

当前我国正进行着劳动人事制度的重大改革。改革向我们提出了一系列问题，这些问题既有经济方面，也有社会方面的，例如，如何通过研究劳动者的需要、动机和行为调动劳动者的积极性？物质鼓励和精神鼓励的关系是什么？在新形势下，如何做好职工的思想工作？人才流动的原因是什么？如何促进人才的合理流动，防止不合理的流动？如何培养工人“爱厂如家”思想和对企业的依赖感？劳动人事制度的全面改革会对人与人的关系产生哪些影响？等等。

这些都是我们面临的劳动社会学问题，需要研究解决。本书在这方面的论述，尽管有些不一定适合我国的情况，但不少是值得我们参考的。

劳动社会学是首先产生于国外的一门新兴学科。我国对劳动社会学的研究起步很晚，近年来，只是随着社会学的恢复和重建，以及劳动科学的发展，才有人着手研究。我们翻译这本书，供广大劳动人事理论和实际工作者研究和借鉴，这肯定有助于尽快建立具有中国特色的我们自己的劳动社会学。

劳动社会学的研究方法[①]

本文不讨论以研究工作为己任的社会学家，而是讨论必须详细了解社会学方法的实际工作者，以便使他们懂得怎样才能取得社会学的研究成果和正确地评价这些研究成果，一旦企业有必要继续进行社会学研究时，能给这一研究工作以内行的帮助。

一、社会学研究的几个阶段

为了进行社会学研究，必须制定研究计划，将整个研究工作分为几个阶段，明确规定各个阶段所要完成的任务。一般来说，全部研究过程可分为准备阶段、基本研究阶段以及对研究结果进行分析和说明的阶段。研究计划还包括必要的物质条件、研究经费和研究期限的说明。

研究的准备阶段十分重要。它奠定了整个研究的基础，决定着整个计划的成败。在准备阶段，首要是正确规定所要解决的研究课题，社会学研究所要达到的目的，以及借助这一研究能否帮助解决所提出的问题。为此，需要听取学术界和实际工作部门的专家们的意见，研究专门的文献或者分析有关的社会学研究成果。

在准备阶段，还应确立计划中的研究课题同现有理论的联系。这样社会学研究才能不仅对实践产生直接的效果，而且通过理论上的概括产生间接的效果。根据现有的理论原理，可以对所研究的各种因素和希望达到的结果作出假设（有

① 摘自1982年鲁·施托伯格《劳动社会学》俄文版，并发表于1986年第2期的《社会学与社会调查》。

科学根据的假设)。也可以不作出假设，而指出所要研究的那些现象之间都有什么样的联系。如果假设是以推论方式作出的，那么研究的目的就是证实或者推翻这种假设。

一般而言，社会学研究就是明确说明所提出的各种假设(例如，假设：在劳动纪律方面，工长对劳动组织的影响要大于他个人在劳动纪律方面的榜样作用)。

理论是应用于研究概念的源泉。应当准确地判断，研究者使用的是什么性质的概念，它同指示器是什么关系(例如，什么叫作“社会主义劳动纪律”？应当研究它的那些特征？)。

整理和比较所取得的资料非常重要。因此，必须正确的规定资料的分组原则。性别、年龄、技术水平和作业班次等是最普遍的分组标志。此外，还要规定，按照什么原则来区分“劳动纪律好”和“劳动纪律不好”,“工长个人的榜样作用大”“工长个人的榜样作用小”，等等。

在准备阶段还要确定收集资料的方法。要分析各种方法的优缺点，看是否有利于解决所提出的课题，然后，对研究材料进行加工整理(例如，汇集问题，制订观察细则等)。通过试验性研究，可以检验所选定的资料的收集方法和具体方案是否适合于既定的研究课题。

确定抽样方法是一个重要的工作。确定抽样调查的人数多少和构成有不同的方法。抽样数目的多少与所反映的各种关系的统计数字的可靠性有关。抽样调查的人数越少，其价值即统计数字的可靠性越小。但这并不是说，抽样调查的人数越多越好。经验证明，在大规模的调查中(而不是像对某工段社会气氛的分析中那样，被调查者的人数等于该工段的全体工作者人数),有300名被调查者就足够了。

抽样调查人数的构成比抽样人数的多少更为重要。原则上抽样调查应具有典型性，就是说，被调查的总人员中的每一个人都有同样被抽中的可能性。例如，要想取得对整个联合企业具有代表性的样本，在被调查的人员中就应当包括联合企业所属各个部门的劳动者。可以按照整群抽样的原则，从20个部门中选择5～6个部门。这就必须保证被挑选的部门能够正确地反映整个联合企业的特征，在技术装备、工资水平或其他方面不能相差过大。在抽样调查中，还要考虑到妇女的比重、技术水平和构成以及其他标志与被研究的所有人员的特征相适应。

选择回答者（被调查者）应严格按照随机原则进行。最好利用干部处的现有材料，从干部卡中每隔 10 张或 20 张抽取一张。不允许委托有关部门的领导者挑选回答者，因为这样可能将一些不能准确反映企业情况（例如，关于社会主义觉悟水平）的人选入样本。

在准备阶段还必须确定分析方法，并要考虑到材料准备上的技术要求，这里所说的技术要求，是指把材料送到初始载体（穿孔卡或穿孔带）上的活动。

资料的收集实际是在基本的研究阶段。要有计划地进行访问、观察和其他工作。收集资料的不同方法各有什么特点，在本文的第二部分将作简要介绍，使用时要加以注意。

当全部资料收集好以后，就要审查它们的可用性。审查在填好的调查表中缺少回答者的资料（这是进行分组的最重要标志），或调查者填好的调查表中的各项是否准确无误。经过审查后，就要根据事先制定的研究计划，对资料进行计算和统计加工。

接着，是对资料进行有步骤的分析，探讨确定问题或者提出假设的系统方法。资料要汇集成图表形式并加以说明，有时要计算几种现象互相关联的相关系数或进行其他的统计分析。

如果发现得到的结果中有差错，而这种差错又不是方法上的错误造成的，为查明原因，应当做进一步的研究。

最后，准备研究报告，其内容包括：研究的目的；呈报研究报告所必需的全部研究资料；研究步骤；以分类和综合的形式阐述研究结果；评价研究结果对劳动社会学理论的意义；评价研究结果（包括管理措施方面的具体建议）对实践的意义；提出课题的研究建议。

二、劳动社会学的研究方法

访谈是最重要的研究方法之一。通过访谈可以用较少的耗费收集到大量的资料。但是应当了解通过访谈所取得的研究结果的价值。就是说，一个研究者绝不能根据某个人的意见或目标就直接对其行为作出结论。目标作为引起行动的愿望，仅是实际行为的一个原因，另一个原因是外部境遇，它可能同目标不一致。例如，如果一个人说，他对一定题目的演讲有兴趣，这并不意味着他一定会出席企业的这类演讲会。调查表中所访谈的一些目标，经常仅与个人的一种社会职能有联系，而没有考虑到他在其他生活领域中的行动。

在对大量的人员进行调查时，宜采取口头访谈和书面调查的方式。书面调查就是把调查表分发给被调查者，然后再收回。这办法比口头访谈省事，而且比口头访谈耗时少，并且能更好地保证为被访谈者隐匿姓名。缺点是，发出的调查表不能全部收回。在企业里进行调查时（调查表在工作地点分发和收回），调查表平均可以收回 85%～90%；邮寄发出的，只能收回 50%～60%。这一缺点可以用学校询问课堂作业的方法，例如，在职工食堂询问的方法加以弥补。书面询问难以保证所提出的问题能够有效地反映目标的稳定性。因为经验证明，被询问者在自己的回答中总是要回避矛盾，如果将调查表交给他们数日，难免不受他人的干扰。

采用口头询问法（访问法）时，难以进行分析的调查表会大大减少，也容易提出问题。询问者可以对询问的事情提供更为详细的情况，防止填表时出现差错。缺点是，询问着的工作量太大时，往往发生所谓的“询问着疲劳”现象。从而可能降低材料填写的质量。同时，训练（指导）和使用询问者的费用也较多。

在询问中，通常提出各种类型的问题。按其内容，问题可以分为事实方面的问题（例如，“目前您是否参加某种进修班？”），信息方面的问题（例如，“您是否知道自己工段的技术发展前景？”），目标方面的问题（例如，“谁可以称得上‘好工人’？”），以及动机方面的问题（例如“您为什么要提高技术水平？”）。

按照形式，问题可分为开放式和闭合式两种。对于开放式问题，被询问者可以用自己的语言来回答。书面询问时，要为被询问者留出余地。不过，开放式问题对被询问者的要求高，回答比较难。因此，采用闭合式问题可提出几个可能的答案，被询问者只要指出他同意的答案就行了。在回答“表列式”问题时，可以从所列答案中指出几个答案。这种情况应当引起被询问者的注意，“多选式”问题应当包括完备的答案。如果被询问者经常提出“另外的”答案，这就证明多选中提出的可能答案不够完备。

问题的提法应当是引导性的、联系性的和检验性的。为此，在访问中，当谈话离题时，要“按问题的重要性”依次提问；当回答不清楚时，要提出一些“试探性”问题。

为了取得良好的调查效果，必须考虑到拟定问题的一系列要求。首先要把问题的主题提法变成若干个测试性、检验性的问题。为了研究劳动态度，只提出一个相应的问题是不够的，要把这个总题目分解为反映劳动态度的各个因素的一系列问题。

另一个重要要求是，问题要提得简单明了，要考虑到被询问者的教育水平。问题提的复杂烦琐，会减少人们回答问题的愿望，并产生不好的结果。问题只有一个答案时，应当明确所指，以便能正确地解释所取得的资料。例如，这样的问题就不明确："您同自己的同事相处好吗？"因为不清楚指的是同谁。

问题的提法，无论是整个题目还是各个组成部分，都不应当带有提示性，不能提示被询问者应当如何回答问题。（例如，"您赞成平均主义，还是赞成根据劳动的成果发给奖金？"，就是一个带有提示性的提法）。要做到这一点，需要有丰富的技巧和经验。不要力求被询问者同意多数人的意见。

在劳动社会学研究中，除了广泛的询问外，还要进行深入访问。这是为了更深入地研究劳动者的生活境况或观点，因而不能加以格式化。深入访问能有效地用来研究轮班制工人的家庭生活方式，研究劳动者对工作和职业的态度。总之，深入访问可以充实广泛询问的结果。深入访问通常由专家们来进行，其任务就是在谈话中提出与所研究的课题有关的一切问题，并尽可能比较完全地把被访问者的观点和意见记录下来。

与鉴定人晤谈类似个别提问，晤谈的对象，是那些能够对研究者感兴趣的问题提供有价值的信息的人。例如，工厂专业进修班的领导者能够提供有关技术水平的重要信息；冲突调解委员会（劳动争议调解委员会）主席可对劳动纪律问题发表见解，等等。同鉴定人晤谈，同样不能格式化。这种晤谈通常是在试验研究阶段进行的，以便正确决定所要研究的问题，检查资料收集范围选择得是否恰当。在基本研究的范围内，这种晤谈也能发挥重要作用（例如，对生产革新者运动进行分析时，必须访问专职从事这一运动的工作者）。

询问的另一种形式是小组讨论。这里所说的不是社会学家参加的讨论。这种讨论不由社会学家主持，而是在工人小组里进行（社会学家只进行观察研究），这是一种有目的的收集资料的方法。讨论小组按一定的原则组成，每组7～12人，讨论会的领导者要力求使参加者就所关心的问题发表意见。社会学家由此就可得到很多重要资料。一般来说，小组讨论能从各种不同观点说明被研究的问题。因为参加者可以互相补充自己的观点，为所研究的问题指出可行的解决方法。因此，这种方式值得重视，企业中的很多现象（如某工段干部的流动性突然增高）可以通过小组讨论得到说明，因而，不要总是采用广泛询问法。

但是，小组讨论对其领导者提出了特别的要求。他们必须保证每个参加者都能发表自己的意见，并采用适当的方式——磁带录音或个人记录——将每个人的发言记录下来。

深入访问、与鉴定人晤谈和小组讨论都要做记录，以作为研究的材料。除富有内容的信息外，记录会包括有关被询问者个人的情况（如年龄、性别，以及对分析研究结果有价值的某些情况和值得注意的事项）。被询问者的姓名，根据无记名原则，不予记录。

在劳动社会学研究中，还采用观察法。科学观察和一般观察不同，一般观察带有偶然性。科学观察是事先计划的一个或几个观察者的有目的活动。

观察可以公开或不公开进行。公开观察时，调查者要不隐瞒自己的身份；不公开观察时，则要隐瞒自己的身份。究竟采用哪种方式，要视危险性大小而定。因为公开观察时，被观察者的行为必然有变化。如果不会出现什么危险（如果被观察者不了解观察的真实目的，就不会出现什么危险），则应进行公开观察。

观察通常是在一定的集体范围内进行的。观察者可以参加这些集体的活动（参与观察法），或者“从外部”完成自己的研究任务（非参与观察法）。究竟选择哪种方法，决定于研究计划和计划的要求。假设，劳动纪律在很大程度上取决于劳动组织，就可以通过参与观察法进行很好的验证。在这种情况下，研究者可在某个时间到集体中去工作，并对与劳动组织有关的破坏劳动纪律的现象作出记录。要了解俱乐部的工作情况就适于非参与观察法，即研究者不必作为俱乐部各小组的成员，就能了解到俱乐部的实际情况。

最近以来，社会实验法对劳动社会学的研究具有越来越大的意义。社会实验法的实质，就是在一定部门进行一些有目的的改变，并确切查明这些改变的影响。社会实验的基础是对两个因素的相互联系的假设，例如，可以提出这样一种假设：各种劳动职能的联系形式对形成社会主义集体关系的影响。按照这一假设，就可以改变各种劳动职能的联系（例如，充实流水作业的任务），并检验这种改变对集体关系的影响。

不言而喻，不论是有意识改变的因素，还是受影响的因素，都应精确地从量上加以查明，但这往往难以做到。要排除与研究计划无关的第三种因素也是不大可能的。因此，除了实验组外，还应当有研究控制组，因为被改变（被研究）的因素在控制组是不变的。在这种条件下，如果控制组出现了变化，很明显，这与被研究的因素无关。例如，劳动报酬形式的一般变化，近期的奖励，等等，可能影响到集体关系。

实验分为实地实验和实验室实验。实地实验的研究单位（集体）是自己的自然环境。实验室实验要建立各种不受“外界”影响的人为条件。实验室实验对于心理学研究有很大的意义。而在劳动社会学研究方面，多采用实地实验，因为实地实验接近实际和日常生活，同时还由于对实验情况的了解，可以引起目标和行为的变化。社会实验作为查明各种影响因素的方法，也可有效地在较小范围内运用。

社会关系测量或者“同组人选择”，是查明集体的社会心理学结构的一种方法。过去，这种方法首先应用于教育心理学。因为分析学生集体的结构，是教师进行教学活动的一个重要方式。近来，在劳动群体中也试行这种方法。社会关系测量的基础首先是分析群体中关系的好坏。通过分析就会发现，在每个集体中都有这样一些成员，很多人都乐于同他们一起工作或者度过闲暇时间；同时也有另外一些人，同事们“无论如何”都不愿意同他们交往，既不想同他们一起休息，也不想同他们一起工作。分析就要对群体的全体成员就上述问题作出评价。首先取得表现所得到的关系结构的社会测量矩阵。这些资料在社会测量图示中也得到更清楚的反映。社会测量图示从集体的结构和团结程度、非正式的或非官方的权威人士及受集体排斥或嫌弃的人（孤立者）的存在情况方面，反映了该集体的关系综合。

劳动社会学领域的研究，还采用文献分析和统计资料分析的方法。这一方法不能作为社会学研究的单一方法，因为它能参考的只是已经发生过的事件和文献中已经确认的材料。但是对这一方法也不能忽视，因为它经常为阐明研究的课题提供不可缺少的信息（例如，分析职工对企业的依恋感时，有关企业干部的流动的资料或劳动力地区流动情况的统计就不可缺少）。因而，在准备阶段，文献和统计资料常常被用来确定研究的目的和对象。

文献一般分为正式文献和非正式文献。正式文献就是统计手册、统计机关和社会组织的资料、科学杂志，等等。非正式文献包括个人书信、笔记和日记等等。这一区分不包括对文献的评价。个人笔记虽具有很大的主观性，但从中可以得到重要的信息。

在劳动社会学研究中，对专题报告这种方法也不能忽视。专题报告一词是指用通俗语言写成的小册子，对一定社会现象和社会环境作详细记述。在劳动问题的社会学研究中，这一方法可以被采用，例如，记录企业实行轮班生产时所发生的全部事件。从收到国家机关第一批消息或工人们的第一批倡议开始，直到所选定的轮班制度正常运转为止，将每一个步骤所发生的问题和解决的方法，都加以详细记录。这样，就可以在“轮班制”这个研究课题方面得到重要启示，在工作者与企业关系等方面得到一些资料。由此也就可以集中好的经验，进一步加以推广。联合企业结构的变化，新技术的采用和新的职业培训计划的贯彻，所有这些都适于用专题报告的方法记录下来。

在社会学研究中，有时也谈到方法上的多元论原则。就是说，社会学研究绝不能局限于某一种方法。一般来说，这一原则是正确的，特别是人们谈到要进行基础科学研究，以求得到新的知识的时候。但是，科学研究的目的并非总是如此。因此，一些小课题的小型研究项目也可只用一种方法，如询问法。当然，在这种情况下，也要利用文献，采用其他方法的某些部分。在任何情况下，方法上的多元论，绝不是要求在同一时间和同等程度上应用所有的方法。

应加强对劳动社会学的研究①

劳动社会学是一门首先产生于国外的科学学科。到目前为止，这门学科还很不成熟，尚处于初期的发展阶段。国内对劳动社会学的研究起步较晚，近年来，只是随着社会学的恢复和重建，以及有关劳动科学的发展，才有人着手翻译和研究。本文是笔者在翻译和阅读国内外这类文献的过程中受到启发而写的。

一、劳动社会学的产生和发展

劳动社会学既是社会学的一个分支。又是劳动科学知识体系的一个组成部

① 本文原载于 1985 年第 4 期的《经济与管理研究》，后经不断修改、补充，发表于 1991 年第 10 期的《北京劳动》。

分，它是跨越于社会学和劳动科学之间的一门边缘科学。

劳动社会学作为劳动科学知识体系的一个组成部分，是随着人们对劳动研究的不断深化而产生和发展的。在19世纪资本主义自由竞争时期，资本家只是凭着个人经验和判断进行企业管理和劳动管理，没有科学的管理方法。所以称为“经验管理”。当时的企业主也就是管理者，他们把工人看成机器的零件，随意靠延长劳动时间和提高劳动强度来增加利润，资本家和工人之间的矛盾相当尖锐。

到了第一次世界大战前后，出现了泰勒倡导的所谓“科学管理”。泰勒对工人在劳动过程中的操作进行长期研究之后，提出要用科学的管理方法代替过去单凭个人经验的管理，创造了劳动定额制度和奖励制度，以提高劳动生产率。泰勒的“科学管理”是当时西方资产阶级的先进事物，对资本主义的发展起了很大的推动作用。但是，泰勒仍然认为工人关心的只是经济收入，金钱是刺激劳动积极性的唯一因素，因而泰勒的管理方法不可能充分调动工人的积极性。

第二次世界大战前后，随着生产力和科学技术的高速发展，现代化生产越来越要求职工发挥主观能动精神，人的积极性对劳动生产力的巨大影响日益显示出来。另外，由于苏联十月革命影响，工人阶级往往用罢工、怠工等方法进行斗争，这样，泰勒那套“见物不见人”的管理办法就失灵了。资本家认识到，在新的历史条件下，除了用金钱刺激工人外，还需要通过改善“人际关系”来缓和劳资关系。于是，“科学管理”也发展到“现代管理”阶段，各种现代管理理论应运而生，而“行为科学”就是现代管理理论的主要流派之一。

行为科学主要是对劳动环境中个人和群体的行为进行分析和解释的心理学和社会学学说。它强调从社会学、心理学的角度去研究劳动管理，重视劳动条件，人的相互关系对提高劳动生产率的影响。“行为科学”学派认为，企业是一个社会组织，工人在劳动过程中不仅有经济方面的问题，而且有社会心理方面的问题。因此，光有对劳动过程自上而下的严格管理和运用物质刺激手段还不够，还必须注意人的因素，从人的内心深处激发出动力，使之产生强烈的工作愿望和劳动动力，以提高劳动效率。这样，行为科学理论就比泰勒的理论前进了一大步，它纠正了“见物不见人”的做法，丰富了企业劳动管理的内容，同时把社会学和心理学引进了劳动管理的研究领域，促进了劳动社会学和劳动心理学的产生。

劳动社会学作为社会学的一个分支也是随着社会学的发展和分化而产生和发展的。社会学在第一次世界大战前后逐渐从其他社会科学区分出来而成为一门学科。第二次世界大战前后，社会学广泛与其他各个专门学科相结合，并且把研究对象扩展到其他专门学科尚未研究的空白领域，从而产生了许多跨学科的社会学分支学科，其中也包括劳动社会学。

法国是劳动社会学产生和发展较早的国家。乔治•弗里德曼是法国劳动社会学的奠基者和创始人。早在20世纪二三十年代，当社会学转向经验方法和分科研究时，他就开始研究劳动社会学。第二次世界大战以后，他着重于人和技术关系方面的研究。1952年，法国建立了劳动社会科学研究所，1959年，创办《劳动社会学》杂志，成为法国劳动社会学研究的主要学术论坛。几乎同时，苏联社会学家也开始使用劳动社会学这一名字。以后劳动社会学陆续在许多国家出现。近几十年来在苏联和东欧一些国家，随着各种专门社会学的迅速发展，劳动社会学学科也发展起来了。

二、劳动社会学的主要内容和特点

在西方，劳动社会学存在不同的派别，各有其不同的理论观点。在苏联和东欧一些国家，对劳动社会学研究的对象和范围意见也不一致。因此，目前还很难确定劳动社会学的研究对象究竟是什么。归纳国外学者的观点，可以概括一下劳动社会学的主要内容和特点。劳动社会学是研究人的劳动行为的科学。劳动行为作为一种社会行为，其产生受两方面因素的影响，一是外部因素即客观条件的影响。其中包括自然条件（地理、气候、资源等）、社会经济条件（工作日长度、劳动报酬等）、技术条件（工具设备等）、劳动卫生条件（照明、噪声、污染）、劳动中的人际关系、劳动组织条件（劳动制度、工作节奏等）。二是受主观条件的影响。如劳动者的生理、心理状态，劳动者的愿望、动机、道德、价值观和目标等。劳动社会学就是通过揭示主客观这两方面的错综复杂的关系，研究劳动者的劳动行为。

劳动社会学主要研究以下五方面的内容：第一，个人的行为。如劳动者的各种需要、动机与其劳动行为之间的关系，劳动的价值观，劳动满意感等。第二，集体（群体）的行动。如劳动集体的社会心理气候，集体中的人际关系，个人与集体的关系，集体中信息的沟通等。第三，领导的行为。如领导者的作风和职能，领导者的素质、领导者的决策行为等。第四，人的劳动态度，劳动性质和内容，劳动环境和条件，劳动态度的测量和评价等。第五，劳动社会学在企业管理和劳动管理中的应用等。

劳动社会学的特点：第一，从社会总体的角度，对劳动行为进行综合性、整体性的研究，这是劳动社会学区别于其他劳动科学的重要标志，以劳动经济学与劳动社会学的区别为例，劳动经济学主要从经济学角度研究劳动活动，即研究如何通过加强劳动管理和贯彻按劳分配来激发劳动者的积极性，提高劳动生产率。劳动社会学除了研究劳动的经济问题外，还把劳动作为一种受多种因素影响的综合性的社会现象来研究，着重探讨劳动活动产生的经济因素以外的社会问题，研究道德、心理、思想、人际关系、劳动条件等对调动劳动者的积极性、提高劳动效率的影响。例如提高劳动生产率问题，劳动社会学不仅仅研究物质技术因素和社会经济因素，还要研究人的主观能动性的发挥，他对生产任务的理解程度和完成任务的信心，以及其他因素对提高劳动生产率的影响。

第二，研究方法的综合性，劳动社会学要求对劳动问题进行多学科的研究，并力求各学科的一体化。为此，它不能离开其他学科的合作，它要吸取和运用一系列有关学科的知识，特别是经济学、心理学的知识。例如，国外对职业的研究，就要求社会学家、经济学家、心理学家和工程师等合作进行。

第三，注重实地调查研究，坚持用事实和材料说话，这是劳动社会学研究的突出优点，也是劳动社会学生命的源泉。劳动社会学在进行调查时，常用的方法有个案调查和抽样调查，以及访问法、观察法、实验法等，并采取用数理统计和电子计算机等现代技术手段对人的劳动态度和劳动行为进行测量。由于调查中采用定性分析和定量分析相结合的方法，不仅能取得丰富的资料，而且能更准确、更全面地反映社会实际情况。

通过以上分析，我们大体上可以为劳动社会学下这样一个定义：劳动社会学是运用社会学的原理和方法，研究劳动过程中人的劳动行为的一门边缘学科，它通过劳动行为产生的原因及其影响因素的社会学分析来解决劳动者在劳动过程中出现的许多社会学问题，调动劳动者的积极性，提高劳动生产率。

三、劳动社会学与其他学科的关系

从对劳动社会学产生与发展的分析中，可以看出它与各专门的社会学学科和各门劳动学学科都有密切的关系。现在再进一步分析它们的联系和区别。

先看劳动社会学与各门劳动学科的关系。劳动是重要的社会现象，也是人类最基本的实践活动。因此许多学科都对它加以研究。研究劳动的学科，大致有劳动经济学、劳动心理学、劳动卫生学、劳动生理学、劳动社会学等，并组成了一个劳动科学的知识体系。这些学科由于共同研究劳动问题，因而有一定的联系。但是它们各有自己的研究侧面，并使用自己特有的研究方法，因而又各有区别。劳动经济学利用经济学的原理研究一定历史中的社会劳动组织；劳动心理学则从心理学的角度研究人的劳动活动的心理特点；劳动卫生学研究劳动过程和周围环境对劳动者身体的影响；劳动生理学则揭示劳动过程中人的生理过程的规律以及生理过程调节的特点，提出相应的建议，以保持人具有长期的高度劳动能力。由于劳动社会学的研究具有综合性、整体性的特点，可以通过多侧面、多角度的与这些学科进行交叉研究，从而将这些学科都联系起来。

再看劳动社会学与社会学的其他专门学科——工业社会学、企业社会学、职业社会学和农业社会学等的关系。劳动社会学与它们有着密切的关系，因为它们具有共同的特点。首先，它们都是社会学的组成部分；其次，它们有一个共同的研究方法，都是在相互联系中对社会过程和社会现象进行综合分析。

它们之间的区别，主要表现在研究的领域不尽相同。工业社会学不仅研究工业劳动的社会问题，而且研究工业发展过程中（如由于科学技术进步）所产生的其他问题。在这一点上它的研究范围要比劳动社会学广。但是，当工业社会学只研究劳动问题时，它又包含在劳动社会学研究范围之中。另外，劳动社会学不仅研究工业劳动问题，还研究包括农业在内的各行各业的劳动问题，在这一点上，劳动社会学比工业社会学的研究范围又宽一些。正因为工业社会学和劳动社会学有这种互相交叉、互相包容的关系，因此在国外大学的社会学课程中，又往往被看成同一门学科。

劳动社会学与企业社会学的关系也类似上述情况。企业社会学把企业看成一个统一的劳动有机体进行研究，主要研究企业集体中的关系和气氛，企业的人员流动问题等。至于职业社会学，目前尚未独立出来，仍包含在劳动社会学之中。农业社会学主要研究的内容是：社会主义制度下工人阶级、集体农民和知识分子的相互接近，以及城乡之间重大差别的克服；集体农民觉悟的提高，农业劳动的社会主义性质的发展，农民生活以及诸过程的相互影响。

上述各专门的社会学学科究竟如何划分，目前国内外学者尚无一致的意见。他们认为，随着整个社会学的进一步发展，学者们分工与协作的加强，加之实际工作的需要，社会学的各门学科将会作出合理的划分。

四、建立具有中国特色的劳动社会学

我国经济社会发展和经济体制的改革，特别是劳动工资制度的改革，向我们提出了一系列问题，这些问题既有经济方面的，也有社会方面的，因此，仅仅对劳动进行经济学的研究还不够，还有待于从社会学的角度去研究解决。

这些问题大致可以包括：如何通过研究劳动者的需要、动机和行为来调动劳动者的积极性，提高劳动生产率。物质鼓励和精神鼓励关系的是什么？在新形势下，如何对职工做好科学的政治思想工作？劳动工资制度的全面改革会对劳动者的人际关系带来什么影响？对职工的职业观、知识观、分配观、消费观、贫富观带来哪些改变？人才流动的原因和流向如何？流动是好事还是坏事？如何促进合理的流动和防止不合理的流动？如何发扬集体中的优良传统，加强青年人和老工人的团结？如何培养职工“爱厂如家”和对企业的依恋感，增加职业自豪感和荣誉感？如何通过对职工的工作时间和业务时间的研究，提出减少业余时间的不合理消耗、增加自由时间的建议？以上都是劳动工资制度改革向我们提出的劳动社会学问题。这些问题的研究和解决，有助于减少劳动工资制度改革引起的社会震荡，增加职工对改革的理解和心理承受能力，从而能促进社会的稳定和改革的顺利进行。由此可见，加强对劳动问题的社会学研究，建立具有中国特色的劳动社会学，势在必行。

如何建立具有中国特色的劳动社会学呢？我认为总的原则是坚持“以我为主，洋为中用，自成一家”的做法，目前，不妨从以下三个方面着手：

第一，吸收西方管理科学和行为科学的合理部分，洋为中用。

行为科学，是西方管理科学的组成部分，它包含着一系列丰富的科学成就，例如行为科学家把社会学和心理学引入劳动管理领域，他们不再把人看作传统的“经济人”，而是“社会人”，认为金钱不是刺激积极性的唯一动力，反对“见物不见人”的观点，注意发挥“人的因素”，给我们这样的启发：在社会主义制度下，应当把劳动者看成是有理想、有抱负、有责任感、有荣誉感的社会成员。从而要了解劳动者的心理状态，帮助他们确立主人翁的地位，做好科学的政治思想工作。再如，美国心理学家马斯洛把人类需要划分为五个层次，但它反映了人类需要的共同规律，并在一定程度上反映了人类需要的多样性，他给我们的启发是不仅要了解人的物质需要，而且要了解人类的精神需要，从而把物质鼓励和精神鼓励有机地结合起来。

劳动社会学与管理科学有密切的联系，因此只要我们结合中国的实际，对行为科学进行具体分析，吸收其合理部分，就可以促进我国劳动社会学的建立。

第二，借鉴苏联和东欧一些国家的学者在劳动社会学领域已取得的研究成果为我所用。

十月革命后，苏联在批判西方社会学的基础上建立了自己的社会学。近几十年来，苏联和东欧一些国家的社会学学科发展较为迅速。20 世纪 60 年代以来，他们十分注意对劳动问题的社会学研究，在这方面发表了大量的文章和著作，并且引进了西方的调查研究方法，逐步建立了他们自己的劳动社会学。1978 年民主德国出版的《劳动社会学》，就反映了他们的研究成果。例如，他们通过对职业内容、职业结构的研究，指导青年选择职业；通过对职业发展的研究，提出克服脑力劳动和体力劳动重大差别的措施；通过对劳动时间的研究，指出缩短劳动时间给劳动者生活方式带来的影响。民主德国的学者提出了劳动动机综合的概念，将劳动者的劳动动机分为四种：第一社会动机（对有社会意义的活动的需要）；第二成就动机（自我肯定的需要）；第三接触动机（对协作和劳动交往的需要）；第四物质报酬动机（对物质保障的需要）。并在此基础上提出了克服单纯物质刺激，用物质刺激和精神刺激相结合的方法调动劳动者积极性的建议。以上研究对我们无疑具有借鉴的作用。

在劳动社会学研究中，他们还吸收了西方劳动社会学和行为科学中的合理部分设计出了劳动行为和劳动态度的测量指标和测量方法。

总之，对苏联和东欧一些国家的劳动社会学，要充分利用他们的研究成果，综合我国的实际情况，注意消化吸收，为我所用。

第三，坚持马克思主义和中国的实际相结合，是建立具有中国特色的劳动社会学的关键。

马克思主义经典作家有丰富的关于劳动人事管理科学、社会学、心理学的精辟论述。新中国成立以来，我们在生产管理和劳动管理以及对职工进行思想教育方面也有不少成功的经验，这些都为建立具有中国特色的劳动社会学提供了有利条件。

党的十一届三中全会以来，随着改革开放方针的实施，我国社会学得到了恢复和重建，劳动科学也得到了繁荣与发展。这些著作和论文涉及的问题是：劳动与人类社会的关系；劳动者的需要、动机和行为；劳动态度；劳动的满意感与劳动积极性；劳动集体与劳动的社会控制；劳动者的自由时间与生活方式；劳动力的流动和劳动力资源的开发等。对这些问题研究的深入和中国化，将为我国劳动社会学的建立奠定基础。

劳动工资制度的改革呼唤着中国劳动社会学的产生。我们相信，只要坚持马克思主义为指导思想，坚持“以我为主，洋为中用，自成一家”的方针，发扬自己的长处，虚心学习别国有用的东西，通过实践，就可以在劳动社会学的研究方面走出一条中国自己的路，建立具有中国特色的劳动社会学。

参考书目

[1] R. 施托伯格. 劳动社会学. 袁伦渠，李步魁，译. 北京：劳动人事出版，1985.

[2] 赵履宽，王子平. 劳动社会学概论. 上海：上海人民出版社，1984.

苏联、东欧国家劳动问题研究

关于苏联劳动制度的一些资料①

一、各个时期劳动力的招收形式

在苏联，不同的历史时期，由于劳动力的来源不同，劳动力的招收形式也不尽相同，六十多年来，大致采取了如下几种劳动力的招收形式：

（一）农业集体化以前的自由招募（1917—1930 年）

十月革命胜利后，沙皇俄国遗留下来数十万失业者。第一次世界大战，外国武装干涉和国内战争破坏了国家经济，使国内失业现象更加严重。1921—1930 年，虽然苏联就业人数不断增长，但仍然存在失业现象。1924 年夏天失业者人数为 134.4 万人，1929 年达 174.1 万人。失业者主要是过去从事家务的妇女、18 岁以下的青少年和农村跑出来的人。

这一时期，苏维埃政权在劳动工作方面的主要任务，是同国内存在的失业现象作斗争。当时的劳动力招收也服从于这一任务，是为改善失业人员状况所采取的措施的一部分。1918 年 1 月 31 日成立劳动职业介绍所，为失业工人介绍工作。当年登记的失业工人近 80 万人。同时，还对失业工人进行培训和职业教育，为他们参加工作创造条件。这种办法，既是改善失业工人状况而采取的措施，又是为各工业部门输送劳动力的形式。1921—1925 年国民经济恢复时期，各经济机关和企业也是通过劳动职业介绍所从失业工人中自由招募。总之，1917—

① 此文应邀供 1979 年国家劳动总局酝酿草拟《中华人民共和国劳动法》参考，载于《经济学动态》1980 年第 7 期第 52～56 页，后刊于国家劳动总局等编的《劳动问题研究资料》（劳动出版社，1981 年第 305 页）。

1930年，在失业现象存在的情况下，劳动力是由各部门从社会上自由招募的。

（二）农业集体化以后到20世纪50年代末的有计劳动力的招收形式

苏联进入20世纪30年代以来，由于实现了工业化和农业集体化，城市失业工人找到了工作；个体农民参加集体农庄后，流入城市的农民没有了。1930年消灭了失业现象。因此，各部门建立在失业工人基础上的劳动力自由招募形式就为几种有计划、有组织的招收形式所代替。

1. 1931年开始的有组织的招收

所谓有组织的招收，就是通过经济机关同集体农庄和集体农庄庄员签订合同的办法招收劳动力。当时负责招收工作的部门是苏联劳动人民委员部。1934年劳动人民委员部撤销，仍由各部门自由招募。于是曾一度出现了一个地方有十几个部门在那里招工，形成抢工挖工，不经农庄许可，私招乱雇集体农庄庄员的混乱现象。因此，从1938年起，苏联政府又决定按指定地区统一招工，严禁互相抢工挖工。1939年又在当时的经济委员会下设立一个有组织招收工人委员会，负责管理招工工作。

在战前几个五年计划里，有组织的招收工人是在农业和国民经济其他部门中再分配劳动力的主要形式，也是补充工业、建筑业和运输业劳动力的最重要办法。1931—1940年，苏联通过有组织招收工人的办法，一共给企业和各建筑工程输送了将近2 900万工人。

卫国战争时期，国民经济各部门所需要的劳动力，国家被迫采取劳动动员方式招收。战后，有组织的招收制度在更高水平的基础上恢复起来。1947—1953年有组织的招收工作由当时的劳动后备部领导。1953年劳动后备部撤销后，这一工作交给各加盟共和国管理。中央没有组织招募工作的统一领导机构。只有国家计委和经委负责编制平衡计划。计划批准后即下达各部、各共和国按计划执行。各部按国家批准的计划向各共和国下达需求劳动力。共和国各级组织根据上级规定的招收任务和本地的具体情况逐级向下级（直到各村苏维埃和集体农庄）布置和分配招收任务。

按照苏联政府规定，招收职工，必须坚持自愿的原则，如果职工不同意，不得强迫。为了保证招收任务的完成，还采取各种办法向职工和居民宣传动员。例如，到居民点、阅览室、电影院等公共场所进行口头宣传，说明哪个企业招收工人，招收什么样的人，到什么地方去，工资待遇、生活福利、劳动条件如何以及这一工作的重要意义等。此外，还采取张贴招收宣传画、刊登招收广告，电台进行招收广播等方式，达到家喻户晓。

如果居民或职工愿意应召，本人也符合条件时，即由有组织招收部门（即区招收站）代替企业与应召者签订劳动合同，送到集中站，集中站按规定发给他们无偿津贴、路费、途中生活补助等，然后派人送到企业。经企业审查合格，即发给护送人员接收证明，付给招收工作中所花去的一切费用，包括无偿津贴、路费、车费、途中生活费等。

在苏联，国民经济各部门所需要的劳动力，除通过有组织地招收进行补充以外，还从劳动后备系统的各种专门学校和工厂附设艺徒学校的毕业生中得到补充，以及从复员军人中得到补充。进入20世纪50年代中期以后，又产生了“社会号召”的新形式，来为工业区和农业区的企业招收劳动力。

2. 20世纪50年代产生的社会号召

20世纪50年代，苏联新建工业区和农业区多数是在东部和北部。这些地区矿藏丰富，土壤肥沃，人烟稀少。苏联政府为了满足这些新工业区和农垦区对劳动力的需要，号召青年自愿到那里劳动和工作。社会号召与有组织招收的不同之点是：第一，社会号召的对象，主要是在企业中工作的青年职工，这些在业青年身体好，有一定的技术专长，一般没有家属，能适应比较艰苦的生活条件，便于尽快开发这些边远地区；第二，不签订合同，只发给派遣证，没有一定的工作期限，以便这些人定居下来。

响应社会号召申请去远方的人，必须经过严格挑选，条件是身体健康，要忠诚地在那工作等。各市、州、区成立选拔委员会，由市、区执委会主席、党委书记、共青团书记、有组织招收全权代表等人组成，具体工作由共青团负责。

响应社会号召的人员，还可享受许多优惠待遇。例如，可领三个月的工资，到达目的地后结婚可以优先领到房子等。

3. 工业移民

工业移民也是补充工业所需劳动力的一种形式，所谓工业移民，就是组织集体农庄庄员和其他居民移居到缺乏劳动力的北方和远东地区的工业企业中去做固定工作。这些工业企业主要是林业和捕鱼业以及一部分建筑业。20世纪50年代中期，在森林采伐业中，用移民办法招收的工人占13%。

工业移民必须具备的条件是：第一，要带家属，要全家移走；第二，每户至少有一两个劳动力；第三，要完全自愿；第四，要自己提出申请，经村苏维埃（因移民主要是农民）签字，然后全家经过体检合格。

移民得到批准后，可以享受以下优待条件：第一，一家大小得到一次无偿津贴；第二，移民到移民区后，免除三年义务交售；第三，给贷款修建住宅；第四，给贷款买牛等。

4. 企业自行招收

苏联各企业，除采用上述各种办法补充劳动力以外，还可以按照国家批准的劳动力增长计划，不必经过有组织招收部门，自己直接招收，有组织招收部门只负责监督检查。

企业自行招收，只准在本市或本居民点就地进行，不许到外地招收。具体做法是：企业张贴广告或登报，说明企业的地址，招收人数和工种，以及必须具备的条件、工资待遇等。凡愿意应招者可自行到企业报名，企业审查劳动手册，体检证件。如果企业和工人都认为合适，就算达成了口头协议（一般不需要签订书面合同），双方就开始发生劳动法律关系，厂长就根据协议颁发录用命令，公布执行。

苏联政府认为，企业在当地自行招收当地居民，可以避免长距离调动，又易解决住房问题，国家也可节约招工费用。因此，它是20世纪50年代苏联招收工人的重要形式之一。

（三）20世纪60年代初至目前的劳动力招收形式

1. 国家统一分配

在固定学校受过专业训练的人，即高等学校和中等专业学校以及职业技术学校的毕业生由国家按计划统一分配。其中大专院校的毕业生，根据所学专业，先做出分配方案，再按分配方案分配工作。大专院校毕业生一般被直接派到基层生产单位中去，要在实际生产中工作几年，才能调任做管理部门的工作。

2. 通过签订劳动合同招收

第一，企业和机关根据劳动合同直接从其他企业流动出来的劳动者，苏军退伍人员、家务劳动者和普通教育学校毕业生中招工。

第二，国家劳动资源利用委员会的地方机关有组织地安排不完全中学和中等综合技术学校毕业生的劳动就业。

第三，从以前工作过的和未工作过的人员中有组织地招收工人、专门人材和职员。

（略）

二、关于劳动合同

（一）劳动合同的内容

在苏联，企业、机关和组织必须通过与劳动者签订劳动合同来招收和使用劳动力，而劳动者也必须通过签订劳动合同实现其劳动权。

所谓劳动合同，就是企业、机关和组织与劳动者之间缔结的一种契约，它规定双方互相承担的义务。根据劳动合同规定，劳动者一方必须在其所在的企业、机关和组织担任一定的工作，并遵守劳动立法和内部劳动规则。例如，勤勤恳恳地工作，认真执行行政命令，提高劳动生产率，改进产品质量，遵守工艺纪律和安全技术、工业卫生等有关劳动保护的规定。而企业、机关和组织则应根据劳动者劳动的数量和质量支付报酬，并保证职工享有劳动立法和劳动合同中规定的一切劳动条件，例如，合理地组织职工的劳动，认真遵守劳动立法和劳动保护规章，关心劳动者的困难和要求，改善他们的劳动条件和生活条件等。

劳动合同既可以由劳动者个人与企业、机关和组织签订，也可由劳动者集体与企业、机关和组织签订，后者叫作集体合同。集体合同由工厂工会委员会、地方工会委员会代表劳动者集体与企业、机关和组织的行政部门签订。

劳动合同可分为三种：第一是不定期的，即不指明工作期限的；第二是定期的，但不超过三年；第三是以完成某项工作为期限。

（二）劳动合同的废除

1970 年苏联劳动法规定，遇有下列情况，劳动合同即行中止：

第一，双方同意解除；第二，合同期限已满或约定的工作已经完成，但是，合同期满后，劳动关系实际上仍在继续或双方都未要求中止的，则合同按原定条件无定期延长；第三，职工应征服兵役；第四，经职工本人同意调动工作或改任选任职务；第五，职工拒绝随同企业、机关和组织迁到其他地方工作；第六，职工被法院判刑。

职工因某种正当理由或因企业、机关和组织的行政违反劳动立法和劳动合同的重要条款时，可以要求提前解除劳动合同。职工也有权解除不定期的劳动合同，但必须在两个星期以前书面通知行政部门。

企业、机关和组织在下列情况下，可以废除不定期的劳动合同和有效期未满的劳动合同：第一，企业、机关和组织撤销，精简编制，减少定员；第二，发现职工不称职；第三，职工无正当理由经常不履行劳动合同或内部劳动规则所规定的义务，而以前已对该职工进行过纪律处分或公开惩戒；第四，职工无正当理由旷工（包括不清醒状态时来上班）；第五，职工因暂时丧失劳动能力连续缺勤四个月以上(怀孕和产假除外)，但因工伤或职业病而丧失劳动力的职工，其工作岗位（职务）可以保留到恢复劳动能力或已确定为残疾时；第六，恢复原来担任该项工作的职工的工作。

三、目前苏联在劳动力方面存在的问题

（一）劳动力的流动

苏联在成立初期，采取了种种措施，克服用人制度上的混乱现象，经过头几个五年计划的努力，那种被称为“追求高薪而经常变换工作的人”很少了。但是，到了20世纪60年代初期，劳动力的流动现象却又变得十分严重。据统计，这一时期，工业中跳厂的职工每年达到300万人次，其中40%的人在跳厂后改变了工种，由于劳动力的流动，每年损失的产品价值达30亿卢布(旧卢布)。劳动力的流动大致有如下四种情况：第一，年纪轻和本企业工龄短的人流动多；第二，主要工种流动多；第三，工业内部流动多；第四，改变产业部门和工种的多。为了解决劳动力流动问题，苏联经济学界在当时曾进行过广泛的讨论。有的主张加强物质刺激；有的主张在劳动立法上加以限制，采取强硬手段；有的主张改进有关制度；也有的主张进行思想教育，等等。

勃列日涅夫当政以来，也采取了一些措施制止劳动力的流动，但是未能奏效，工人跳厂现象至今仍经常发生。劳动力的流动现象不仅给个别企业，而且给整个国民经济造成了重大的人力和物力浪费。

苏联农村劳动力盲目流入城市的现象也很严重。有关部门支出，转入城市的劳动力大大超过了计划，而且在很大程度上是自发的，不是在社会的控制下转入的，这使得全国许多地区的农业劳动力十分紧张。

（二）劳动力不足

近年来，苏联国民经济各部门普遍感到劳动力不足，主要原因是劳动力来源的贫乏。进入20世纪60年代后，苏联劳动力来源主要有两个，一是进入劳动年龄的青年，即16到25岁的人，二是从家务劳动和个体副业中解脱出来的人。1961—1970年，国民经济所增加的职工，前者占1/3，后者占2/3。

从发展的趋势看，从事家务劳动和个体副业的劳动力已日趋减少，据人口调查，从事个体副业的人，已由1959年的1 790万人减少到1970年的590万人；在家务劳动方面，由于苏联家庭生活方式的完全改变，除了抚育幼儿以外，很少有人专门搞家务，再加上妇女劳动技能的提高，少子女家庭的增加，也使得苏联从事家务劳动的人日趋减少。1961—1965年，从家务劳动和个体副业中吸收到社会生产中去的有1 000万人，而1966—1970年，吸收的人则减少到360万人。因此，最近十年，正在成长的一代几乎成了补充国民经济劳动力的唯一来源。但是，近年来，由于中等教育的普及，高等学校学生人数增加以及参军服役，16～25岁劳动适龄的青年能在国民经济各部门工作的不到一半人。参加社会生产和学习的人占劳动适龄人口的比重，1959年为82%，1965年为87%，1970年以后已达到92%以上。因此，国民经济各部门补充劳动力受到了极大的限制，普遍感到劳动力紧张。尽管物质生产部门的扩大再生产可以靠提高劳动生产率解决一部分问题，但在服务部门，由于机械化程度不高，却迫切要求增加劳动力。

在这种情况下，那些超过工作年龄但尚有劳动能力的人口（退休者），即所谓“亚老年”人也成了补充劳动力的一个来源。为了吸收和保留这些亚老年人参加工作，苏联当局反复说明这些人参加工作的客观必要性和可能性，研究解决他们参加工作的理论问题和实际问题。目前，正研究如何为亚老年人挑选最合适的工种和工作，改进技术和工艺，以适应亚老年人工作，减少工作量，缩短工作时间，做轻便工作，以及如何建立亚老年人的特殊车间等。

民主德国社会学家谈“劳动异化”问题[①]

在科学中，任何理论研究的对象也许都不会像劳动那样占有如此重要的地位。劳动的地位是由其对于个人和整个社会存在与发展的意义决定的。

劳动的首要的和最重要的原理是：劳动创造了人并且决定着人的本质。人只是由于劳动才脱离了动物界而成为真正的人。劳动决定人的本质，因而劳动作为人类本质力量的使用和表现的原理，对于劳动社会学具有很重要的意义。它能回答：应当如何理解把劳动变成人的生活需要？如今劳动能满足人的何种需要？随着社会的发展，劳动又将能满足人的何种需要？

关于劳动的意义的第二条原理是：劳动是社会财富的源泉。在劳动过程中，即人与自然的相互作用中，创造着社会存在和继续发展的物质前提。只有劳动生产率提高了，首先是生产资料增加了，社会财富才能增长，社会需要才能得到满足。

关于劳动意义的这两条马克思主义原理，就其内容来说，还是一般的和抽象的概念，因为它们只是将劳动作为个人和整个社会的一般生活条件来评价的。至于这两条原理以什么具体形式来实现，则以占统治地位的社会关系为转移。

劳动的社会形式，也就是它的社会经济性质，是以占统治地位的生产方式为转移的。因此，关于劳动对于人和社会的意义的一般原理，应当具体地历史地来考察。在不同的社会制度下，人们在不同程度上发展着自己在劳动中的本质力量。在一切建立在剥削关系上的社会形态中，劳动对大多数劳动者来说是一种负担，甚至是痛苦，其原因是统治阶级对被统治阶级的剥削。这种剥削主要表现为劳动的强制性，即表现为劳动力为剥削者所榨取，以及恶劣的劳动条件、脑力劳动与体力劳动的分离、劳动强度过大和统治阶级竭力延长劳动日。这样，劳动对劳动者来说，便不再是真正的人的自由的活动，而成了与他们格格不入的东西。劳动的这种异化造成了社会中人与人关系的异化，这充分表现

① 摘译自民主德国 P.施托伯格 1982 年出版的《劳动社会学》，标题系译者所加，载于中国社会科学院《国外社会学参考》1984 年第 2 期。

在资本主义的生产中。在这里。劳动的异化首先表现为劳动工具的异化，劳动工具作为剥削手段而与工人相对立，并加强了工人的自愿的奴隶地位；其次，劳动的异化还表现为产品的异化，因为这种产品不属于工人而属于资本家；最后，劳动的异化表现为劳动过程的异化，因为劳动过程服从于最有效地使用资本的目的，并把工人当成生产机器的普通零件。只有在社会主义条件下才能消除劳动的异化。在这里，劳动发展成为人的自我实现的手段，因而成为真正的生活需要。

如何利用劳动所创造的社会财富，也取决于社会制度的性质。在剥削阶级社会中，劳动创造的财富是统治阶级及其走狗进行剥削和用来满足寄生生活需要的手段。只有在社会主义制度下，社会财富才被用来满足整个社会的需要，社会财富的增加才能成为全体人民物质文化生活水平提高的基础，劳动成果才能成为衡量社会财富（作为部分国民收入）分配和满足每个社会成员需要的尺度。

关于劳动意义的第三条原理是：劳动具有具体的历史规定性。这一原理直接涉及劳动社会学的劳动造就着人并促进人的个性发展。人是在劳动过程中发展的，甚至在存在剥削的条件下也是如此，但是只有在一定的生产目的所允许的范围内才能做到，只有消灭了剥削制度，工人的个性才能得到自由发展。在社会主义制度下，尽管还存在阶级，但阶级利益一致，目的相同，因而不再相互对立，人们通过自觉地加入工人集体和积极参加集体的生活，建设新社会，建立和巩固自己的阶级地位，加强自己的修养，发挥才能，增长知识，从而在这些方面不断地得到完善和提高。在这里表现出社会主义类型的个性特点，实际上也就是劳动者的个性特点，它代表着作为社会主义领导力量的工人阶级，由此产生了社会主义的劳动态度、对工作的热爱以及没有劳动者的生活就没有真正价值的信念。这样，认真的诚实的有益于社会的劳动就会发展成为社会主义生活方式的基础。

关于劳动意义的第四条原理是：劳动对工人个性发展的作用。个人最重要的社会联系，是个人与社会的联系，只有劳动中才能得到实现。如果说资本主义制度下这种联系的特点是人在社会中的异化，那么在社会主义制度下，这种联系便具有整体化的性质。在资本主义制度下，工人的劳动与社会的联系被完全割断，二者之间存在的只是作为资本主义唯一生产目的的利润。劳动条件成了剥削的条件,劳动的物质条件作为统治和压迫工人的社会力量而与工人相对立。劳动过程中社会整体化被社会的解体所代替，异化成为劳动的性质。社会主义生产从根本上消除了劳动异化，使劳动完全有可能成为社会整体化的因素。社会主义生产的目的是满足整个社会的需要，因此，与资本主义相反，社会主义的劳动者在劳动过程中与自己的社会有着紧密的联系，这种联系表现在最能说明社会主义社会关系本质的社会主义劳动态度中。劳动者懂得，要达到和实现整个社会生产的目的，只能靠他们个人的劳动。

只有在社会主义条件下，劳动才能完全获得自己的主要性质——决定人的本质。马克思列宁主义经典作家也正是根据这一原理作出了劳动在共产主义社会将变成生活第一需要的预言。但是，不能把生活的“第一”需要理解为吃饭和睡觉，而应当看作是人——社会的人——的社会生活的第一需要。

将劳动变成生活的需要，这直接关系到要消除劳动的异化问题。马克思谈到，在资本主义社会，由于劳动异化的结果，劳动不再成为人的需要，而是受处于劳动之外的需要所推动，即通过出卖劳动力获得维持劳动力再生产和保证家庭生存所必需的货币基金的需要所推动。资产阶级的思想家不仅经常摘引马克思早期作品中的个别词句对马克思进行片面的攻击，而且利用马克思的主张达到自己不可告人的目的。他们还往往把这种观点强加给马克思，硬说劳动的异化如同一般的异化一样，是人类生活的普遍现象，与一定的社会制度无关。

这些资产阶级的思想家就是这样企图将当代的问题作为全人类的问题提出来，并企图回避现实的社会矛盾及其产生的客观基础和条件。随着社会主义社会的建立，人在社会中的异化、人的自身异化以及人的劳动异化的原因实际上正在消除之中。总的来说，研究异化问题，还应当从劳动的性质，其中包括劳动的社会经济本质出发，而不能从劳动内容或者劳动者还有不满意的感觉出发。因为这在原则上是同马克思主义对异化实质的理解相对立的。当然，在社会主义生产中,还存在着一些为人的自我肯定和提高人的自尊心而工作的劳动。但是，在社会主义条件下，即使遇到这种情况，劳动的社会经济本质也发生了变化，首先是在工人的意识中，劳动活动的目的发生了变化。

在社会主义社会，劳动摆脱了异化，变成人在展示其本质力量过程中进行自我表现的手段。因此，劳动（作为社会的劳动）不能用于“劳动以外”的目的。在这里，需要（人的本质力量的发展）与满足需要的途径（劳动活动）是一致的。但是，这并不排除人的本质力量发展的本身具有各种不同的方面，而这些方面可能成为特殊的需要。

如果说在目前条件下，人对劳动的需要的本性还仅仅在形成，劳动还没有成为每个个人的需要，尤其是生活第一需要的话，那么，我们就应当认为，社会主义的生产关系正在消除劳动异化的原因，而且最重要的是正在把劳动变成人的需要。

列宁在 1920 年谈到共产国际劳动时这样写道："共产主义劳动，从比较狭窄和比较严格的意义上说，是一种为社会造福的无报酬的劳动，这种劳动不是为了履行一定的义务、不是为了享有取得某种产品的权利、不是按照事先规定的法定定额进行的劳动，而是自愿的劳动，是无定额的劳动，是不指望报酬、没有报酬条件的劳动，是根据为公共利益劳动的习惯、根据必须为公共利益劳动的自觉要求（这已成为习惯）来进行的劳动，这种劳动是健康的身体的自然需要。"①

但是，列宁同样强调说，在目前的社会情况下，"我们……还远不能广泛而真正普遍地实行这种劳动。"②

苏联学者对劳动资源等几个概念的看法③

当前，关于"劳动力""有劳动能力的人口""劳动资源"这些概念的内涵没有一致的看法。这给研究和管理工作带来了一定的困难。因此，首先必须准确地分清这些概念，确定其中每一个概念的使用范围。什么是劳动力？马克思说："我们把劳动力或劳动能力，理解为人的身体即活的人体中存在的，每当人生产某种使用价值时就运用的体力和智力的总和。"④

根据这个定义可以推断出，劳动力——这是几方面的统一体——包括两层含义：（1）人所具有的体力和智力的总和，即人的劳动能力；（2）生产使用价

①《列宁全集》中文版第 30 卷，人民出版社 1963 年版，第 475 页。

② 同上。

③ 根据苏联萨鲁哈诺夫所著的《劳动力管理的经济问题》第一章编译，载于《社会学与社会调查》1988 年第 1 期。

④《马克思恩格斯全集》第 23 卷第 109 页。

值的能力。

人作为体力和智力的总和，在劳动中表现自己时，“在实际上成为发挥作用的劳动力，成为工人，而在此以前，他只不过在可能性上是工人”。[①]

劳动力是一个社会经济范畴，以上援引的有关劳动力的定义适用于一切社会经济形态。但是，在不同的社会经济形态中，劳动力的社会经济形式不同，并由此产生了由生产资料所有制决定的经济关系。尽管劳动力首先在劳动使用领域中得到体现，可是它所形成的经济关系存在于再生产过程中的一切阶段。

劳动能力的体现者，即主要的生产力是人。没有人也就没有劳动力。劳动力在社会生产体系中所处的地位决定着人在生产使用价值时其体力和智力利用的性质，正是在这个意义上劳动力是一种经济范畴。

有一些经济学家一向不承认“劳动力”这一范畴，认为它不是社会主义所固有的东西。例如，佳普金断定，“在社会主义社会没有，也不能有‘劳动力’这种经济范畴”。但是很明显，在社会主义条件下存在人的劳动能力，它在劳动过程中，即生产使用价值时表现出来。这就是说，在社会主义的实际经济生活中存在“劳动力”概念总和的现象。因此，否定社会主义政治经济生活中存在劳动力这一概念的任何尝试都是违背现实生活的，并导致从社会主义生产力和生产关系中排除其主要因素的错误。在社会主义社会，“劳动力”概念充满了崭新的社会经济内容。

很显然，问题不在于社会主义政治经济中是否固有“劳动力”这一范畴（我们认为不可争辩的固有），而在于社会主义制度下劳动力的社会阶级内容是什么。在社会主义条件下劳动力表现着社会主义的生产关系，它不是买卖对象，不是商品，而是直接和生产资料结合起来并且重新和每个人的个性融为一体。

“有劳动力的人口”是单个劳动力的体现者，每个社会具有劳动能力的所有成员，即所有劳动人口是劳动力总和的体现者。在这个意义上，“劳动力体现者总和”和“具有劳动能力的人口”这两个概念是一致的。但是，二者也有一定的区别，“有劳动能力的人口”这一概念含义较宽，它包括各式各样的人的总和。

这里应当着重指出，人只有劳动能力的体现者才是经济理论研究的对象。

---

① 《马克思恩格斯全集》第 23 卷第 201 页。

劳动力是经济范畴，即表现为生产关系的范畴，而人却不是，因而具有劳动能力的人口也不是。

可以同意 A.Э. 科特利亚尔的这种观点，即劳动力是有劳动能力的人口、劳动资源等概念的核心。但是他认为劳动力的体现者只是“由于自己的社会地位应当从事劳动”的有劳动能力的人口，我们认为这是错误的。

苏联学者认为，应当将一般劳动能力和专业劳动能力区分开来。一般劳动能力以人所具有的体力的、心理生理的、年龄和其他条件为前提，它是一定的不需要专门培训，即不熟练的劳动的能力。专业劳动能力是在一定的国民经济部门中具体劳动的能力，它需要专门的培训，也就是从事需要专门技术的能力。在生产发展的现代条件下，专业劳动能力具有特殊的意义，因而它是我们研究的对象。

马克思指出：“要改变一般的人的本性，使他获得一定劳动部门的技能和技巧，成为发达的和专门的劳动力，就要有一定的教育或训练。”[①]由此得出结论，只有参加（或者能够参加）具体的劳动过程，具有适应这一劳动过程的体力与智力条件，并受过一定的专门训练的人才是有专业劳动能力的人。

那么，能否将还在学习某种职业的人，也像受过训练的正在生产中工作的人一样，算作有劳动能力的人口？绝对不能。因为目前前者还没有准备好在国民经济的一定部门参加劳动，还只是一种潜在的劳动力的体现者。

因此，苏联学者认为，有劳动能力的人口应当包括一切在体力和智力上具有劳动能力的人，即劳动年龄之内（男人 16～59 岁，女人 16～54 岁）和超过劳动年龄但还有劳动能力的人。在这里应当包括从事社会生产以及在家庭和个体副业中工作的人，甚至不在任何地方工作的人。社会上有劳动能力人口的实际范围应当这样统计。

“劳动资源”这一概念是 20 世纪 20 年代初期产生并开始使用的，当时，C.Г. 斯特鲁米林根据 1920 年的人口普查资料进行了人口预测，并编制了 1920—1941 年间国家劳动平衡表，从而把劳动力资源的概念引用到经济科学中，从此，劳动资源这一术语就在计划统计中起到度量劳动力的作用。劳动资源包括劳动年龄内具有劳动能力的人口（残废者和不工作的领退休金者除外）以及到

① 《马克思恩格斯全集》第 23 卷第 195 页。

了退休年龄尚在工作的人和未满 16 岁的从事生产的少年人。在 1959 年人口普查之后，劳动资源开始广泛应用于指令性的文献和经济书籍中。但是，关于这个概念的内容直到今天还没有一致的意见。有些作者一直否认劳动资源是一个经济范畴，认为它是劳动年龄内人口的机械总和。相反，吉利茨基和其他许多学者有根据地提出这一范畴的社会经济本质，指出劳动资源具有历史的规定性，是一个社会经济的概念，而不是一个徒具形式的统计总和。还有一些看法，其中有的把劳动资源与劳动力混为一谈，或者从部门角度看待劳动力，从地域角度看待劳动资源。还有些学者把劳动力看成劳动资源的组成部分，并断定劳动资源概念比劳动力更加广泛。

在制定苏联国民经济发展的国家计划工作方法指示中规定，劳动资源包括：（1）在劳动年龄内具有劳动能力的人口，即 16～59 岁的男人和 16～54 岁的女人；丧失劳动能力的残废工人和一、二级残废军人以及按优惠条件提前领取退休金的 50～59 岁的男人和 45～54 岁的女人[①]除外。（2）正在国家企业、机关、群众团体和集体农庄等公有经济中工作的 60 岁及 60 岁以上的男人和 55 岁及 55 岁以上的女人和未满 16 岁的少年。

所以，为了估计全国，一个地区和一个国民经济部门拥有多少有劳动能力的人口，即劳动力的体现者，在编制计划工作中便采用了劳动资源这一概念。但是苏联学者认为，用劳动资源的概念来统计劳动力数量是不准确的，因为：第一，它一方面将在劳动年龄内有劳动能力的人口和正在生产中工作的人无法律根据地混为一谈，另一方面将不工作的人和正在学习的人混为一谈。第二，它统计的不是全部超过劳动年龄但尚有劳动能力的人，而仅仅是其中正在工作的人。第三，将 16 岁以下的少年看作是劳动资源，其理由也不充分。因为现在他们在工作者总数中所占的比重已经微乎其微，并且还有继续减少的趋势，直至减少到零。与此同时，从有劳动能力的人口中划分出劳动年龄内（男人 16～59 岁，女人 16～54 岁）有劳动能力的人口这种做法似乎比较合理。

有时，人们还把劳动资源说成劳动储备，但是，在这种情况下，劳动储备只能包括具有劳动能力的人口中，当前不参加社会生产的人，而对于参加工作

---

① 指从事井下工作等繁重体力劳动和在有毒有害劳动环境中工作的人以及生过 5 个以上孩子并把他们养育到 8 岁的妇女。

的人只能包括其兼职工作的那部分体力和智力资源。劳动储备（资源）应当用来说明现实存在的，但在当前还没有被利用的有劳动能力的人口。

由上所述，苏联学者认为，劳动资源这一术语是有多重意义，因而也是不确定的，它是一个不具有自己所特有的经济内容的概念。劳动力是一个经济范畴，而劳动资源仅仅是劳动力的数量表现。

社会主义所有制的更新

内容提要：本文是作者留苏期间译自苏联《经济报》的一篇文章，回国后发表在《劳动与人事》1989 年第 5 期上。作者系苏联科学院经济研究所所长、院士阿巴尔金，本文反映了 20 世纪 80 年代初他对苏联经济体制和政治体制改革的观点。

我们生活的这个时代，处在一个最复杂和最紧要的改革关头。过去的一段时期里，我们有可能在经济和社会思想方面进行了一些变革，但也感到我们面临的任务十分深刻和复杂，以及工作上将会遇到的困难。

当前看来已十分明显，如果不触及公有制的深层，就不可能将改革顺利推向前进。而且，如果不采取所有制关系的根本变革来巩固改革的初步成果，就有可能后退。因此，采取措施更新社会主义所有制，就显得十分重要。

抛弃简单化的公式

不言而喻，为了解决当前的问题，经济科学无论就其发挥的作用还是就其承担的责任来说，都在不断增强。经济理论面临的任务，不是简单的推进，而是从质量上的突破。历史的经验，我们对过去和当代问题的大量思考都要求这种突破，要求马克思列宁主义经济理论领域从根本上实行新的变革。我们不应当为此而困扰，而应当经常明了列宁主义的这一原理："我们决不把马克思的理论看作某种一成不变的和神圣不可侵犯的东西；恰恰相反，我们深信：它只是给一种科学奠定了基础，社会主义者如果不愿意落后于实际生活，就应当在各方面把这门科学向前推进。"

这句话应当成为认识理论的进一步发展，总结历史经验，重新评价现实理论和简单化公式的先导。

苏联科学院经济研究所通过分析社会主义经济体制方面的理论遗产，得出这样的结论：列宁关于社会主义经济的概念是在不断发展、明确和不断丰富的，换句话说，任何一种科学其固有的特点是，向前发展，修改陈旧的公式，补充丰富新的内容。我们不可能在列宁著作中去寻找解决问题的现成答案和处理问题的万应灵药。我们的任务是掌握列宁主义分析问题的方法，善于研究和批判性的理解历史经验。

因此，最迫切的一项任务是形成一种科学的和普遍的新型经济思维。这就需要一种突破，由简单的公式，由双向思维向多向思维转变，以反映社会现象的丰富性、复杂性和多样性。

认清发展的辩证法

按照非此即彼原则推理的双向思维不可能理解所有制关系的多重性质，即所有制的多主体性问题。例如，如果国家是所有者，那么集体就不是所有者；如果集体是所有者，那么国家就不可能是所有者。要掌握这个过程的辩证法，理解复杂的在国家不是所有者情况下集体是所有者这种现象的矛盾结合，在传统的双向思维的框子里是不可能的。

新思维要求形成真正的科学道德。社会科学学者们应当养成坚持真理的习惯，养成除了真理什么也不相信的作风。如果科学中有上帝的话，这个上帝就是真理。为真理服务，这是唯一的宗旨，它赋予科学之所以为科学的权利，并使科学能行使对社会的重大使命。我们曾为改变这种状况付出了高昂的代价，今后不应当再犯错误。

要形成一个完整的社会主义所有制的概念，找出其发展的规律性，以及经济上实现的形式和机制，需要很长时间，这样一个重大问题的解决不是一蹴而就的。

解决所有制问题的锁钥不在于对它的孤立的分析，而在于以组织经济的、社会政治的关系的全部总和为背景对它进行研究，应当从理解社会过程的规律性和人类文明的发展开始。现在具有丰富历史教训的我们懂得，社会过程既包括否定的因素，也包括继承的因素，即继承性。在未来社会发展的每一阶段都应当吸收已往积累的一切好东西。这涉及诸如合作制、市场、民主制度等。我们应当学会准确地区分经济过程本身中哪些是反映社会前进的社会经济因素，哪些是社会过程和特殊的社会经济形式，区分某种社会结构固有的特点。

形式和结构的多样性

社会进步的一个根本特点就是形式和结构的合乎规律的复杂化和日趋多样化。而过去的科学文献却曾宣传这样一种观点：社会进步导致简单划一，导致形式和结构的单一化。以至将社会主义的发展理解为由多种形式的所有制向单一形式所有制的简单过渡。

今天我们接受了过去的教训，得出了这样的结论：社会进步的规律性乃是社会关系、社会结构和形式的日趋多样化与复杂化，其中包括所有制的发展，即所有制形式的丰富化、经济生活组织和经济核算方法的多样化。

但是旧的观念不会自行消失，我们往往提出这样一个重要而又尖锐的问题，即如何将第一种和第二种不同的经济核算模式比较评价，现在又出现了租赁制这个第三种经济核算模式。学者们的争论常常围绕这种问题进行：这些模式或形式哪一种好？不过这种争论是无的放矢的，因为它们不承认合理的多样性，都想找出一种对现实生活的各方面都使用的整齐划一的模式。

在新的经济机制形成过程中，还出现过这种观点，就是试图找出一把万能钥匙，立即将所有的问题都加以解决。例如，一谈到租赁制，就希望将一切经营方式都变成租赁制，并以此解决一切问题，显然这是一种过了时的思维方式。我们还曾绞尽脑汁，试图找出一种统一的模式，找到一个救命的拐棍，这也是一种传统的陈旧的思维方式。不考虑当地居民的经验和文化素养，不考虑生产的技术组织状况，不考虑历史传统等方面的因素，要找出一种统一的经营管理方式，使之既适用于波罗的海沿岸又适用于中亚，既适用于俄罗斯的欧洲部分，又适用于亚洲部分，既适用于大企业又适用于小企业，这显然是不可能的。

采取灵活多样的方法处理问题，这是还在党的二十七大就提出的改革的一项基本原则。党的二十七大提出，与已往历次经济改革不同，我们这次改革不想寻找一种统一的经营管理形式和方法来适用于我国的一切部门和地区。这种合乎规律的多样性在客观上可以促进人的真正的独立自主和首创精神以及社会生活的民主化，使之可以根据当时当地的具体条件将各种不同的方案进行自由的对比和选择。

关于形成系统的方法

但是，当我们谈论形式和结构的多样性时，应当避免将这些形式和结构加以混淆，正是这种形式的多样性和客观上的发展逻辑迫切要求形成系统的研究经济现象的方法。

在对所有制的研究中，需要将所有制的结构形成的形式或者主要形式，同各种次要的派生的混合和过渡的形式区分开来。善于区分主要的结构并看到过程的完整性对于理解所有制关系的社会本质特别重要。离开有系统形成的联系而抽象地谈论任何一种所有制形式（无论是小集体合作社还是个体劳动所有制），谈论其特点和社会类型，这就意味着取消逻辑分析。

与所有制形式多样性相适应，产生了一个所有制形式的评判标准问题。只有这些标准的全部总和才可以评价某种形式是不是社会主义所有制的形式。采用多样性的评价标准可以确定，如果所有制表面上看来是国家的，但经营不好，效果很差，那么这种所有制就不能认为是社会主义的。

可以考虑将评价所有制形式的社会主义性质的全部的标准区分为两大类，一是属于反映一般进步逻辑，并证明这种所有制形式比以往形式更进步的社会经济性质的标准，这一普遍观点反映在马克思关于在集体生产条件下节约时间规律仍然是首要经济规律的著名原理中，以及列宁关于提高劳动生产率是保证新社会制度胜利的决定作用的原理中，我们应当严格坚持这些评价，以免从总体上失去社会主义所固有的特点。

另一个是解决普遍就业，建立社会保障，坚信未来等所有制的社会主义性质的特殊评价标准。但是在这方面需要进一步提出，如果存在劳动者与所有制的分离；如果现实中劳动集体不是生产资料的真正主人，不是生产资料的绝对支配者；如果劳动者感到自己是一个短工，临时工；那么这种所有制就未必称得上是社会主义的。

社会主义与进步

这里所谈的问题，在行将进入20世纪末期时，随着人类社会的进步，已成为注意的中心。在两种制度的历史对抗中，产生了非此即彼的抉择，其中一种社会制度能保证生产的高效率，产品的高质量，消费品和劳务的丰富市场，以及由于科技革命所造成的迅速而灵活的改革。但是它却也为此付出了高昂的代价：失业，社会保障的缺乏，社会对人类命运的冷漠，对未来信心的丧失。另一种社会制度能保证充分就业，人的社会保障，没有人感到孤独的集体主义。但也需要为此付出代价：生产的低效率，消费品市场的不平衡，对新科学技术成果的反应迟钝。

社会主义能否解决这个非此即彼的抉择问题？社会主义社会能否保证生产的高效率而不失去自己的社会价值？对这些问题的回答不仅决定着我们的未来，而且决定着整个人类文明的未来。

我们认为，可以从三个方面来回答这个问题。第一，社会主义不可能依靠历史上形成的、当前仍存在的经济组织、社会管理、政治结构形式来解决这个问题，我们已经证明了这一点。在保留旧有结构而缺乏革命性改革的情况下，不能期待有什么好的结果。

第二，从根本上说，社会主义如果能找得一种比资本主义更好的方式来鼓励人的社会和劳动积极性，找到一种更强有力的刺激因素来促进社会改革的话，它是能够达到社会生活的人道主义的高效率的。而这些激励方式和刺激因素的形成只能依靠对各项事业建立真正的经济关系，根据这种经济关系的发展水平就可以评价所有制关系的社会主义性质及其成熟程度。

第三，社会主义只有吸收并继承人类文明创造的一切优秀成果，才能完成上述任务。

总之，要对所有制，对全部社会关系的革命性更新制定出规划，这就是我们的回答。

经济改革与政治体制

对所有制的研究不能脱离政治体制、社会关系、社会的道德和文化价值而孤立地进行。

经验证明，如果不进行精神生活、价值观念和道德范畴的变革，所有制关系的改变不会独立取得重大进展。我们今天经济上的改革遇到了来自传统的价值观念、需要结构以及与此有关的劳动活动动机的顽强抵抗，以致我们往往不得不用行政的强制手段建立某些新的经营管理形式。不破除这些障碍，不消除这些需求结构，不建立新的价值和定向体系，不发展人的需要，我们就不能顺利解决经济改革的问题。

在很多关键的现代科学技术部门，我们遇到的困难，不是缺乏投资或者新的技术思想，甚至也不是官僚主义的管理方法，而首先是极低的劳动文明程度。

需要研究，如何借助所有制关系的更新来实现这些必要的变化。只有互相补充、互相丰富，才能产生效果。经济学者应当看到问题的多样性和复杂性，不能将自己和社会面临的任务的性质简单化。

正是在这个广泛的背景下产生了经济改革与政治体制改革的相互影响问题。政治体制改革，这是一个重大的特别深刻和多样性的过程，不能把它简单地说成是选举制度的变化或者组织机构相互关系的改变。

应当懂得这样一个著名的列宁主义原理："政策应当是从千百万人着眼，而不是从几千人着眼。只有从千百万人着眼，才会有实事求是的政策。"不改变所有制关系，能否调动千百万人的政治积极性？不调动千百万人的政治积极性，能否改变所有制关系？解决政治主体的问题并不比解决所有制主体的问题来得简单。群众，特别是革命时期的群众，应当成为政治的主体，而不是政治舞台上的旁观者。

政治体制改革，这是一件相当严峻的事情，它是一场深刻的根本变革，比经济改革更为重要。在这里不能将一切问题都推给行使政权的国家而将问题简单化。马克思在《哥达纲领批判》中指出："权力永远不能超出社会经济结构以及由经济结构所制约的社会的文化发展。"权力国家是社会发展的产物。"市民社会是全部历史的真正发源地和舞台"，这种社会组织"在一切时代都构成国家的基础以及任何其他的观念的上层建筑的基础。"

不应当将权力准则强加给生活，应当从社会发展的客观逻辑中得出结论。这并不意味着权力是消极的，权力起着积极的作用，它对社会进步的影响取决于它在多大程度上能充分而准确地反映市民社会发展的逻辑和规律性。

回忆 讲演 发言 访谈

永远的怀念[①]

——纪念邓小平百年诞辰

今年八月二十二日是中国改革开放政策总设计师邓小平同志的百年诞辰纪念日。中国人民怀念他，世界人民也在怀念他。时至今日，人们难以忘怀的是他的伟大思想和丰功伟绩，是他的人格魅力、他的伟人风范、他的平民本色。他具有世界胸怀和全球眼光，虽然经历了革命的轰轰烈烈和命运的动荡坎坷，他依然在古稀之年放眼全球清醒认识到世界和平与发展的大势，果断作出对内改革、对外开放的决策。

邓小平的理论思想博大精深，涵盖了社会、政治、经济等各个方面。在他复出之后不久，就对“文化大革命”进行拨乱反正。在 1978 年举行的十一届三中全会上提出共产党的主要任务和工作要转向经济建设和实现四个现代化上来。1978 年 3 月在全国科学大会上，他提出知识分子是工人阶级的一部分，要尊重知识尊重人才，使被极左路线压抑多年的知识分子欢欣鼓舞。小平同志还提出了科学技术是第一生产力的论断，大胆地吸收国外先进科学技术和先进的经济管理方法；他坚持发展是硬道理，提出让一部分人先富起来，又要防止社会两极分化；他提出建设具有中国特色社会主义的理论，主张发展生产力使人民共同富裕。而 1992 年的南方谈话最终确立了毫不动摇的改革路线，从此中国经济进入了一个持续稳定快速增长的发展时期。为了实现中国的统一大业，小

① 本文发表于 2004 年 8 月 25 日的国务院参事室《参事工作通讯》纪念邓小平同志百年诞辰专刊。

平同志提出了“一国两制”的构想，顺利解决了香港回归问题。在外交方面，他提出和平与发展是当代世界的两大“主题”，使中国与周边国家建立了睦邻友好关系，为中国的发展创造了良好的外部环境。

改革开放25年过去了，邓小平的伟大思想和丰功伟绩使占世界人口总数1/4的中国人民走向富裕，越来越多的中国人民过上了小康的生活。

在小平同志百年诞辰纪念日的时候，一件终生难忘的往事又浮现在我的面前。那是1977年8月4日，我作为教师代表在出席全国工资会议，晚间接到通知，敬爱的小平同志第二天要接见与会代表。这一消息使大家欢喜雀跃，我也兴奋得一夜没睡好。我们出席的这次会议是贯彻中央和小平同志整顿工作精神的会议，在“文化大革命”中，劳动工资领域也是“重灾区”之一。劳动管理被诬蔑为“修正主义分物资刺激”，社会保险被污蔑为“毒害工人的诱饵”。这次会议的任务之一就是消除“四人帮”对劳动工资工作的恶劣影响，拨乱反正，同时研究提高10余年未升过级的职工的待遇问题。小平同志在“文化大革命”磨难后刚刚恢复中共中央副主席、国务院副总理、中央军委副主席和解放军总参谋长的职务、面对“四人帮”的破坏、整个国家问题成堆，需要全面整顿，可以说是日理万机。可是在他老人家复出后只有一个月时间就过问劳动工资工作，接见会议代表，充分说明他对劳动工资工作的重视和对劳动人民的关怀，怎能不叫与会代表欢欣鼓舞呢？

第二天上午代表们早早集合到人民大会堂等待小平同志的接见。大约是在上午十点钟，大厅里忽然响起了一阵掌声，只见小平同志身着军装，神采奕奕，在其他中央领导同志的陪同下，迈着矫健的步伐，边挥手边向我们走来。我激动得心怦怦直跳，眼里含着泪水。小平同志停在我们面前，满面笑容，和蔼可亲，慈祥地看着每一个人，向大家问好。代表们齐声问候小平同志好，掌声经久不息，经工作人员再三示意，掌声才停息下来。然后他老人家回转身去在代表前落座，与我们合影留念。合影后小平同志和大家挥手告别，代表又以热烈的掌声，依依不舍地目送他老人家离去。这是我一生中经历的最光荣、最幸福、最难忘的时刻。

转眼27年过去了，我一直将小平同志接见我们的照片挂在墙上。每当看到他老人家那温和的目光，慈祥的面容，我内心就充满了敬仰和温暖。这张珍贵的照片成了我20多年来坚持劳动经济教学和科研工作的动力。

回忆在“首期社会学讲习班”学习的日子①

时光飞逝，转瞬“首期社会学讲习班”结业已经 20 年了。作为讲习班的一名学员，这段时光是我一生都难以忘怀的美好回忆。讲习班所学的课程至今仍深印在我的脑海里，老师们讲课的声音仍时时回响在我的耳畔，同学们的音容笑貌仍历历闪现在我的眼前。

一、走进“首期社会学讲习班”

1980 年 5 月，由我的恩师、时任北京经济学院劳动经济系主任的袁方教授推荐，我开始成为“首期社会学讲习班”的一名学员。

“首期社会学讲习班”的开办有其深远的背景。由于受苏联学术界历史唯物主义可以代替社会学理论的影响，1952 年我国的各高校停办了社会学专业，学术机关停止了社会学的研究。1978 年党的十一届三中全会以后，在邓小平理论的指引下，人们逐渐认识到社会学对社会主义建设事业的重要性。于是，在胡乔木同志的倡导下，我国开始恢复社会学研究。1979 年中国社科院成立社会学所，为了重新培养社会学研究人才，便举办了社会学讲习班。因为后来陆续还会有第二期、第三期讲习班，所以习惯称这次讲习班为“首期社会学讲习班”。可以说，讲习班是在国家的改革开放政策的阳光下开办的。后来的事实证明，讲习班的学员为我国社会学的建立和发展起到了承前启后的作用。

“首期社会学讲习班”于 1980 年 5 月底开办，7 月底结业。在整整两个月的时间里，来自全国不同高校、研究机关和政府部门的 40 名素不相识的莘莘学子便成为同窗好友，开始了紧张的学习生活。全班 40 名学员分为四个组，每组 10 人，各选一名组长。我荣幸地担任了第一组的组长。

我们的老师几乎都是国内外最著名的学者、教授和社会学家，其中有费孝通、雷洁琼、于光远、吴文藻、吴泽霖、袁方、戴世光、全尉天、王康、李沛良、刘创楚，以及美国匹斯堡大学的杨靖昆、霍尔兹那和叶尼瓦萨，等等。

我们所学的主要课程有：“社会学概论”，由费孝通教授主讲；“社会学与

① 本文选自沈阳出版社 2000 年 7 月出版的《我与中国社会学 20 年——中国社会学第一期讲习班回顾》。

现代化”，由杨靖昆、霍尔兹那和叶尼瓦萨教授主讲；“社会学统计分析”，由李沛良教授主讲；“社会学调查”由刘创楚教授主讲；“中国劳动问题”，由袁方教授主讲。此外，80 岁高龄的吴文藻教授还给我们讲述了“北方社会学”；吴泽霖教授给我们讲述了抗战前的社会学，等等。

二、我所接触的费孝通先生

我早就仰望费孝通先生的名字，而真正认识恩师费孝通先生是从参加这次讲习班开始的，至今我还清楚地记得初次见到他的情景。大概是在开班不久，一位精神矍铄、面目慈祥、头发斑白的老人走上讲台，不用介绍，大家都知道这就是我国著名社会学家费孝通教授。

费先生操着浓重的吴江口音给我们讲授了社会学基本知识、社会学的产生与发展以及他在中国研究社会学的经历。令我们十分感动的是他深入广大的穷乡僻壤进行社会调查而失去亲人的事迹。那是在 20 世纪 40 年代的一天，费先生和他的夫人王同惠女士深入广西瑶山的深山老林进行社会调查，他不慎跌入猎人捕捉老虎的陷阱里，王同惠女士去找人搭救，谁知竟一去不复返，后来王同惠女士的遗体在河里被人发现。费先生为献身社会学事业而失去妻子这一悲痛的经历感动了我们全体学员，也一直激励着后来的社会学者。

费先生当时虽已 70 岁高龄，但仍不辞劳苦，白天讲课，晚上进行耐心的辅导，有时还同我们一起整理录音、笔记。在两位美国教授讲授“社会学与现代化”时，费先生坐在第一排，当我们遇到难懂的问题，他便亲自为我们当翻译，或者对译员翻译的不妥之处加以纠正。

费先生讲课言辞隽永，谈笑风生，往往用一个形象的比喻就能深入浅出地道出一个深奥的道理。比如，他将汽车众多的美国称为“轮子上的国家”；在讲述中西方不同的代际关系时，他形象地将中国的代际关系比喻为“反哺型”，将美国的代际关系比喻为“接力型”，这就入木三分地将中西代际关系的不同实质揭示出来。为鼓励我们同学之间互相学习、互相欣赏、共同进步，他还用自己总结的 16 个字教导我们：“各美其美，美人之美，美美与共，世界大同。”这 16 字箴言让我们终生难忘，并从此成为青年学子和读书人的座右铭。费先生学贯中西，对语言的运用达到了炉火纯青的地步。正是他第一次将 community 这个难译的英文字创造性地译为“社区”，这个恰如其分的译法很快被国人所接受，现已被广泛地使用于政府的文件甚至法律条文中。费先生虽已年事已高但仍思维敏捷，三五千字的文章，他不打草稿，只需伏案思考片刻后便一气呵成。

除了聆听费孝通先生的“社会学概论”课程外，我们还学习了他的《乡土中国》《江村经济》等著作。他在书中表现出的渊博的知识、严谨的学风、注重实地调查的态度使我们受益良多。

三、找到了社会学与劳动科学的结合点

讲习班胜利结业后，40 名学员回到各自的岗位，用所学的知识为社会学在中国的恢复和重建努力工作。回到工作岗位以后，我也一直考虑如何将所学的社会学知识和我从事的劳动科学结合起来。为此，我查阅了北京图书馆几乎所有的社科目录，竟然意外地发现了三本不同版本的劳动社会学：一本是苏联 1981 年出版的马赫纳雷洛夫的《劳动社会学》，一本是民主德国 1978 年出版的 R. 施托伯格的《劳动社会学》（俄文版），一本是南斯拉夫 1982 年出版的马尔科维奇的《劳动社会学》。这是我第一次看到劳动社会学这个名字。浏览了三本书的目录后，我十分高兴，因为我终于找到了社会学与劳动科学的结合点——劳动社会学。德国是马克思的故乡，曾产生了黑格尔和费尔巴哈等哲学家。于是我于 1983—1985 年牵头与人合译了民主德国的《劳动社会学》并于 1985 年由劳动出版社出版。为了进一步将这一门新兴学科介绍给我国读者，我细心钻研了这本书，从 1984 年开始，陆续公开发表了《一门新兴的学科——劳动社会学》《应加强对劳动社会学的研究》《民主德国社会学家谈劳动异化问题》《建立具有中国特色的劳动社会学》等论文。这些论文的主要观点和内容是：劳动社会学是从社会学分化出来的一门年轻的学科，它运用社会学的原理和方法研究人的劳动活动，既是社会学的一个分支，又是劳动科学知识体系的一个组成部分。它研究的主要内容包括劳动的性质和内容、人的劳动态度和劳动行为、劳动的满意感和劳动集体中的社会心理气氛、领导者的领导方法和领导作风、职业选择和人员流动、技术革命对劳动内容和劳动条件的影响等。劳动社会学的特点是：（1）从社会总体的角度对劳动问题进行综合性、整体性研究；（2）用经济学、社会学、心理学的知识对劳动进行多学科的研究；（3）注重实地调查，坚持用事实和材料说话；等等。

劳动社会学认为，企业是一个集体组织，工人不但有经济方面的要求，而

且有社会心理方面的要求，因此，单纯对劳动者进行物质刺激的手段还不够，还必须注意人的因素，研究劳动者的愿望、动机、价值观和追求的目标等，从人的内心激发出动力，使之产生强烈的工作愿望，以提高劳动效率。这就冲破了传统劳动管理中那种见物不见人的做法，提出了做好人的思想工作对调动劳动者积极性的作用，从而丰富了企业劳动管理的内容。

上述这些论述不仅拓宽了劳动管理的内容，也使对劳动管理研究向对人力资源管理研究的转变迈进了一步。

除了翻译和介绍、研究劳动社会学之外，我还积极进行劳动社会学的教学与科研活动。从1985—1990年，我还应北京大学社会学系主任袁方和潘乃谷教授之邀，多次为北京大学社会学系的研究生和本科生讲授劳动社会学和劳动问题，将自己的研究成果与北京大学师生共同切磋，受到师生的欢迎。从北京大学社会系讲授劳动社会学开始，国内各高校陆续开设劳动社会学课程，从而将这门新兴学科引进中国学术界。

1988—1989年，作为高级访问学者在苏联莫斯科国民经济学院劳动经济教研室进修和讲学期间，我也总是抽时间进行劳动社会学交流。我曾去苏联科学院社会学研究所和远东研究所访问，与他们共同研究社会学和劳动社会学问题。并且克服了重重困难去民主德国哈勒市的马丁·路德大学找到了《劳动社会学》的作者，时任该校哲学系主任的R.施托伯格教授，将我翻译的该书的中译本赠给他，当时59岁的R.施托伯格教授高兴得像孩子一样拥抱着我，中断了他主持的系务会议，同我进行了长时间的学术交流，并一起合影留念。

自“首期社会学讲习班”结束以来，我一直进行着社会学和劳动社会学的介绍和研究工作，作为最早接触劳动社会学的学者之一，对劳动社会学在20世纪80年代引进中国和以后在中国的传播作出了自己的贡献。

“首期社会学讲习班”结业已经20年了，老师们传授我的知识使我受益终生。他们当中不少人已经作古，健在的老师还在社会学园地里辛勤地耕耘着，他们追求真理、献身教育的精神永远激励着我们。就在我写这篇文章的时候，惊悉我的恩师、中国著名的社会学家和劳动经济学家袁方教授逝世的噩耗，我五内俱焚。我从20岁就做他的学生，此后他老人家耳提面命教导了我几十年。我还记得20年前我与他同住一个单身宿舍，他常同我促膝长谈到深夜，教导我做学问和做人的道理。我今天取得的成就都浸透着他的心血。没想到一年前北京大学一见，竟成永诀。袁先生为中国社会学的恢复和发展耕耘了一生，直到最后一息。我决心化悲痛为力量，继承袁先生遗志，为中国的社会学和劳动经济学的发展奋斗终生，以告慰他的在天之灵。

访苏见闻①

北京经济学院袁伦渠同志受国家教委的派遣，以高级访问学者的身份，于1988年6月—1989年3月去苏联访问讲学。近一年时间，他先后访问了莫斯科国民经济学院、列宁格勒财经学院和基辅国民经济学院，以及苏联科学院经济所和远东所，苏联国家劳动科学研究所等学术单位，同时在苏联各地进行了参观和考察，见闻不少，感触颇多。本刊特约他撰写访苏见闻数则，分期刊载，供读者参考。

蒙古掠影

8月31日早晨，我由北京站登上了开往莫斯科的国际列车，傍晚到达中蒙边境的中国城市二连浩特市。在这里列车经过吊装换底盘（因蒙苏铁轨比中国的宽）和海关检查后，即驶入蒙古人民共和国境内。列车在这个平均海拔1 500米、布满粗沙和砾石的戈壁滩上奔驰了十几个小时，于9月1日中午到达了蒙古人民共和国首都乌兰巴托。这是一座群山环抱的城市，由于刚下过一场透雨，显得十分整洁和美丽。由乌兰巴托向北，渐渐出现了起伏的丘陵，列车像一条游龙在群山中蜿蜒穿行，窗外牧草茂密，流水潺潺，大草原犹如一张皱褶的绿毯向天边伸延，远处那片片白云一样的羊群，那朵朵白花一般的蒙古包，正是这个以畜牧业为主的国家的象征，也反映出这个世界上最大的内陆国的多彩多姿。

列车进入蒙古人民共和国北部山地，这里降水较多，沿铁路有一条河，河水清澈见底，人烟也开始稠密起来，不时看到身穿黄坎肩的铁路工人和过往行人向我们微笑和招手，洋溢着中蒙两国人民互相理解的轻松气氛。显然，这是党的十一届三中全会以来，中国的外交政策和改革开放赢得了蒙古人民的友谊

① 本文发表于1989年第12期的《北京民建》。

和支持的缘故。

苏联——地域辽阔的国家

列车在蒙古人民共和国境内急驰了一天一夜，于 9 月 2 日上午 10 时半进入苏联边境城市多卓尔内。

苏联的领土横跨欧亚大陆，西濒波罗的海，东临白令海峡，北靠北冰洋，面积 2 200 万平方千米，人口约二亿八千万。记得 20 世纪 50 年代有一首苏联歌曲唱道："我们的领土多么辽阔广大，她有无数田野和森林。"这次乘车赴苏，使我对这个世界上面积最大的国家有了真实感受。在列车 15 分钟停车时间，我们都将目光投向窗外，紧张地等待着在这个熟悉而又陌生的国家里将会发生的一切。不一会儿，边防军、海关和检疫人员鱼贯登上车厢，出人意料的是，这些头戴大檐帽、脚蹬长筒靴的大个子士兵十分和气而有礼貌，在我们按照要求交验护照和黄皮书（检疫书）填写入境卡片和携带物品申报单后说声"谢谢，再见"就离开了。那位金发碧眼的白衣小姐还不时地向我们示以亲切的微笑，一切都很顺利。这使我们紧张的心情顿时轻松下来。"三检"过后，一位 50 多岁的苏联车长还特意来到我们中国人的车厢，逐个包厢看望，互赠些小礼品，他还不时地开些幽默的玩笑，车厢里洋溢着中苏人民的友好气氛。

11 时左右，车到纳乌什基，停车两个多小时，由于我们大多数人都是第一次踏上苏联的土地，所以决定下车去看看。这是一个十分整洁而宁静的边境小站，候车室是一座典型的尖顶俄罗斯建筑，红的墙蓝的房顶在秋阳下格外醒目。室内餐厅、售票处和小卖部收拾得整整齐齐。正厅内的一排排长椅上有几十个人在候车。令人奇怪的是，这些男男女女竟是如此的安静有序，正襟端坐，连小孩子也规规矩矩地偎依在大人身边。没有人吸烟，没有人吐痰，没有人乱扔纸屑，地面上干干净净。很少有人说话，即使交谈，也是轻声细语，让对方听清为止，就像学生在上课。离开纳乌什基，列车在茫茫的西伯利亚急驰。一觉醒来，已是次日早晨 8 点钟（莫斯科时间 3 点钟，与北京时差为 5 小时）。"快看呀，贝加尔湖！"不知是谁孩子似地叫了一声。我兴奋地一跃而起，从右侧窗外映入眼帘的是一片汪洋，万顷碧波，遥接着湛蓝湛蓝的天空。车窗离湖最近处只有几米远，湖水澄澈清冽，岸边湖底的鹅卵石历历可数，据说透明度可深达40米。少时学地理知道，这个有“西伯利亚明眸”美称的天然大湖是好几十万年前由于地层断裂陷落而形成的，从地图上看，它就像一条啃吃桑叶的卧蚕，面积有三万多平方千米，相当于中国台湾那么大，最深处达1 620米，是世界上最深和蓄水量最大的淡水湖。据中国古书记载，贝加尔湖称为“北海”，曾是中国古代北方民族的主要活动地区。汉朝使节苏武出使匈奴，被扣在此，饮雪吞毡，牧羊一十九年，最终返回祖国。这个古老的故事更增加了贝加尔湖的神奇和梦幻般色彩。如今斗转星移，但这位古代民族英雄出使异域，不屈使命的凛然爱国气节，仍使我这个出国学子钦佩不已。

火车沿着湖岸走了约四个小时，到了下午，只见铁路两旁青山环抱，大片大片的森林连绵不绝，白桦、白杨、冷杉、落叶松等形成一道道森林屏障，从西伯利亚，经莫斯科直到东欧平原北部，绵延数千千米。其中尤以白桦树惹人喜欢，那高耸的树干笔直挺立，那洁白的树皮在阳光下闪着光，难怪苏联人常用“小白桦”当作剧团、歌舞团的名字，而一些高档的特供商店更被冠以“小白桦”的美名。

据资料记载，苏联拥有22%的世界森林资源，森林面积7.47亿公顷，森林覆盖率为33%，木材总蓄积量为795亿立方米，占世界木材总蓄积量的32.3%，居世界之首。为了保护和发展森林资源，苏联政府采取了许多政策和措施：建立专门机构对采伐工作进行严格监督和检查；对过熟林和成熟林进行有计划的砍伐，以保证幼林的充分发展和增加国民收入；动员全体人民积极开展植树造林活动（近几年苏联造林活动取得成效，每年增加森林面积200万～290万公顷）；对护林和造林成绩突出者进行奖励，对破坏森林者进行批评和处罚，情节严重者要受到法律制裁。可惜的是，苏联的森林虽然丰富，而以木材为原料的造纸业却非常落后，每年要花费大量外汇进口纸张，苏联年人均用纸量为35千克，仅为美国的1/8，居世界第42位，与一个工业大国的地位实在不相称。这也许是苏联在传统上不重视轻工业的缘故。

列车经过了西伯利亚铁路和航空中心，拥有100万人口的工业城市伊尔库茨克，于9月3日凌晨到了叶尼塞河。苏联地形，以叶尼塞河为界分为东西两部分，西部主要是平原，东部多高原山地。火车穿过叶尼塞河，折转向西，由人烟稀少的中西伯利亚高原进入一马平川的西伯利亚平原。这里地势平坦，人口较为稠密，是苏联农业较发达地区。在一道道绿色的林荫带里镶嵌着大片大片的农田，宛如一幅幅美丽的油画，间或有被翻耕的土地闪着黑黝黝的亮光。据统计，苏联有耕地34亿亩，由于苏联劳动力不足，利用土地采取广种薄收、粗放型的经营方法，加之管理不善，以致产量很低，1935年粮食产量只有1.9亿吨，只相当于美国的55%。每年不得不从国外大量进口粮食。

9月4日晨7时，列车开到秋明，这里石油储量丰富，是苏联著名的石油城。在秋明，我们看到铁路旁的一座小木房子上写着："实行改革人人有责"的标语，这是我进入苏联境内看到的第一条标语，接着又看到第二条、第三条标语："改革是巩固和发展社会主义的唯一道路"，"越是改革，越是接近列宁主义"……，我十分高兴，这是一个来自改革开放的社会主义中国的学者对一个实行改革政策的邻邦产生的共鸣。

在车站的一旁，一些提着小篮子卖东西的老大娘正同旅客讨价还价，篮子里有榛子、野葡萄、胡萝卜、西红柿、黄瓜等。还有的在一旁摆摊，出售各种花花绿绿的俄罗斯工艺品。她们都说自己是拿养老金的老太太，在家闲着没事，出来挣些零花钱。她们凭经验知道我们这些中国人往往光看不买，但同我谈话时还是面带笑容，不怕耽误生意。

车站的另一旁，有几处小棚子，里面一些小伙子和姑娘们一边做大饼、烤羊肉串，一边高声叫卖。这些坦率的苏联人还主动地自我介绍说，他们都是新开张的个体户。我看着那一张张兴高采烈的脸，心想他们也许是苏联经济体制改革的第一批受益者吧。

列车经过斯维尔德洛夫斯克城不久，即穿过乌拉尔山的欧亚分界线进入苏联的欧洲部分。这里人烟稠密、土地肥沃，充满了生机，是苏联政治和经济的核心地区，全国3/4的工业和人口，以及大部分城市包括莫斯科都集中在这里。

列车急驰了六天五夜，穿过了广袤的西伯利亚，波状起伏的东欧平原，跨过了叶尼塞河、鄂毕河、伏尔加河三大河流，行程7 800千米，终于在9月5日11时45分准时抵达苏联首都莫斯科。我将在这里度过近一年的学习和工作生活。（待续）

莫斯科印象（一）①

——访苏见闻（续一）

苏联首都莫斯科位于苏联欧洲部分的中部，是苏联的政治、经济、文化和交通的中心。莫斯科又是个古老而现代化的城市，它自从1147年人们第一次提起它的名字起，至今已有842年的历史。近几十年市区的面貌发生了巨大变化，特别是在郊区一幢幢现代化高层建筑拔地而起，如今的莫斯科已是一个辖31区、南北长40千米、东西宽30千米、面积879平方千米、约800万人口的特大城市。

绿荫掩映的城市

莫斯科留给我印象最深的是出色的环境保护。如果你从高处俯瞰大地，就会发现莫斯科掩映在莽莽苍苍、一望无际的大森林里。郊区小丘上数不清的绵延的防护林带，形成一道道绿色的屏障，一座座青砖红瓦的小别墅就如万绿丛中的点点红花。到了深秋，大片大片树林红、黄、绿相间，斑驳陆离，莫斯科简直成了金黄的世界。

住在莫斯科，你不会感到大都市的喧嚣，市内到处都有街心公园、花坛和草地，很少有地表裸露的地方。在一些住宅区，房舍之间也种植树木和草坪，树丛中摆放着一排排长椅，或者架设一些别致的小木屋、秋千、平衡木什么的，供老人休息和孩子玩耍。在市内还辟有森林公园，园中树木草地都不加修剪，任凭自生自落，那情形就像是原始森林保护区，据说这是为了使市民足不出城就能领略到大自然的情趣。

苏联拥有22%的世界森林资源，森林覆盖率为33%，木材总蓄积量居世界之首。但苏联人对林木从不滥采滥伐，莫斯科人对大自然更是爱护备至，从未见过人随意攀折损害树木，在公园里，也很难看到践踏草地和攀摘花木的现象。

莫斯科的居民还喜欢种草养花。在家家户户的阳台上都可以看到一盆盆花草争奇斗艳。工作人员的办公桌上的瓶内也总是插着几束鲜花，或种些青藤，

① 本文发表于1990年第1期的《北京民建》。

任其在室内攀缘附生，借以美化工作环境。出色的环境不仅表现在卓有成效的环境绿化方面，还表现于对污染的治理。莫斯科是苏联最大的综合性工业中心。可你在那里看不到冒黑烟的大烟囱，也看不到被污染的河水和池塘，马路上也较少闻到汽车排放的呛人气味，空中透明度也高。站在高楼上极目远眺，可清晰地看到远处鳞次栉比的建筑群，教堂上的十字架在阳光下闪闪发光。市里空气新鲜，没有风沙，一件白衬衫穿上几天不换还是洁白的，有时到外地出差，一周后回来，办公桌还很干净。

优美的环境自然会招引各种益鸟良禽来此栖息。郊外，你看到最多的是乌鸦和喜鹊。一天我乘车外出，看到公路两旁树上黑压压的鸦巢，连成一片，其中一棵树上竟有几十个鸦巢。那些乌鸦又肥又大，羽毛发亮，有时数以千计，在空中盘旋，这情景使人有置身于原始旷野之感。中国有句俗话："天下乌鸦一般黑"，可奇怪的是我竟然在那里看到不少全身洁白的黑脖子乌鸦。还有很多乌鸦飞到城里栖息和觅食，它们大摇大摆旁若无人地横过马路，甚至飞到卧室的窗台将人吵醒。那丑陋的样子、聒耳的叫声固然惹人心烦，但也为都市增添了不少野趣。

莫斯科市内则是鸽子的天下，成千上万只在空中飞翔，时而落在你脚下觅食。如果你拿出一块面包，马上就会有几十只甚至上百只的鸽子朝你飞来，将你包围，甚至落在你的手上、肩上，比家养的还温驯。

著名的莫斯科河流经整个莫斯科市，并联通东欧平原上的伏尔加等诸多河流。当你乘坐大型游艇饱览两岸秀丽景色时，可以看到河水清澈，游鱼历历可数，那些自由自在的野鸭水鸟或成双成对，或三五成群，依偎漫游，时而相啄而嬉，显得悠然自在。

莫斯科的大人小孩都有爱鸟的习惯，不但没有人伤害、捕杀，就连吓唬一下的现象也没有。而且，他们总是设法保护鸟。有的鸽子误飞到地下过街道里或地铁站里，他们就捉住放飞。我还看见一位小车司机把车停下来驱赶前面一群贪吃的鸽子，以免将它们碰伤。这些鸟大概凭经验知道，人类是愿意与它们"和平共处"的，所以它们才不躲人、不怕人，做人的好朋友。

莫斯科印象（二）①

——访苏见闻（续二）

世界上第一流的地铁

莫斯科还是一个交通方便、四通八达的城市。它有十一个火车站，十几条铁路呈放射状通向全国的四面八方。郊外则有电力火车（实际上是大型的有轨电车）环莫斯科而行，通往各个名胜古迹。

市内交通除了公共汽车、电车和有轨电车承担48%的客运任务外，剩下的就要靠地铁了。莫斯科地铁堪称世界一流。它于1935年开始动工兴建，目前由一条环线和七条直线交织而成，状如蛛网；总长度约为220千米。沿线有130个站，每隔50秒即有一列车到站，一昼夜客运量为600万人次（北京地铁节假日高峰时一昼夜为112万人次）占莫斯科客运总量的43%，居世界第一位。在两条以上线路的交叉处，车站分为三层，乘客由自动电扶梯上下，并可经过天桥随意转车，不用出站即可到达莫斯科任何一个街区，所以你如果在莫斯科迷了路，尽可以往地铁里跑，就能到达目的地。现在莫斯科地铁还在扩建，预计到2000年，建成一个直线和环线相结合的地铁系统，长度达到360千米。

莫斯科地铁也是世界上最漂亮的地铁之一。走进站内，仿佛置身于一座富丽堂皇的地下宫殿。车站高大宽敞，四壁和一桩桩巨大支柱用大理石镶砌而成。栩栩如生的浮雕和五颜六色壁画目不暇接，各式各样的吊灯和壁灯，令人眼花缭乱。每个站式样各异，无一雷同，展示着俄罗斯和苏联的历史和文化，也反映着苏联劳动人民的智慧和才能。

莫斯科居民拥有私人小汽车50万～60万辆，平均每3～4家有一辆。这些小汽车全部是苏联国产货，多为“拉达”和“伏尔加”。每辆车价格8 000卢布左右，相当于一个副教授两年的工资，所以很多莫斯科人是买得起的。但由于产量少，据说要排队10年才能买到一部。

由于莫斯科形成了一个以地铁为主的四通八达的交通网络，所以平时并不

① 本文发表于1990年第2期的《北京民建》。

太拥挤，一般车上都有座位。但到上下班高峰时公共汽车和电车上人也很多，特别是地铁站内乘客如云，即使在这时，人们也都能遵守纪律自觉排队，先下后上，互相照顾似乎已成了社会公德。车厢内写着“年长者与残疾人专座”也能做到名副其实。一些中小学生自觉为老年人让座也已成了习惯。我还不止一次地看到佩戴两杠四星肩章、手提公文箱的大校军官也自觉站着，不与老百姓争座位。即使乘客再多，车内也是安静的，许多人都利用乘车时间阅读书报杂志，从不大声喧嚷，更无吵骂打架现象发生。

莫斯科的公共交通全是自动化服务，而且票价低廉，不管是公共汽车票、电车票，还是地铁票，每张一律五戈比（相当我国五分钱），而且可以坐遍全程。公共汽车、电车没有售票员，只有一名司机开车兼管售票。乘客可向司机购票，或者到售票亭（站）去买，一些商业网点或摊位也出售车票，一联 10 张，共 50 戈比。乘客上车后自动到车内打票器上打一下孔就算交验票了，如果你离得远，会同时伸出几只手帮助你。在地铁入口处，你只要将一枚 5 戈比硬币塞进小铁门一旁的小孔里，绿灯一闪就可以通过；你如果不交钱，红灯一亮，你的一条腿就被夹住。

当然，由于车上无人售票，靠乘客自我服务，个别逃票现象还是有的。据说，苏联有的地方对公共汽车票实行了抽彩出售的新办法。中彩者可持中彩车票领到彩电、收录机等贵重物品。实行抽彩后，不但逃票者明显减少，而且车站也很准见到随地乱扔废票的现象了。

对诚信问题的几点思考①

近几年，诚信已经成为我国社会最热门的话题之一。如果诚信问题不能很好地解决，那对我国现代市场体系的建立和完善，对实现全面建设小康社会的目标都将会产生不利的影响。党的十六届三中全会指出：“建立健全社会信用体系。形成以道德为支撑、产权为基础、法律为保障的社会信用制度，是建设现代市场体系的必要条件，也是规范市场经济秩序的治本之策。”最近，胡锦涛总书记提出的以“八荣八耻”为主要内容的社会主义荣辱观，也明确提出了“以

① 应邀在北京大学举办的诚信问题论坛会议上的讲演，2006 年 4 月 6 日于人民大会堂。

诚实守信为荣”。我从以下几方面谈一谈对诚信问题的思考。

一、什么是诚信

在中国传统道德体系中，诚信是一种重要的道德规范，诚信是人与人之间交往的基本道德准则。诚信是诚与信的统一，《说文解字》中解释说：“信，诚也”，“诚，信也”。《管子·枢言》云：“诚信者，天下之结也。”意思是说诚实守信，是治国的关键，是人与人之间连接的纽带，是凝聚人心的保证。

诚信是道德范畴和制度范畴的统一。作为全体公民都应该遵循的基本道德规范，诚信基本内容是诚实、诚恳、信用、信任，也就是忠诚老实、诚恳待人、严守信用、信任他人。

依据现代经济学的视角，诚信是市场经济领域中的基础性行为，是基于特定条件下经济主体间普遍遵守和履行契约的均衡状态。诚信度对市场经济的交易成本有着重要的影响，如果没有这种信用基础，市场中的交易就无法完成。

二、当前我国诚信危机的种种表现

由于经济主体违背诚信原则，打破了普遍遵守和履行契约的均衡状态，造成社会效率的损失与交易成本的上升，产生了诚信危机。近些年来，由于经济体制转轨、公共政策缺位等多种原因，诚信危机几乎渗透到我国经济社会生活的方方面面。各种不讲诚信的表现主要可分为以下几类。

（1）经济生活的诚信危机。例如：在商品、金融领域中制售假冒伪劣商品、各种虚假的广告宣传、侵害知识产权、价格欺诈、非法集资等现象；受利益驱动，在会计审计、法律服务、评估监理等领域中，出现违反独立、公正、诚实的基本职业道德的现象，损害了国家和群众利益。

（2）公共管理的诚信危机。一些地方和政府部门，还存在以权谋私、权钱交易、形式主义、浮夸虚报、朝令夕改等现象，干扰了社会发展的正常秩序，破坏了公共政策的权威。

（3）教育领域的诚信危机。部分学生乃至教师诚信缺失，存在学术失范、拖欠助学贷款、评选奖学金弄虚作假、考试作弊等不良现象。

（4）个人交往中的诚信危机。许多人急功近利，言而无信，甚至坑蒙拐骗，导致人与人的交往缺乏相互信任，造成诚信危机。

三、我国现阶段诚信危机的成因

（1）经济体制转轨引起的诚信危机。计划经济时期，资源分配集中，一方面压抑了人的物质需求，另一方面损人利己、谋取私利的空间较小。市场经济使人们欲望得到极大的张扬和释放，在利益机制驱动和政策缺位的情况下，损人利己、谋取私利的机会增多，导致失信行为的发生。

（2）失信成本低，守信者未得到有效的保护。失信者未得到严厉的制裁，以致形成逆向淘汰。

（3）存在政府职能错位、缺位、越位现象，造成政府的信用缺失。政府对信用资源的垄断和对企业的隐性担保助长了企业失信（如地方保护主义对失信企业的保护等现象）；政策稳定性差，承诺不能兑现；法律制度不健全等。

（4）其他文化道德、社会心理方面的原因。

四、"软""硬"兼施，构建诚信社会

诚信可以降低交易成本、减少投机行为，是确保市场经济得以高效运行的基本要素，建设和谐社会、建立市场经济体系，必然要解决各种诚信危机。诚信问题不是中国独有，也不是经济转轨国家独有，西方发达国家也存在有关诚信缺失的现象（如"安然事件""巴林银行事件"等），但由于这些国家具有完善制度体系，各种失信行为存在较小的生存空间。结合中国国情，我认为，建设诚信社会需要"软""硬"兼施。

（一）"软约束"——诚信的诱致性制度安排

诱致性制度安排是一种自发的渐进性制度安排，是一种"软约束"。在潜在收益诱导下，经济主体通过守信与失信的收益权衡和长期博弈，逐步形成覆盖全社会的诚信规则，实现信用均衡。失信的经济主体因诱致性制度安排丧失生存空间，自发遵循诚信规则。例如：企业以次充好，欺骗消费者，造成产品积压，利润的下降迫使其遵守诚信，逐步重新建立企业信誉。诱致性制度安排的效果具有长期性，有利于整个社会诚信体系的建立；其缺点在于作用速度较慢、交易费用较高、安排效率较低，往往在产生巨大的效率损失后才回归诚信均衡。

（二）“硬要求”——诚信的强制性制度安排

构建适应市场经济要求的强制性制度安排是解决诚信问题的“硬要求”。由政府依法建立社会信任框架，运用国家强制力推动建立诚信规则。失信的经济主体因强制性制度安排产生较高的失信成本，被迫遵循诚信规则。由于国家强制力的优势，诚信的强制性制度安排具有效率高、交易成本低、作用速度快等优点。例如：国家制定实施《消费者权益保护法》，强制假冒伪劣产品退市，维护商业诚信。强制性制度安排存在政府理性的可靠性、政策的滞后性、知识的局限性等问题，不一定能够及时建立最有效的制度安排。

（三）“软”“硬”兼施，构建诚信社会

构建符合市场经济要求的诚信社会，必须“软”“硬”兼施，诱致性制度安排与强制性制度安排并存互补、自律与他律相结合，要充分重视舆论的导向作用、政府的规范作用，加强诚信教育以及诚信制度和社会信用体系建设，使经济主体自觉遵循诚信规则。

当前我国诚信危机的产生原因很复杂，建设诚信社会的要求也非常迫切，可喜的是社会各界已经认识到诚实守信的重要性（如《北京市社会信用体系建设方案》于去年（2005 年）年底颁布实施），各种失信行为必将丧失生存空间，我们一定能够建成符合市场经济要求的诚信社会。

五年实现国民收入倍增①

从深层次对收入分配进行调整，已经成为深化改革的当务之急，也将是决定“结构调整之年”成败的关键环节。有人提议中国也应该搞“国民收入倍增计划”，预计在未来 5～6 年使居民收入翻一番，美好蓝图引来广泛关注，为此，本刊记者与国务院参事、北京交通大学经济管理学院博士生导师袁伦渠教授进行了对话。

记者：对于在中国搞“国民收入倍增计划”的提议，您怎么看？

袁伦渠：我认为很有必要。这一计划是日本于 1960 年提出并实施的，效

① 2010 年 7 月 3 日接受人民日报社主管主办的《民生周刊》记者崔靖芳的采访，此文发表在该刊 2010 年 7 月 3 日（试刊）。

果还不错，从 1960 年到 1973 年，日本人均实际国民收入甚至增加了两倍。近年来，我国国内生产总值迅速增长，但居民收入占 GDP 的比重和劳动报酬占初次分配的比重却逐年下降，提高居民收入已迫在眉睫，当前的中国适时推出“国民收入倍增计划”可以达到类似的效果。但是我认为就我国的社会制度而言，该计划称“居民收入倍增计划”更合适。

记者：您认为 5 年内可以实现居民收入倍增的目标吗？

袁伦渠：完全可以实现。按照国家统计局 2009 年统计年鉴提供的最新数据计算，2008 年我国居民年平均收入为 11 436.38 元，居民可支配收入占 GDP 的比重为 50.39%。依据我国目前的经济增长速度及相关部门预期，到 2015 年我国经济平均增长速度为 8%左右，那么，2015 年 GDP 约为 51.9 万亿元，如果到 2015 年居民可支配收入占 GDP 比重达到 60%左右，居民年平均收入也将达到 22 388.40 元，基本实现人均可支配收入翻一番的目标。

记者：有人认为国家不可能通过行政手段干预企业的工资标准，唯有通过首先提高公务员的工资标准，来带动整个社会的工资上涨，您认为这一计划是否应该首先考虑公务员？

袁伦渠：公众对公务员相对完善的社会保障早已颇多热议，首先考虑公务员恐怕不妥，会引起不安定的因素，我认为首先应该考虑低收入者，如农民工。提高最低工资标准，并保证每年 20%～25%的增长比例。

记者：过多使用行政手段干预经济是否会造成新的市场扭曲，产生额外的风险，例如导致通胀？

袁伦渠：我认为国家通过行政手段只是对利益关系的调整，实际上是从富裕阶层手中拿出一部分货币给低收入者，而总的货币量并没有增加，不会导致通胀。

记者：有部委拟建言通过减税助企业提高工资，您认为这是调节收入的好办法吗？

袁伦渠：对于那些充分竞争行业的中小企业的确应该降低税收，但对某些群体我认为应该增税。

记者：增税？这个说法很新鲜，能否谈谈您的理由？

袁伦渠：这一计划不能只看重平均数的增长，更要重视增长的质量与内涵。唯有逐步缩小不同群体的收入差距，使其协调发展，才是“居民收入倍增计划”的最终目标。社会财富总量是有限的，唯有控制高收入者的收入，才更有利于使财富流向低收入者。我建议实行个人收入累进税率。在英国，年薪在 4 800 英镑以下的低收入者不用纳税，超过部分分三个等级按不同比例纳税，最高税率为40%；目前，美国个人所得税采用六级超额累进税率结构，最高税率为35%，芬兰高收入者的最高税率高达 60%，仅累进税一项，就使得最低和最高收入群体的收入差距大幅度缩小。

在中国开征遗产税和赠与税也是缩小收入差距的重要手段。日本现行遗产税率从 10%～70%共分 13 个档次，通过这两项税的征收，防止财富集中到少数人手中，对建设橄榄型社会起到至关重要的作用。

记者：除此之外，您还有哪些建议？

袁伦渠：首先，提高劳动收入在初次分配中的比重。通过提高最低工资标准，逐步缩小农民工与城镇职工之间、劳动派遣工与企业正式职工之间的收入差距；尽快制定和发布全国工资指导意见，建议将工资性收入之外的资本性收入、股权收益等纳入工资指导线的调控范围；积极推进行业性集体协商制度；控制国有企业高管，特别是垄断行业高管的收入，将其收入和福利全部货币化，隐性收入显性化。

其次，通过提高个人收入调节税的起征点，来完善个人税收制度，同时不断健全社会保障体系，使蛋糕在第二次分配中切割得更合理。

庆祝《人口与经济》创刊30周年暨全国“人口、就业和社会保障”学术研讨会致辞[①]

各位领导，各位学术前辈，各位教授，各位同学，各位朋友，大家上午好！

我怀着十分兴奋的心情，参加庆祝《人口与经济》创刊30周年暨全国“人口、就业和社会保障”学术研讨会。

大家记得，党的十一届三中全会以后，学术界受科学春天的鼓舞，被压抑蛰伏多年的学术刊物如雨后春笋破土而出，争艳斗丽，1980年创刊的《人口与经济》正是这个学术百花园中的一枝奇葩。回想《人口与经济》创刊的日子，真叫我激动不已，仿佛又会到30年前我年富力强、朝气蓬勃的岁月，就在那一年，1980年9月15日出版的《人口与经济》第一期（创刊号）上刊登了我与人合译的《人口知识体系导论》（共6页约9 000字），1986年第3期上又刊登了我写的《世界主要国家老年退休制度》一文，这两篇文章是我“文化大革命”后初次发表的文章，虽然水平不高，但承蒙《人口与经济》编辑部厚爱，使我受到极大的鼓舞，从此《人口与经济》杂志如一个助推器使我焕发了勇气和热情。先后在中国社科院《中国工业经济》杂志创刊号上，以及和于光远先生主持的《经济研究参考》发表了一系列与人口经济有关的文章。我感激《人口与经济》，我热爱《人口与经济》。30年来，我辗转了几个单位，搬了多次家，其他书籍丢了不少，唯独这两本《人口与经济》如宝贝一样留在我身边，尽管发了黄（当时在大会上展示《人口与经济》1980年创刊号时引起百余与会者的热烈鼓掌）。

《人口与经济》自1980年创刊以来，始终坚持“学术民主、繁荣发展中国人口科学”的宗旨，本着公平公正的办刊原则，形成了自己的风格和特色，成为我国学术界有重要影响的核心刊物，立于中国学术刊物之林。

人口学是研究人类自身生产和再生产的科学，他研究人口的质量和数量，研究人口变动及其规律，研究人口问题和人口政策。但是人口学的研究并不是孤立的，他和社会经济有着密切的联系。例如，他研究人口变动与经济发展的

① 在中国人口学会首都经济贸易大学举办的《中国人口与经济》创刊30周年庆祝会上的发言，2010年10月23日于北京会议中心。

关系，研究城乡统筹发展中的人口问题，研究人口老龄化与社会养老保险的关系，研究人口与就业的关系等。30年来，《人口与经济》正是在研究人口理论、介绍人口知识、宣传国家的人口政策和计划生育政策、维护社会的和谐和稳定方面发挥了其他刊物不可代替的作用。

最近召开的党的十七届三中全会和会上通过的《经济社会发展十二五规划纲要》都提出了计划生育作为基本国策的原则。今年，适逢“中共中央国务院关于控制我国人口增长问题对全体共产党员、共青团员公开信”发表30周年，信中曾提出“到了30年后，目前特别紧张的人口增长问题就可以缓和，也就可以采取不同的人口政策”，这时的计划生育政策再次为社会和公众所关注，许多人就稳定生育政策提出了建议，也有人主张有必要改变生育政策，放开二孩生育。在这种情况下，如何保持人口的基本稳定，成为人口学家研究的问题。

我祝愿我们的《人口与经济》今后越办越好，刊登更多更好的理论文章，提供更多的人口研究信息，为人口决策部门提供理论上的支持和实际操作的手段，成为引领人口学术研究的基地。我也希望能在这次学术会议上，向专家们学到更多的有关人口、就业和社会保障的理论与知识。

最后，祝《人口与经济》创刊30周年暨全国“人口、就业和社会保障”学术研讨会圆满成功！

在“新形势下劳动标准与人力资源管理研讨会”上的发言①

各位领导，各位专家，各位教授：

大家上午好！非常高兴参加今天的研讨会，说起定额定员，我真地不如孙义敏教授那样进行过深入的研究和探讨，更不具备各位领导的实践经验。但是我几十年一直从事劳动经济学的教学和研究，对劳动定额定员的研究及应用十分关注。主办单位邀请我参加此次研讨会，引起我对劳动定额定员的一系列的联想。劳动定额与劳动定员，其实就是劳动标准。劳动定额原为美国工程师泰

① 在全国劳动定员定额标准化委员会、中国劳动保障科学研究院、首都经济贸易大学劳动经济学院举办的学术会上的讲演，2010年11月20日于北京会议中心。

勒的发明和使用，劳动定额的概念是从20世纪50年代初苏联教科书中引用而来，而编制定员则是我国自己的创造。20世纪60年代的教科书认为，劳动定额定员是劳动组织的组成部分，而劳动组织又是劳动经济学的重要内容。我第一次知道劳动定额定员的概念是在大二时，在北京经济学院陈平老师的讲堂上。所谓定额，是指在一定的生产技术条件下，采用科学合理的方法，对生产合格产品或完成一定工作量所预先规定的劳动消耗量标准。还记得关于定额水平的表述，究竟用先进合理还是平均先进表述为好，大家引起了争论。陈平老师说，还是先进合理好！那就是在正常条件下，多数工人经过努力能够达到，部分工人能够接近，少数工人能够超过的水平，并且用”跳一跳摘果子”来打比方，这是多么简明易懂的表述。还记得在学习技术测定法时，我们学生手握秒表对工人的一举一动进行测时，甚至跟到厕所里去测时间，这些似乎不近情理的做法说明了当时做学问的认真和科学态度。还有的说“赚钱不赚钱，全靠定额定员”，这就说明定额定员的重要性。这些50年前近乎幽默活泼可笑的情景，恍若隔世却又如在眼前。以后又读过孙义敏教授的专著，总觉得劳动定额是和陈平、孙义敏的名字连在一起。后来我们又听过建设部曹瑛司长、煤炭部赵汝晶司长、铁道部徐蓟昌司长的定额演讲，大四时我又随铁道部徐蓟昌司长去铁道部戚墅堰车辆厂实习，并在闻潜老师和赵经甫工程师的指导下，写出了《铁路企业劳动定额制定方法》的毕业论文。1964年，毕业分配到劳动部办公厅《劳动》杂志社工作，负责编写《劳动》杂志定额定员栏目。1978—1981年，我在翻译苏联劳动经济学教科书中又接触到劳动组织、劳动定额的翻译；我1987年撰写的《劳动经济学概论》、1988年撰写的《劳动组织学》都涉及定额定员的章节。1988年我留苏时，又听到导师伊万诺夫教授劳动定额的讲授。1990年，我撰写的《中国劳动经济史》又从历史角度叙述了我国劳动定额和劳动定员的沿革和发展变化。2001年，我作为《中国铁道百科全书——经济与运输卷》编委时，又组织编写了劳动组织、劳动定额、劳动定员等多个词条。2005年，又参与劳动部苏海南教授主持的《劳动标准研究》以及铁路公务系统劳动定员定额等工作的研究。

以上的经历使我感受到劳动定额定员的重要性，它对改善劳动组织、优化配置人力资源、搞好工资分配和提高企业效率发挥着十分重要的作用。劳动定员、劳动定额以及劳动组织本来就是劳动经济学研究的重要内容，可惜近些年由于某些经济研究领域向西方经济学过度的一边倒和食洋不化、玩弄脱离实际的花拳绣腿，将复杂的经济现象采用简单的模型公式曲线来表述。在劳动经济学研究中，竟将最具应用价值的定额定员删除，而用工作分析加以代替。在经济学、劳动经济学和人力资源管理的课堂上，再也听不到劳动定额、劳动定员的声音，在相关杂志上，也很少看到类似的文章，它只是在个别行业和企业发出微弱的声音。

我对劳动定员和劳动定额缺乏实际劳动经验，但我对它充满感情。所以得知全国专业标准化委员会成立时非常高兴，并欣然参加本次研讨会，希望在研讨会上向大家学习，获得一些关于劳动定额定员研究和应用的新进展的信息。比如最近听到一些令人困惑的说法：劳动定额产生是苏联计划经济的产物，与市场经济不适应，可以用工作分析代替它；劳动定额仅仅适用于工人，不适用于干部等。我正是带着这些疑问来此参加会议的，希望得到研讨会的关注。

在“北京师范大学人力资源圆桌研讨会”上的发言①

首先感谢北京师范大学经济与工商管理学院人力资源管理学院邀请我参加圆桌会议，并预祝会议圆满成功。

圆桌会议的召开很有意义，很有必要。过去我们常说，凡是有人的地方都有劳动管理问题，今天我们说，凡是有人的地方都有人力资源管理问题。因为政府机关、事业单位、企业组织、非政府组织都需要人力资源管理方面的人才，尤其需要高端人才。而人力资源管理人才的成长则需要人力资源管理专业的培养。当前人力资源管理专业的需求甚旺，人力资源学科的发展迅速，已有 200 余所学校开设人力资源专业。人力资源管理的研究涉及经济管理、公共管理、管理工程、劳动经济、人事心理及组织行为的理论和知识。既包括社会经济学科，也包括自然学科。但长期以来，人力资源管理的交流多在社会科学和财经院校之间进行，多涉及社会经济研究领域，在综合大学、理工大学之间交流较少。今天北师大人力资源管理学院特邀请北大、清华、人大、北理工、华北电力大学等著名高校的教授举行圆桌会议，共同交流和研究人力资源管理学科的

---

① 2011 年 4 月 22 日，在北京师范大学经济与工商管理学院主办的人力资源圆桌研讨会上的讲话。

建设问题，发挥理工科背景的人力资源学科的优势，我认为非常及时和必要。

本次圆桌会议拟订的五个议题反映了当前人力资源管理学科建设和学术研究的焦点及前沿趋势。可以通过与不同学科的对话交流，取长补短，优势互补，知识共享，进一步展开各校之间的合作。

本次圆桌会议提出在人力资源管理学科领域，开展的心理学、组织行为学、人力资本理论、教育经济、劳动经济学、制度经济以及跨文化管理的综合研究，加强彼此合作，从不同的角度研究人力资源管理，可以使人力资源管理研究视野拓宽，理论和实践深化。尤其值得一提的是，北师大人力资源管理学院依托北师大百年老校深厚的文化积淀，享誉国内外的心理学、教育学的优势，又有学院扎实的经济学基础、整齐的人员结构、合理的雄厚的师资队伍，以及丰富的教学科研成果和为社会服务的经验，相信很快将发展成为国内著名的、相当有影响力的人力资源管理学院。

我还想说一说心理学和教育学对人力资源管理学科的影响。在传统上，人力资源管理是依附于劳动经济学和企业管理学的，也就是说是从劳动经济学和企业管理学中分化出来的。20 世纪 60 年代，在我所学的劳动经济学专业当中，其主要课程《劳动经济学》中包括两部分内容，即劳动经济和劳动管理，在苏联劳动经济学中也是如此。当时人民大学企业管理系的《企业管理》课程中也有劳动管理部分（当时认为企业管理就是人财物的管理，即劳动力管理、财务管理、物资管理），北京经济学院劳动经济系和人民大学的企业管理系还存在究竟劳动管理属于谁、谁为主的争论，各有各的道理，结果是各开各的课。总的来说，劳动管理是劳动经济和企业管理的一部分。当时对劳动管理的认识仅限于通过劳动组织的整顿、管理来节约劳动力，而且管理的对象主要是指体力劳动者和工人。

改革开放后，随着市场经济体制的建立，引进西方的理念，叫“人力资源开发”，将人力资源开发代替了劳动力管理，扩大了内容，不再只涉及工人、农民等体力劳动者，还包括了脑力劳动者等所有劳动者，也不再把劳动者当作被管理的对象，而当成可开发利用的资源。这比过去单纯的劳动力管理先进了一步。将心理学和教育学理论引进人力资源管理，提出了开发和管理，使这一学科又有了新的进展。人力资源管理的对象是人，人是有思想有心理活动的，可以通过心理学的研究激发人的积极性，可以通过教育培养提高人的素质。这才使人力资源管理中有了开发的内容。将心理学与教育学引入人力资源学科的重要意义，可以通过一个例子来说明。去年，富士康“十二跳”的悲剧为什么会发生？不仅仅是因为劳动报酬低的问题，更重要的是员工的心理造成的，试想那些打工仔和打工妹成年累月地在流水线上工作，日复一日地重复同一个动作，单调枯燥产生的职业“倦怠”，看不到工作前景和前途会产生的绝望，人与人之间不能接触和交流甚至睡在一个房间里彼此也不相识、互不说话，所产生的寂寞与压抑，没有安全感、没有归属感、没有自尊所产生的生不如死的感觉，这些因素才促进了跳楼悲剧的产生。由此可见，在人力资源管理中引入心理学研究是多么重要。北师大人力资源管理学院有著名的心理学和教育学背景，可谓得天独厚的条件。

建筑节能，构建环境友好型社会①

环境是人类社会、经济、文化发展的重要基础，保护环境是人类最崇高、最有价值的行为，是落实科学发展观、构建环境友好型社会的重要举措。改革开放30多年来，我国经济发展保持了年均约10%的增长速度，综合国力跃居世界第二，人民生活水平不断提高。但也不能不看到，高速增长也付出了巨大的经济和环境代价。我国的经济增长方式落后、粗放，GDP的高度增长是靠高耗能、高污染，牺牲环境和生态换来的。有数据表明，2005年我国用世界上31%的煤、29%的石油、49%的水泥只产生了占世界6%的GDP。为了保证我国经济的可持续发展和人民的根本利益，国务院从2006年开始，正式启动“十一五”节能减排计划，制定了一系列节能减排政策，温家宝总理亲自担任节能减排工作领导小组组长，狠抓节能减排工作，完成了“十一五”期间国家下达的节能减排任务。我国“十二五”规划中提出，单位GDP能耗降低16%，这又是摆在我们面前的繁重任务。为落实完成这一任务，政府部门、企业、团体和个人开始行动起来，积极参与环保活动，其中北京光恒金泰工程技术有限公司举办的建筑节能研讨会就是这一活动的具体表现。

建筑业是我国产生GDP、提供税收和就业岗位的大户，也是国民经济的重

① 2011年6月15日在北京光恒金泰工程技术有限公司建筑节能研讨会上的发言。

要支柱产业。但是又是耗能大户。我国既有建筑面积约400亿平方米，随着经济社会发展和城镇化的进程，每年还要新增20亿平方米，超过所有发达国家每年建成面积的总和。我国建筑耗能占全国能源消费总量的28%。既有建筑中只有1%为节能建筑，80%以上属于高耗能建筑，由此可见，建筑节能在我国节能减排中承担十分重要的任务。建筑节能是实现节能减排和低碳发展模式的重要措施。

“十二五”期间节能减排任务的落实，除国家一系列方针、政策的落实外，还要靠采取一系列科学技术措施，特别是靠新技术的推动。北京光恒金泰工程技术有限公司提出：建筑节能具体指在建筑物的规划、设计、新建、改造和使用过程中执行节能标准，采用节能型的技术、工艺、设备、材料和产品，提高保温隔热性能、采暖供热和空调制冷系统效率，加强建筑物用能系统的运行管理，利用可再生能源，在保证室内热环境质量的前提下，减少供热、空调制冷制热、照明热水供应的能耗。北京光恒金泰工程技术有限公司提出的采暖空调节能、建筑排水节能设备和技术不仅能够减少能耗，而且能保证安全。不久前，央视新址大火、上海胶州路居民楼大火、沈阳皇朝万鑫国际大厦的大火等一系列建筑物特大火灾，给国家和人民群众生命财产带来重大损失。通过灾难事故的分析，我们发现，除了监督管理不利之外，在建筑物外墙使用了不当的易燃保温材料是造成这些建筑物发生火灾的共同原因。北京光恒金泰工程技术有限公司推出的设备和技术措施是既节能又安全的正确选择。

最后，我想介绍一篇我校一位博士生的博士论文，题目是《产业与环境——基于可持续发展的产业环保研究》。著名环保专家、原国家环保总局局长曲格平为此文写了序。这篇论文认为在实践中应该把环保与产业发展有机结合起来进行研究，该学生基于环境库兹涅茨曲线，提出了“假象拐点”的可能性。因为中国的资源条件不允许坐等人均国民收入1万美元时才出现环境质量的根本改善，新的发展模式的选择和新的环保技术的推广应用会使中国“环境拐点”大大提前。他基于环保经济效益的分析，论证了环保内生于产业发展，使产业主体在内部利益机制和外部导向机制的双重作用下，实现由被动到主动、由抵触到自觉进行环保转变的必要性。从理论和实践上，这是把环境和发展有机结合起来的新的和最有效的发展模式，因为环境经济本质上是一种生态经济，它要求运用生态学规律来指导经济活动，这与传统经济模式根本不同。传统经济是一种由资源—产品—消费—污染排放所构成的物质单向流动的线性经济，而循环经济是一种建立在不断循环利用基础上的发展模式，它要求把经济活动按照自然生态系统模式，组成一个资源—产品—消费—再生资源的物质反复环流的过程，要实现循环经济必须要有符合循环经济的设计，把经济效益和生态效益统一起来，充分使物质循环利用做到物尽其用。这必须依靠科技进步，更多地采用无公害新工艺、新技术，大力降低原材料和能源的消耗，实现少投入、高产出、低污染，尽可能把环境污染物的排放消除在生产过程中；必须充分利用资源，实行废弃物资源化、减量化和无害化，把有害环境的废弃物减少到最低限度。

因此可以说，在循环经济模式下，环保不仅仅是增加成本的投入，更是可能产生经济效益的源泉；经济与环境不是绝对的矛盾与对立，更有其内在的统一性，经济发展和环保是可以实现协调发展和双赢的，这种双赢有利于解决中国发展面临的矛盾与问题，有利于促进人与自然的和谐。

关于工人阶级的若干问题①

一、关于中国工人的主力军地位

在全国总工会十五届五次会议上，王兆国主席精辟概括的、胡锦涛总书记在全国劳模表彰会再次肯定的三十二个字可以深刻反映中国工人阶级的伟大品格，那就是：信心坚定、立场鲜明、艰苦奋斗、勇于拼搏、胸怀大局、纪律严明、开拓奉献、自强不息。

这种伟大品格也决定了中国工人阶级坚持和发展中国特色社会主义事业的主力军地位。具体表现在以下几方面。

（1）工人阶级是领导阶级。中国共产党章程指出：中国共产党是中国工人阶级的先锋队，中国共产党执政就是中国工人阶级执政。2004 年通过的《宪法》指出：中华人民共和国是工人阶级领导的，以工农联盟为基础的人民民主专政的国家。我国工会法也将维护工人阶级的权利，提到很高的地位。

① 应中宣部某刊物邀请，2011 年 4 月 30 日五一节前接受访谈。

（2）工人阶级是物质财富的主要创造者。近5年来，国民生产总值每年以10%以上的速度增长，2010年国民生产总值已达到39万多亿元，工人阶级功不可没。正如一首歌所唱的："我们工人有力量，盖起了高楼大厦，修起了铁路煤矿……"

（3）在新的历史时期，我国工人阶级具有主人翁责任感和使命感，勤奋学习，锐意进取，掌握新知识，练就新本领，如"抓斗大王"包起帆就是中国工人阶级的典型代表。

（4）工人是科学技术转化为现实生产力的关键人才。我们常说，科学技术是生产力，那么是谁将科学家的发明创造转化为现实的生产力呢？那就是技术工人。技术工人是将科学技术转化为现实生产力的实践者和操作者。

二、关于倡导劳动观

劳动创造了世界，劳动创造了人类，劳动是人类最基本的实践活动。可是近几年来，轻视体力劳动，轻视劳动人民的现象越来越严重，我们教育中的大问题是劳动观的缺失。从小学到中学，以至大学，很少有热爱劳动、热爱劳动人民的教育，很少宣传让学生当工人的，中小学生的课余活动就是吹拉弹唱，绘画跳舞。大学生不参加劳动，打扫卫生全部由农民工担任，评奖指标中，劳动因素几乎为零。这种轻视体力劳动的现象再也不能继续下去，为此建议：第一，各级学校都应进行热爱劳动、热爱劳动人民的教育。第二，尽可能组织学生参加各种社会实践和社会劳动。

三、关于工人阶级的层次问题

据中国青少年发展报告显示，当今我国只有4%的青少年愿意当技术工人，想当老板的青年是想当技术工人的青年的4倍。在中国很多家长要求孩子"非大学不上，非名牌大学不上，非热门专业不上"，很少考虑社会的需要和学生的特长。第一线的技术工人不被重视，职业教育不受重视，在源头上堵塞了技术工人的产生。重学历轻技术，鄙薄技术工人，忽视技术工人的培养。因此必须首先更新观念，加快技术工人的队伍建设。技术工人是分层次的，不同层次的技术工人构成人力资源缺一不可的体系，没有高低贵贱之分。高级工程技术人员是人才，高级管理人员是人才，技术工人同样是人才，也都是工人阶级。应当大力宣传和表彰技术工人在国家经济建设、企业技术革新、解决生产技术难题中发挥的重要作用，促成全社会尊重工人阶级、尊重技术工人的风气。

政府要创造机会，让不同层次的工人有上下流动的机会，让工人有终身学习的机会。

“十二五”规划的目标是转换经济发展方式，调整经济结构，通过科技进步和产业优化升级实现经济的增长。推动生产力发展是中国工人阶级先进性的具体表现。实现“十二五”规划的宏伟蓝图，离不开以工人阶级为主的广大劳动者的共同奋斗。中国工人阶级具有强烈的主人翁责任感，具有忘我劳动、爱岗敬业的精神，具有积极主动，勇于创新的大智大勇，具有顾全大局、艰苦奋斗、与时俱进的优秀品格。这是我国实现“十二五”规划的基本保证。

我们党和国家尊重工人阶级的劳动、知识和创造精神，正通过实施重点行业和领域的创新人才培养工程提高工人的劳动技能；通过制定劳动法、劳动合同法、社会保险法、安全生产法等一系列法律法规，以及坚持和完善企业职工代表大会制度等，维护工人阶级的合法权益。采取以上政策措施，保证了工人阶级在实现“十二五”规划蓝图中发挥主力军的作用。

雇主品牌构建之浅见[①]

时下有这样一种说法：三流的企业做产品，二流的企业做市场，一流的企业做品牌。这是人们对现代企业发展趋势和社会效应的直观的评价和描述，也说明品牌对企业发展的重要性。

一、企业品牌的构建应有自己的特色

所谓企业品牌是指企业对其提供的货物和劳务所定的名称、术语、记号、象征或其组合，主要供消费者识别所用。企业将其品牌在政府有关主管部门注册登记后即成为商标。以上是我对企业品牌含义的理解。不可将品牌简单理解为公司的招牌、一种产品的牌子。好的品牌应有自己的特色，品牌特色是品牌

① 在第七届中国雇主品牌论坛学术会上的发言，2012 年 12 月 7 日于北京会议中心。

的个性和生命力，因为在“天下熙熙皆为利来，天下攘攘皆为利往”的物欲横流的年代，各种广告的喧嚣、信息的杂乱往往会造成鱼龙混杂、以假乱真，因此品牌的特色和个性就显得十分重要。

品牌是消费者对产品质量和服务的认知。麦当劳品牌虽然是大众品牌，但它们以自己的特色取胜。一个小小的汉堡包风靡全球。当你走进麦当劳，会感到一种活泼、洁净、轻松的氛围，其标准化在全世界独一无二。在国外，你如果感到内急找不到卫生间，你尽可以往麦当劳店里跑，他们不会拒绝你，这就是他们的特色。可口可乐之所以称为全球最成功的品牌之一，是他们将代表着美国文化的精神揉进了品牌之中。迪士尼公司的产品并不便宜但受欢迎，是因为他们的产品融进了米老鼠和唐老鸭的浪漫、忠诚、可爱、憨厚、亲如一家的气氛。西门子品牌涉及多个行业，但它严谨、可靠的特色却代表着德国一丝不苟的民族特色。红豆品牌借唐人王维“此物最相思”的亲切浪漫的诗句，使一个名不见经传的制衣小厂获得巨大成功。这都是它们的特色所在。

二、雇主品牌的构建

雇主品牌是企业品牌的一个重要组成部分。对它的研究似乎较晚，有人认为它是20世纪90年代开始，近年来随着竞争的加剧受到关注。优秀的雇主品牌是由雇主的魅力和对员工的亲和力以及对社会的责任感打造而成的，它表现为在人力资源市场上的吸引力和在企业内部对员工的凝聚力。我对打造最佳雇主品牌有以下三点认识。

（一）善待员工构建和谐的劳动关系

在当前强资本弱劳动的情势下，构建和谐劳动关系，第一雇主应怀仁爱之心，平等待人，对员工进行人性关怀；第二应持劳动与资本共创财富的观点，尊重员工合法权益，实行利润分享；第三应以雇主与员工互利共存的理念达到雇主与员工双赢的局面。这方面日本企业的经验值得借鉴。他们实行的员工终身雇佣制、年功序列工资制和企业工会制，形成了和谐的劳动关系，成为日本经济发展的三根支柱。我国台湾富士康员工“十三跳”的悲剧就直接砸了雇主的牌子。2012年12月4日汕头制衣厂就因为劳资冲突造成了大火，烧死了14个无辜的年轻姑娘。这些惨痛的教训都值得我们深思。

（二）建立企业的诚信文化

营造雇主品牌必须建立企业的诚信文化，企业应恪守商业道德，决不能搞假冒伪劣商品。有人说，真正的雇主品牌可以将生意人、商人和企业家不同的经营理念和价值取向区别开来，生意人是能赚钱的事就做，没什么是非观念，商人有可为有可不为，有所取舍，有一定的生意原则。真正的企业家则不考虑眼前利益，把建立品牌当成企业的核心任务，实现自己的抱负和自我价值。我国有着悠久的诚信文化传统，同仁堂所坚持的“炮制虽繁必不敢省工，品味虽贵必不敢减力”的理念获得广大消费者的信任，历经百年而不衰。只是在我国传统诚信文化遭到破坏的情况下才出现了三聚氰胺、毒奶粉、苏丹红等给自己雇主品牌抹黑的恶性事件。

（三）承担社会责任

按西方经济学理论，企业的目标就是追求利润最大化和个人收入最大化，但是真正的企业家也应有追求承担社会责任的目标。

所谓社会责任，一是经济责任，为国家提供利润和税收，为劳动者提供就业岗位，为社会提供优质产品和服务，维护消费者的利益。二是法律责任，遵法守纪，不污染环境保护生态文明，遵守国家有关法规，如《劳动法》《劳动合同法》《社会保险法》《女职工特殊劳动保护法》等法律和法规。三是要科技创新，使企业担当国家科技创新的基础责任。

最后，提一点建议，希望将企业品牌和雇主品牌的研究成为人力资源管理著作或教材的一章。

弘扬中国传统文化，塑造诚信道德规范①

“百行以德为首”，在源远流长的中华文明中，对道德情操的完善和不懈追求是中国人引以为豪的优良传统和精神财富。道德，源自人类对美好心灵的守望，道德的魅力在于能够释放出质朴的人性光辉，为他人和社会奉献人世间最可宝贵的爱和善，更在于“送人玫瑰，手有余香”，为人类照亮前程、纯粹心灵、

① 在国务院参事室举办的建立我国转型期道德文化座谈会上的发言，2011 年 9 月 25 日于双沟会议中心。

提升素质、升华境界。在中国传统道德体系中，诚信是一种重要的道德规范，诚信是人与人之间交往的道德准则。孔子说："人而无信，不知其可也"，曾子将交友守信作为每日必须检讨自己的三省之一。诚信是诚与信的统一，古代先贤把"立德、立信、立言"作为为人处世的准则。可见忠诚老实、待人诚恳、严守信用、信任他人是全体公民都应当遵守的基本道德规范，是做人的根本，是人与人之间连接的纽带，是凝聚人心的保证，是社会经济正常运行的基础。我们党和国家一向提倡中华道德传统，尤其重视诚信道德建设。2006 年 3 月 4 日，胡锦涛总书记提出的"八荣八耻"为主要内容的社会主义荣辱观，也明确提出了"以诚实守信为荣"。温家宝总理在中央文史研究馆成立六十周年座谈会上指出"国家发展和民族振兴，不仅需要强大的经济力量，更需要强大的文化和道德力量"。

改革开放后，我国逐步实行的社会主义市场经济带来了高效率，经济发展也驶入了快车道，综合国力大大加强，GDP 占世界第二位，成为世界上第二个经济大国，人民生活水平大大提高。但与此同时，在社会生活中也出现了不少令人担心的问题，其中最突出的表现之一是一些人道德滑坡、诚信缺失，发生了信用危机。在经济领域，假冒伪劣商品充斥、虚假广告宣传、价格欺诈、侵害知识产权、中介组织违反独立公正的基本职业道德现象层出不穷。在我所研究的劳动经济政策领域，由计划经济向市场经济转型的过程中，由于对市场经济的不正确理解，加之法律不完善，以及某些人诚信的缺失，出现了一些扭曲的现象。例如，在分配制度方面，由中央集中统一的工资分配制度向企业自主分配的过程中，便出现了企业领导和工人收入的高低悬殊；由国家统一用工制度向企业自主用工与企业和劳动者双向选择的转型中，便出现了工人多次跳槽与企业和工人互炒鱿鱼的现象；在实行按劳分配和按生产资料分配制度中，出现了强资本对弱劳动的剥夺。以上种种倾向，造成劳动关系的紧张、劳动争议和群体性事件层出不穷，影响了社会的稳定。要化解以上矛盾，除了以法律和相关制度加以约束外，还可以通过弘扬传统诚信美德，唤起人们的良知良能，大家以诚相待，使劳动关系双方都得到公平的经济回报和预期利益的增长，企业将劳动者视为可创造财富的人力资本，使劳动者实现自身的价值进而得到更多的回报，这样，企业与劳动者形成一个共同体，实现劳动关系的双赢局面。在公共管理领域，一些地方和政府部门，以权谋私、权钱交易、浮夸虚报、破坏公共政策权威。在文教卫生领域，也存在着弄虚作假、学术腐败、营私舞弊等行为。在这里我想说说社会上弥漫着的庸俗、低俗、媚俗的坏风气。从侮辱残疾人的卖拐开始的一系列小品，讲的都是骗子的鬼把戏，他或者拿老人的婚姻开涮，或者拿自己的父母耍笑，甚至拿自己的妻女开心。庸俗、低俗、媚俗的恶搞加以复加。这种庸俗、低俗、媚俗的文化传开来，简直是中国的灾难。

以上诚信的缺失，严重影响了社会主义和谐社会的建立，破坏了社会主义市场经济的运行，污染了社会风气。为了实现我国经济社会健康有序的运行，必须建立诚信体系，在全社会形成维护诚信的有效约束机制，建立起我国完善的信用体系。为此，我提出如下建议：

第一，加强公民的道德修养和道德建设。从小学开始，设立公民课程和中华文化传统道德课程，以人类的普世价值和礼义廉耻、温良恭俭让的中华道德熏陶和教育他们，使之从幼童开始就能遵纪守法，识别美与丑，塑造真善美的心灵。

第二，加强法制建设，改善社会管理，夯实诚信的法制基础。

第三，提高市场组织化程度，打造诚信的组织基础。诚信是市场经济中的基础行为，是基于特定条件下的经济主体间普遍遵守和履行契约的均衡状态，诚信度对市场经济的交易成本有重要影响。如果没有这种信用基础，市场中的交易就无法完成。

第四，形成企业有效的博弈规则，构建诚信的制度基础。

在中国劳动学会适度劳动分会第四届年会上的发言①

“适度劳动”是相对“过度劳动”而提出的一个新概念。提出这一概念（命题）非常重要。因为随着我国从传统社会向现代社会的演变，从计划经济向市场经济的转变，社会文明程度有所提高，经济实力大大增强，但同时也产生了一些社会矛盾和经济问题。过度劳动就是其中之一。过度劳动表现为工时的过度延长（“五加二”“白加黑”），劳动强度的加大，以及劳动者在恶劣环境中的

① 2015年5月20日。

身心疲惫，造成劳动者的亚健康、早衰甚至死亡。

造成过度劳动的原因是多方面的，既有企业追求利润造成的劳动者身心的负荷超支，也有劳动者为追求高收入主动过劳，或为生计、怕失业而被动过劳。

还有一个重要原因造成的过劳，就是有的单位领导同志长期以来一直强调辛勤劳动、无私奉献、勇挑重担、争创一流的一面，往往忽视了对劳动者从法律上、制度上和行动上的以人为本的关怀。习近平主席在今年“五一”国际劳动节表彰劳动模范和先进工作者的大会上指出：要弘扬劳模精神，弘扬劳动精神，要始终实现好、维护好、发展好劳动者的根本利益。这其中当然就包含着对劳动者体面劳动、舒心劳动、适度劳动、全面发展的人本关怀。

党的十八大以来，我国经济发展放弃了两位数的增长速度，提出转变经济发展方式，将创新作为经济社会发展的引擎，提出 GDP 约 7%的增长速度，使经济发展方式进入结构优化、中高速前行的“新常态”。因此，政府可以通过宏观调控，适当缩减劳动时间、减轻劳动强度，使劳动者分享科技创新和劳动生产率提高带来的成果，放松身心进入适度劳动的“新常态”。

几点建议

（1）对过度劳动问题应进行劳动科学体系的多学科研究。

① 劳动经济学，通过对雇主（企业）追求利润最大化和雇员（职工）追求收入最大化的研究，提出工作时间与闲暇时间合理分配的建议。

② 劳动关系学研究劳资双方和谐劳动关系的建立，使劳资双方都能得到公平的经济回报和预期的利益增长，企业（雇主）将劳动者视为可创造财富的人力资本，劳动者通过企业利润的增长实现自身价值进而得到更多的回报。企业与劳动者结成一个利益共同体，实现劳资双赢的局面。

③ 劳动社会学对过劳问题进行综合研究，对劳动时间、劳动强度以及劳动成就感、劳动价值观、收入观、消费观的研究，使劳资双方放弃对财富和收入的过度追求。

④ 劳动生理学、卫生学研究如何更好地消除劳动过程中劳动者身心遭受的孤独感、寂寞感、单调、焦虑感，以及身心疲惫。

⑤ 劳动保护学研究消除劳动过程中的不安全、不卫生（硅肺、尘肺），改

善恶劣环境，增进劳动者的幸福感。

⑥ 劳动法学研究贯彻执行劳动法、劳动合同法、带薪休假等一系列法律法规消除过劳的影响。

（2）对过劳问题的研究应当对不同劳动群体区别对待。城乡劳动者、国企与民企、城镇职工与农民工、机关公务员与事业单位员工、体制内与体制外劳动者以及不同行业劳动者的过劳问题表现是不同的，应当分别进行研究。

（3）通过以上研究，提出关于劳动时间、劳动强度等适度劳动标准的建议。

附录A　作者主要著作和主持课题

1. 著作和编著

（1）《劳动经济学》，2002 年第一版，2021 年 3 月第六版，东北财经大学出版社出版。

（2）*Labor and Social Insurance Legislation in China:Trends and Developments For Operating in The New Economy. PDI Global Research Consortia*（中译文《中国劳动和社会保障立法的发展与趋势》），英文版著作，2001 年在美国出版。

（3）《社会保险概论》，1999 年，中国铁道出版社出版。

（4）《劳动经济学教程》（3 人合著排序第 2），1997 年，西南交通大学出版社。

（5）《社会保险大全》（编著，副主编），1994 年，河南人民出版社出版。

（6）《中国劳动经济史》，1990 年，北京经济学院出版社出版。

（7）《现代劳动组织学——宏观论与微观论》（袁伦渠、潘功胜、熊敏鹏合著），1988 年，中国财政经济出版社出版。

（8）《当代中国的职工工资福利和社会保险》（重要成员），1987 年，中国社会科学出版社出版（《当代中国》丛书之一卷，邓力群、马洪主编）。

（9）《新中国劳动经济史》，1987 年，劳动人事出版社出版。

（10）《劳动经济学概论》，1987 年，劳动人事出版社出版。

（11）《新中国工资史稿》（3 人合著排序第 2），1986 年 7 月，中国财政经济出版社出版。

（12）《劳动工作基本知识》（2 人合著），1982 年，劳动出版社出版。

（13）［民主德国］《劳动社会学》（2 人合译排序第 1），1985 年，劳动人事出版社出版。

（14）［苏］《劳动经济学》（3人合译排序第1），1981年第一版，生活·读书·新知三联书店出版。

2. 课题

（1）铁路行车主要工种教育培训研究（主持），铁道部项目，2006年。

（2）我国老龄产业发展研究（主持），教育部高等学校博士点基金项目，2003年。

（3）沂蒙老区农村剩余劳动力的开发利用的研究（主持），沂蒙地区劳动局委托项目，2002年。

（4）铁路企业实施减员增效与再就业工程研究，1998—2001年。

（5）九五期间铁路职工总量控制和用工制度研究（主持），铁道部项目，1996—1998年。

（6）中国养老保险改革与立法研究（劳动部主持，作为重要成员参与，国际合作项目英文版），1996年6月。

（7）中国社会保障体系的建立与完善（参与），劳动部课题，1994年。

（8）社会保障体系研究（主持），国家教委课题，1993年。

后　记

——八十岁感言

2020年底，接到北京交通大学经济管理学院不再继续返聘的通知，我这才真正意识到，自己已经八十高龄，到了耄耋之年，应该彻底退休，安度晚年了。

遥想1964年7月，我作为中国最早开办劳动经济专业的北京经济学院（首都经济贸易大学前身）的第二届毕业生走出校门，先后开始了在劳动部（现人力资源和社会保障部）、北京经济学院（现首都经济贸易大学）、北京交通大学和国务院参事室工作共52年的工作生涯，直到2020年底学院返聘4年工作的结束，我实际上在教育战线度过了56个春秋。在这漫长的岁月里，除了因"文化大革命"蹉跎几年时光，可以说我的一生都献给了劳动经济的教学和科研事业。

在我成长和工作的56年中，我首先应当感谢我的母校首都经济贸易大学，是您给了我醍醐灌顶的滋养，圆了我的出国留学梦。我要感谢国家最高劳动管理机关劳动部，是您给我参与劳动工作实践的机会，使我认识到劳动工作的伟大，从而开始了一生劳动经济工作的征程。我要感谢我工作了近26年并成为我最终归宿的北京交通大学，是您提供了宽松的工作和学术环境，支持我和全体同仁组建了劳动经济系，全系培养了数以百计的博士、硕士研究生。我要感谢国务院参事室，是您让我有幸以国务院参事身份亲耳聆听两位总理的教诲与指导，并以直通车的形式参与国家政策的研讨，写出10余篇得到国务院领导同志批示的参事建议。我还要感谢北京交通大学经管学院劳动经济系的同仁和我们的学生们，与你们数十年的朝夕相处，切磋砥砺，教学相长，为劳动经济学科的发展贡献力量。

本论文集的30余篇文章是从我公开发表的100余篇文章中挑选的，除个别论文联合署名外，绝大部分都是我亲笔撰写的。本论文集按照发表时间先后由远及近编排，分别组成了劳动就业、收入分配、社会保障与人力资源管理等既独立成章又相互联系的四部分。我并没有拘泥于教育部的学科分类，而是将这四部分统一归属于劳动经济学的研究范畴，进而将本书冠名为“劳动经济研究论文集”。劳动就业是民生之本，收入分配是民生之源，社会保障是民生之基；有了就业，才能参与收入分配，就业状况决定收入分配格局；社会保障在劳动者丧失劳动能力时给予支持，不仅直接关乎民生福祉，还会通过影响劳动力供需影响就业与收入分配；而人力资源管理是劳动就业、收入分配与社会保障得以运作的微观基础。这四者在理论和现实中均紧密联系，相互交织，构成广义的劳动经济学科体系。除学术论文之外，本书还收录了我对苏联劳动经济和东欧国家劳动社会学的研究、编译以及我个人的回忆、讲演、访谈文稿数篇供读者参考。

还要说明的是，这30余篇论文反映了我国改革开放40余年不同时期的研究成果，由于成文的时间跨度大，只能反映各个时期观点。然而这也使得读者能看到改革开放以来我国劳动经济学理论发展和实践探索的历史演进，进而从历史视角对当今我国实现更高质量更加充分的就业、更加公平的收入分配和更加完备的社会保障体系，落实“六稳”“六保”政策提供启示与借鉴。如果读者在认可文章的学术水平之余，还能感受到这些文章的历史参考价值和现实借鉴意义，我就得偿所愿、倍感欣慰了。

我一生以书为伴，教好书、带好学生是我最大的快乐，劳动经济学科研教学是我终生的追求。现在我就要离开熟悉的讲台，放下手中的笔，惜别弦歌一堂的学生了，怎能不感慨系之呢！谨以我这最后的一本书，怀念逝去的教书时光，也作为一份礼物献给培养、教导、帮助过我的领导、老师、学生与读者。

最后，我要对本书整理、编辑、出版过程中提供帮助的人们表示感谢。感谢北京交通大学领导的支持，以及北京交通大学哲学社会科学文库的资助。感谢我国著名劳动经济学家、现任中国人民大学荣誉一级教授、博士生导师赵履宽先生对我的鼓励和对论文集的推荐，并亲手写下长篇序言。感谢北京交通大学经济管理学院的彭兆祺副教授、中国劳动关系学院经济管理学院的刘盾老师、首都经济贸易大学的博士后耿元、北京交通大学硕士研究生晋紫薇同学对本书的策划、整理付出的辛劳。感谢北京交通大学出版社领导和责任编辑田秀青老师认真细致的工作，使得本书得以面世。

北京交通大学经济管理学院　袁伦渠

2020年12月